Microsoft® Excel
Spreadsheet Design

John M. Nevison

Brady

New York   London   Toronto   Sydney   Tokyo   Singapore

BRADY

A Division of Simon & Schuster, Inc.
15 Columbus Circle
New York, NY 10023

Manufactured in the United States of America

10 9 8 7 6 5 4 3 2 1

Library of Congress Cataloging-in-Publication Data

Nevison, John M.
    Microsoft excel spreadsheet design / John M. Nevison.
        p.   cm.
    ISBN 0-13-585019-3
    1. Microsoft Excel (Computer program) 2. Business—Data
processing. 3. Electronic spreadsheets. I. Title
    HF5548.4.M523N48 1990
    650'.0285'5369—dc20   90-35218
                                         CIP

To John and Dorothy and Susannah, Laura, and Nancy.

Contents

Acknowledgments   ix

Preface   xi
   The Need for Rules of Style   xi
   Novice Reader, Experienced Reader   xii
   How to Use This Book   xii
   Particular Excel Versions   xiii
   Spreadsheets as Tools   xiii
   Nursery Rhymes   xiv

Chapter 1   Introduction: Form Follows Function   1
   A Song of Sixpence   2

Chapter 2   The Basic Form   11
   The Introduction   11
      Rule 1: Make a Formal Introduction   11
      Rule 2: Title to Tell   12
      Rule 3: Declare the Model's Purpose   15
      Rule 4: Give Clear Instructions   17
      Rule 5: Reference Critical Ideas   19
      Rule 6: Map the Contents   20
   The Initial Data Area   26
      Rule 7: Identify the Data   26
      Rule 8: Surface and Label Every Assumption   31
   The Model Area   33
      Rule 9: Model to Explain   33
      Rule 10: Point to the Right Source   38
      The Dual Role of the Model Area   39
   Using the Basic Form   39
   Spreadsheets That Do Not Have Model Areas   42

Chapter 3   The Mind's Eye: Design   47
Rule 11: First Design on Paper   47
Rule 12: Test and Edit   49
Rule 13: Keep It Visible   51
Rule 14: Space the Spreadsheet for Easy Reading   52
Your Own Reader   54

Chapter 4   Other Functions, Other Forms   55
Rule 15: Give a New Function a New Area   55
Rule 16: Report to Your Reader   58
Rule 17: Graph to Illuminate   66
Rule 18: Import with Care   78
Rule 19: Verify Critical Work   79
Rule 20: Control All Macros   82
    Macros and Computer Programming   88
Rule 21: Focus the Model's Activity   91
Conclusion   94

Chapter 5   The Submodel   97
Rule 22: Enter Carefully   98
Submodel: The Reuse of Tools   104
The Submodel Focuses Attention   113
Collections of Spreadsheets   127

Chapter 6   Two Worked Examples   129
Building a New Spreadsheet: PROGRESS   129
Modifying an Old Spreadsheet: GROWTH   155
    First Work Session   165
    Second Work Session   168
    Third Work Session   170
    An Explanation of the Ideas in the Revised GROWTH   174
    The Value of Experience   174
    The Integrated Model   175
    The Spreadsheet Model GROWTH   175
    The Results of the Model   184
    The Implications of the Model   186
    An Afterword on Experience Curve Mathematics   192
Conclusion   194

Chapter 7   Examples   195
The Model QUEST   195
The Model LADY   200
The Model RAINCOAT   204
The Model PIETEST   209
The Model SEASON   212
The Model TASKTIME   218
The Model ACTIVITY   224
The Model PRESENT   229
  Present Value   229
The Models SIMPLPAY and PAYMENTS   236
The Model BUYBORO   246
The Model RAISES   255
The Model Template JMNRULE   258
The Model TODO   260

Chapter 8   The Wider World   267
The Work Group and Its Concerns   268
The Librarian's Requirements   269
Final Moves   271

Annotated References   273

References   275

Appendix A: Checklists for Action   277
Building the Initial Data Area and the Model Area   277
How to Link Cells   278
Linking Labels   279
How to Protect Your Spreadsheet   279
  When You Protect   280
How to Print Your Spreadsheet as Formulas   280
Future New Products for Spreadsheets   281

**Appendix B: Business Spreadsheets—Templates for Action,
              Tools for Use   283**

Management Tools   285
    References   286
Strategic Business Tools   286
    References   287
Financial Tools   288
    References   289
Personal Business Tools   290
    References   291
Other Spreadsheet Tools   291
    Reference   292

Index   293

Acknowledgments

The ideas that began the journey toward this book arose in discussions with John Kenower, Timothy Stein, and Julie Bingham. The ideas were given their first field tests in courses at CIGNA Corporation and at the Boston Edison Company. Students contributed ideas in other classes taught at Arco, CBS, Chesebrough-Ponds, Coca-Cola, GTE, Gillette, General Electric, Lotus, Melon Bank, and Westinghouse. Information Mapping, Inc. provided valuable format ideas. The manuscript profited from the careful reading of Jim Chelini, Joe Gwinn, Bill Schillhammer, Steve Shapse, and Tim Stein. Michael Vitale of the Harvard Business School (now of Prudential) and Ted Standish of the Gillette Company had kind words when they were needed most. Elva Wohlers generously extended the "two week" loan of her Compaq computer to several months. Special thanks to Ty Carlson of Microsoft Corporation for suggesting several Excel features that aid good decisions. Brady's Michael O'Brien, Tom Dillon, and Kristin Brooks each gave the manuscript a critical reading (and Michael gave it a new rule, Test and Edit). Carol Barth of Modern Design added grace and clarity with her design. Burton Gabriel of Brady has steadily supported this book and efforts to get it to the retail reader. My two daughters Laura and Susannah, continue to provide hugs as needed. My final and largest debt of gratitude is to my wife, Nancy Ross McJennett, who collaborated on the typographic design of this edition's spreadsheets and who assumed the extra family responsibilities that allowed me the luxury of this work. The mistakes that remain are unavoidably the responsibility of the author.

John M. Nevison
Concord, MA

Limits of Liability and Disclaimer of Warranty

The author and publisher of this book have used their best efforts in preparing this book and the programs contained in it. These efforts include the development, research, and testing of the theories and programs to determine their effectiveness. The author and publisher make no warranty of any kind, expressed or implied, with regard to these programs or the documentation contained in this book. The author and publisher shall not be liable in any event for incidental or consequential damages in connection with, or arising out of, the furnishing, performance, or use of these programs.

Trademarks

The name Excel is a registered trademark of Microsoft Corporation.

Preface

Writing a good spreadsheet requires the kind of careful thought you would devote to writing a good letter. Editing either document demands further patient attention. The purpose of this small book is to help you write and edit a spreadsheet. Will Strunk once wrote a book on how to write clear English. E. B. White added a section on style and republished the book as *The Elements of Style*. This book takes its inspiration from that book.

The rules are short, the discussion is limited, and the examples are simple in the hope that the ideas will be easy to read and reread.

The Need for Rules of Style

The need for these rules of style is larger than the technology. A word processor cannot make a good writer, nor can Excel make a sound analyst. There is no technological fix for sloppy thought or poor expression. You need to know that writing a good spreadsheet is hard work, that this work can be rewarding and fulfilling, and that the rules of style in this book can help you to do this work well.

These 22 rules are not intended to set brittle standards of performance. They are intended to encourage you, the spreadsheet author, to think seriously about the purpose of your work. All spreadsheets must first be correct. If they are to maintain this correctness over time, they must be clear. If they are to maintain this correctness when they are modified by others, they must be clear and well structured.

If these rules help you form the habits of careful spreadsheet construction, of reflection and revision, and of precision and focus, they will dramatically enhance your professional productivity.

The examples that accompany the rules show weak and strong versions of the ideas in practice. The terms "weak" and "strong" were chosen to indicate that these are merely examples on a continuum: Examples can be worse than the weak and better than the strong. As you work on your spreadsheets, you very well may improve on the examples provided here.

Novice Reader, Experienced Reader

If you are new to spreadsheets, before you use this book you must learn Excel. You must know how to build and copy formulas, how to move areas about on the spreadsheet, and how to make graphs. You may find parts of this book helpful without knowing Excel, but you will want to read the rules again after you have mastered it. In short, you should know something about your paints and brushes before you begin to explore the problems of composing a picture.

As a novice spreadsheet user, **please follow the rule before you break it**. After you use an apparently inconvenient rule on a few spreadsheets, you may find it has become an absolute necessity. You may also find that, because you do not have to unlearn a lot of bad habits, your work may quickly achieve a higher standard than that of your more experienced colleagues.

If you are an experienced user of spreadsheets, you may have difficulty with some of the rules in this book. However, if you strongly disagree with a rule it should be for the same reason that the rule was advanced: There is a better way to build a clear, correct spreadsheet. Few, if any, experienced readers will agree with all of the rules, but every experienced reader will find at least one new rule that will improve his or her spreadsheets. That one rule will repay the cost of the book and the effort to read it.

As all readers become experienced they should heed the other unwritten rule: **When you have a good reason, break the rule**. These rules should encourage thoughtful activity, not blind obedience.

How to Use This Book

The following table illustrates how you can get what you want from this book.

If you want to...	Read...
Get a quick overview of the idea	This preface and Chapter 1
Design a small spreadsheet	Chapter 2
Get all 22 rules	Chapters 2, 3, and 4
Design a big spreadsheet	Chapter 5
See a new spreadsheet written using the rules	Chapter 6
See an old spreadsheet modified to satisfy the rules	Chapter 6
See a lot of business ideas	Appendix B
Get some pointers on office use	Chapter 8
Find out what else to read	Annotated References and References
Learn some step-by-step Excel moves	Appendix A

Particular Excel Versions

The spreadsheets in this book will run as shown in almost all versions of Excel. Some of the typeface conventions will require Version 2.2, or greater, on the Macintosh and Windows or PM Version 2.0, or greater, on the IBM PC.

NOTE: Some of the graphs in this book were created by hand editing Excel graphs. Do not try to blindly reproduce the charts and graphs as they appear in the text.

Spreadsheets as Tools

This book extends its predecessor, *The Elements of Spreadsheet Style* (Brady, 1987), by expanding the number of working spreadsheets to more than 30. In order to make these tools accessible they have been cross-referenced extensively in the Appendices. The general categories of tool are illustrated in the following diagram.

The Business Spreadsheet Toolkit

Management Tools	
Financial Tools	Strategic Business Tools
Personal Business Tools	
Other Spreadsheet Tools	

So, in addition to learning more about spreadsheet construction, you can use the examples in this book to construct a considerable variety of personal spreadsheet tools.

Nursery Rhymes

The nursery rhymes in the book are intended to relieve the somewhat sober nature of the subject. Rhymes that are puzzles introduce some of the chapters. Rhymes that are about historical personages appear in the text and have dates that loosely correspond to the character about whom the rhyme was written. For example, in the spreadsheet SIXPENCE, the King is Henry the Eighth, the Queen is Catherine of Aragon, the maid is Anne Boleyn (who eventually had her head, not just her nose, snapped off), and the blackbird is Cardinal Wolsey; the date is 1536, an arbitrary year during the reign of Henry the Eighth. Mary, Queen of Scots, figures in several rhymes, and so does Queen Elizabeth the First. Other English royalty can be guessed by the dates. For those who like historical puzzles, Humpty Dumpty's spreadsheet contains the only specific historical date in the book. The date on the spreadsheets ascribed to Mother Goose herself (she has no known tie to an historical personage) is 1386, the year when Chaucer is believed to have begun his *Canterbury Tales*.

1

Introduction: Form Follows Function

FINGERS AND TOES
Every lady in this land
Has twenty nails, upon each hand
Five, and twenty on hands and feet:
All this is true, without deceit.

A spreadsheet should be of good character. It should be straightforward to build, easy to read, simple to use, receptive to change, and, above all, free of error.

The first step toward achieving this goal is to construct a spreadsheet that has an appropriate form. This form is the cornerstone of correctness. When each function is carried out in an appropriate location, its activity can be verified by eye and reviewed by a thoughtful reader. The appropriate form also denies errors a place to hide. When something is out of place, it looks out of place.

Because the appropriate form focuses your attention on the proper detail at the proper place, it is easy to remember and you do not get lost. A user engaged in the small changes of normal use knows where to alter an initial "what if" assumption, where to slip in a new calculation, and where to modify a printed report.

When a spreadsheet must undergo a major overhaul to meet a new need, the appropriate form will suggest where you can make the additions and deletions.

Finally, the appropriate form not only reveals the completed thought, it supports and guides the unfolding thought. A completed spreadsheet often can be reused as a template for subsequent work. Such a template saves a significant amount of start-up time on a new project, ensures that you will not forget an important section of the spreadsheet, and provides a guiding framework for thinking about the problem under examination.

A Song of Sixpence

To understand what this appropriate form might look like in practice, consider the spreadsheet model below. While it is small, it raises several questions. Who wrote it? What is its name? When was it written? What is its purpose? Why is it so hard to read? Is it complete? Is it accurate? What are its units?

	A	B	C	D	E	F
1		Income	Rent	Tax	Poor tax	Real inc.
2	King	90000	15000	20700	180	54120
3	Queen	75000	12000	17250	180	45570
4	Maid	12000	1000	2760	180	8060
5	Blackbird	3000	200	690	180	1930
6	Totals	180000	28200	41400	720	109680

Now, take a look at a second version of the same model.

	A	B	C	D	E	F
1	Twopence 10 December 1536 King Henry					
2						
3	To show how income is distributed in the kingdom.					
4						
5		KINGDOM INCOME DISTRIBUTION 1537				
6		(dollars)				
7	Person	Income	Rent	Tax	Poor tax	Real inc.
8						
9	King	90,000	15,000	20,700	180	54,120
10	Queen	75,000	12,000	17,250	180	45,570
11	Maid	12,000	1,000	2,760	180	8,060
12	Blackbird	3,000	200	690	180	1,930
13		---------	---------	---------	---------	---------
14	Totals	180,000	28,200	41,400	720	109,680

Twopence is a clear improvement. You know its name, when it was created, and who created it. You have been thrust into a nursery rhyme kingdom. You know the model's purpose: to show how income is distributed in the kingdom. The results have been laid out in an easy-to-read fashion. The units of measure are dollars. You have some idea of how this model might be used.

However, this apparently complete version is not complete. Twopence is hiding information. While you expect a spreadsheet to work with formulas you can't see (for example, the Totals row or the Real Income column), you do not want formulas to contain hidden numbers. Hidden numbers are buried threats. Unknown to the viewer, and hard to find for the user, these surreptitious figures can sabotage the best-intentioned effort. In the case of Twopence, the hidden number is the tax rate that is buried in the formulas in the Tax column. You are being denied access to important information about this model. The third version reveals this small, but highly significant, detail.

	A	B	C	D	E	F
1	**THRPENCE (Threepence)**			10 December 1536	King Henry	
3	Description					
4			To show how income is distributed in the kingdom			
6	Assumptions		23%	Tax rate		
7			180	Poor tax		
8	Model					
9		KINGDOM	INCOME DISTRIBUTION 1537			
10			(dollars)			
11	Person	Income	Rent	Tax	Poor tax	Real inc.
12						
13	King	90,000	15,000	20,700	180	54,120
14	Queen	75,000	12,000	17,250	180	45,570
15	Maid	12,000	1,000	2,760	180	8,060
16	Blackbird	3,000	200	690	180	1,930
17		---------------	---------------	---------------	---------------	---------------
18	Totals	180,000	28,200	41,400	720	109,680

Threepence tells you that the tax rate is 23 percent. Now what you see is what you get. All of the information on which the model depends is visible.

Notice that the Poor Tax appears as an assumption too. While it was visible before (it was repeated four times), now, by appearing as an assumption and having the four occurrences in the model all tied to the assumption, the Poor Tax may be changed by changing only one number instead of four.

You can also change the tax rate for the whole model by changing one number, the 23 percent at the top of the model. In addition to making the information accessible, the visible assumptions allow you to modify the program without digging into the formulas.

For many purposes Threepence may be satisfactory. However, if King Henry knows he will be off on a quest and wants to leave things in a fashion that will be easy for Queen Catherine to handle, he might rearrange the model for another person to use.

	A	B	C	D	E	F
1	**FORPENCE (Fourpence)**			10 December 1536	King Henry	
3	Description					
4			To show how income is distributed in the kingdom			
7	Initial data					
8			Beginning assumptions			
10		23%	Tax rate			
11		180	Poor tax			
12						
13		Income	Person (dollars)	Rent	Dwelling (dollars)	
15		90,000	King	15,000	Counting House	
16		75,000	Queen	12,000	Parlor	
17		12,000	Maid	1,000	Garden house	
18		3,000	Blackbird	200	Garden	
21	Income distribution model					
22		KINGDOM INCOME DISTRIBUTION 1537				
23		(dollars)				
24	Person	Income	Rent	Tax	Poor tax	Real inc.
26	King	90,000	15,000	20,700	180	54,120
27	Queen	75,000	12,000	17,250	180	45,570
28	Maid	12,000	1,000	2,760	180	8,060
29	Blackbird	3,000	200	690	180	1,930
31	Totals	180,000	28,200	41,400	720	109,680

Fourpence extracts all the raw numbers from the model, collects them, and labels them in the initial data area near the top of the spreadsheet. Fourpence changes all the numbers in the model area to formulas. For example, the King's $90,000 income in the model is no longer a number; it is a one-term formula that refers to the raw value in the initial data. All the apparent numbers in the model are formulas that refer to the raw values in the initial data or formulas that construct other values, such as the tax, from these numbers. Fourpence separates all the raw data from the formulas.

Having this separation allows a split in how the model is handled. The original author, the King, can work anywhere in the spreadsheet. But, when he is finished, he can lock up the formulas in the model itself. The second user of the model, the Queen, never has to touch a formula. She may exercise the model by simply changing figures in the initial data. Providing an area for the initial data allows the raw data to be not only visible, but fully labeled. In this case, you find out that the parlor rents for $12,000 and you can infer that the Queen is in the parlor (eating bread and honey).

The King wants to prepare some clear, concise reports: one for the Queen on the spending of the royal funds and one for the maid on the distribution of the royal burden. He extends his model to include these two reports.

	A	B	C	D	E	F
1	**FIVPENCE (Fivepence)**		10 December 1536 King Henry			
3	Description					
4		To show how income is distributed in the kingdom				
6	Contents					
7		Introduction: title, description, contents				
8		Initial data				
9		Income distribution model				
10		Report on kingdom's spending for the year				
11		Distribution of royal burden				
14	Initial data					
15			Beginning assumptions			
17		23%	Tax rate			
18		180	Poor tax			
19		1537	Year of report			
20						
21		Income	Person (dollars)	Rent	Dwelling (dollars)	
23		90,000	King	15,000	Counting House	
24		75,000	Queen	12,000	Parlor	
25		12,000	Maid	1,000	Garden house	
26		3,000	Blackbird	200	Garden	

(continued)

	A	B	C	D	E	F
29	Income distribution model					
30						
31		KINGDOM INCOME DISTRIBUTION		1537		
32		(dollars)				
33	Person	Income	Rent	Tax	Poor tax	Real inc.
35	King	90,000	15,000	20,700	180	54,120
36	Queen	75,000	12,000	17,250	180	45,570
37	Maid	12,000	1,000	2,760	180	8,060
38	Blackbird	3,000	200	690	180	1,930
40	Totals	180,000	28,200	41,400	720	109,680
43	Report on kingdom's spending for the year			1537		
44						
45		$28,200	Funds for the maintenance of the buildings and grounds			
46		41,400	Funds for the defense of the kingdom			
47		720	Funds for the poor			
49		70,320	Total spent			
52	Distribution of royal burden			1537		
53						
54				Burden as		
55		Person	Burden	% of income		
57		King	$35,880	40%		
58		Queen	29,430	39%		
59		Maid	3,940	33%		
60		Blackbird	1,070	36%		
62			70,320	39%		

Now that the model has grown beyond what can be seen on one screen, the King has added a table of contents. The contents gives the reader a quick idea of the full extent of the model. The King also has added two new regions to the spreadsheet. Each region is intended to be a report that can be printed out independently of the rest of the model. By giving each report its own area, the King has made it easier for either report to be modified. Because he wanted the year to appear in both reports as well as in his original model, he has added the year of the report to the initial data.

Looking at Fivepence you might wonder whether the whole effort has been overdone. Clearly, this model is more work than the already satisfactory Threepence. Is Fivepence worth the trouble? To answer this question, consider for a moment how it might be used.

Late in 1537 the King was away on a quest and he wrote home to the Queen suggesting that they increase the tax rate to whatever was necessary to cover an anticipated $50,000 expense in the defense of the Kingdom. The rye crop had been good, so the Queen knew everyone would receive an increase in their income. The Queen wanted to increase the poor tax if she could do it without increasing the overall royal burden on the population.

The Queen called up Fivepence and:

1. Entered the new incomes—$100,000 for the king, $88,000 for the Queen, $15,000 for the Maid, and $4,500 for the Blackbird.

2. Held rents the same.

3. Increased the tax rate until the total tax exceeded $50,000.

4. Increased the poor tax until the overall burden equalled the previous year's burden.

When she was finished, she retitled the model Sixpence.

	A	B	C	D	E	F
1	**SIXPENCE**		15 November 1537	Queen Catherine		
3	Description					
4		To show how income is distributed in the kingdom				
6	Contents					
7		Introduction: title, description, contents				
8		Initial data				
9		Income distribution model				
10		Report on kingdom's spending for the year				
11		Distribution of royal burden				
14	Initial data					
15			Beginning assumptions			
17		25%	Tax rate			
18		471	Poor tax			
19		1538	Year of report			
20						
21		Income	Person (dollars)		Rent	Dwelling (dollars)
23		100,000	King		15,000	Counting House
24		88,000	Queen		12,000	Parlor
25		15,000	Maid		1,000	Garden house
26		4,500	Blackbird		200	Garden

(continued)

	A	B	C	D	E	F
29	Income distribution model					
30						
31		KINGDOM INCOME DISTRIBUTION			1538	
32			(dollars)			
33	Person	Income	Rent	Tax	Poor tax	Real inc.
35	King	100,000	15,000	25,000	471	59,529
36	Queen	88,000	12,000	22,000	471	53,529
37	Maid	15,000	1,000	3,750	471	9,779
38	Blackbird	4,500	200	1,125	471	2,704
40	Totals	207,500	28,200	51,875	1,884	125,541

	A	B	C	D	E	F
43	Report on kingdom's spending for the year			1538		
44						
45		$28,200	Funds for the maintenance of the buildings and grounds			
46		51,875	Funds for the defense of the kingdom			
47		1,884	Funds for the poor			
49		81,959	Total spent			

	A	B	C	D	E	F
52	Distribution of royal burden			1538		
53						
54				Burden as		
55		Person		Burden	% of income	
57		King		$40,471	40%	
58		Queen		34,471	39%	
59		Maid		5,221	35%	
60		Blackbird		1,796	40%	
62				81,959	39%	

Because the structure of Fivepence made it convenient for a second person to use, the model was successfully integrated into the regular work habits of the administration. If the King set out to build a model to help rule the kingdom, he achieved his goal. The Queen could carry on in the King's absence.

What is the moral of these six versions? **Form follows function**. What form is appropriate depends on what function the spreadsheet is intended to fulfill. This moral does not mean all forms are adequate for some purpose. Onepence and Twopence are clearly unsatisfactory. Threepence, Fourpence, and Fivepence, however, each satisfy a different purpose. If you wish to have a personal model you can quickly build and change, then Threepence is fine. If you are going to let another person use your model, Fourpence is a sound approach. If you find that your model is composed of several parts, Fivepence is appropriate. Sixpence is evidence that Fivepence works.

To understand in more detail how spreadsheets should be fashioned, you need to know the rules for the basic form and the rules for extensions to the basic form. With these rules you can fashion forms appropriate to your functions. The next four chapters will present these 22 rules.

2

The Basic Form

AN EQUAL
Read my riddle, I pray.
What God never sees,
What the king seldom sees,
What we see every day.

The basic form divides into three fundamental parts:

- the **Introduction**, where you tell the reader what is about to appear;

- the **Initial Data Area**, where you present the raw material of the model; and

- the **Model Area**, where the spreadsheet performs its work in an informative and attractive manner.

Even a spreadsheet that ends up omitting or abbreviating one part should begin with a plan that includes all three.

The Introduction

Rule 1: Make a Formal Introduction

The top of the model introduces the reader to the model. The reader must get his bearings here, and the work of the spreadsheet must be fit into larger contexts. The top ties the model to the outside world. Several devices play introductory roles:

- The title line telegraphs critical information.
- The description declares the purpose.
- The directions say how to use the model.
- The references offer collateral information.
- The table of contents maps the spreadsheet's organization.

By the time the reader leaves the Introduction he should have a good idea how the model fits into the activities of the real world and where to go in the model to explore the details.

Rule 2: Title to Tell

The first thing the reader encounters is the title of the model. Make it tell. It should be short, apt, and memorable. In conjunction with the first few lines of the introduction, the title should allow the reader to decide whether to quit or to continue. All of the remaining reading will be colored by the title's first impression. Make sure it is the right impression.

Weak

	A
1	Sim3x5
2	Pies
3	Tuff13.6

Strong

	A	B	C
1	Simple	4 March 1620	S. Simon
2	Tuffet	15 May 1560	M. Muffet
3	Lost Sheep	22 June 1563	B. Peep

The title line telegraphs critical information. A strong title line contains at least the name of the model, the date it was completed, and the person who wrote it. Plain names are more informative than abbreviations. Nouns or verbs tell more than adjectives.

Choosing the right name for your model is especially important when your model will immediately become the property of several people or must fit into an existing scheme of documents. Others can immediately identify how your contribution fits into the group effort if the name follows the local convention. Suppose your model is the third one supporting a proposal to Acorn Corporation. You might want the title to be:

	A	B	C
1	Acorn Proposal #33 Model #3		

But if it must fit in a limited number of characters, it might require some abbreviation. Here is what one standard might look like.

Weak

	A
1	ACP33M03

Strong

	A	B	C	D
1	ACP33M03	(Acorn Corporation Proposal 33, Model 3)		
2	24 May 1488 T. Tucker			

Terse titles that follow an established abbreviation standard need a decoded explanation in the spreadsheet itself. The strong example shows how a two-line title can meet a terse naming standard and yet remain comprehensible to a busy reader. Naming conventions also need the support of:

- A list of the current conventions posted on the wall near every computer that will use these names;

- A regular, attentive review and update procedure; and

- A manager (called a librarian) to oversee the function.

A very useful bit of information to have along with the title is the date the current copy was printed. You may add this to your spreadsheet using the NOW() function and the label "Date Printed."

Weak

	A	B	C
1	**Sheep**	22 June 1563	B. Peep

Strong

	A	B	C
1	**Sheep**	22 June 1563	B. Peep
2		4-Nov-89 Date Printed	

The strong title area tells you that, while the spreadsheet was written a long time ago, the copy you are reading was printed rather recently. The date printed warns you to be on the lookout for undocumented revisions. If you are using a copy several times a day, you might consider including the time of day.

Strong

	A	B	C
1	**Sheep**	22 June 1563	B. Peep
2		4-Nov-89 12:56 Date Printed	

There is no magic in having only one or two lines for the title. When the critical information grows to several lines to meet work demands, the title line can become a title area. The title area should be so familiar that it can be read like a title line. The title, line or area, should telegraph critical information.

Strong

	A	B	C	D	E	F
1	**NURSERY KINGDOM CONFIDENTIAL INFORMATION**					
3	Name:	SILBELL (Silver Bells)				
4	Date:	12 August 1560				
5	Author:	M. Contrary				
6	Dept:	Garden				
7	Division:	Outdoor				
8	Date Printed:	30-Aug-89				
10	**Date last modified:**	23 Sept 1561				
11	**Last modified by:**	M. Contrary				

Several critical pieces of information appear in Silver Bells. The formal heading identifies the owner of the information and notifies the reader that this information is confidential. Not only do you have the name, date, and author, you know the department name, the division name, and the corporation name. On August 12, 1560, Mary Contrary completed the spreadsheet Silver Bells while she was in the Garden Department of the Outdoor Division of the Nursery Kingdom.

A modification is also mentioned here. You know that Mary Contrary revised the model on September 23, 1561. Another style of doing the revision history could allow for the insertion of further updates.

Strong

	A	B	C	D	E	F
1	**NURSERY KINGDOM**		*CONFIDENTIAL INFORMATION*			
3	Name	SILBELL2 (Silver Bells Number 2)				
4	Date	12 August 1560				
5	Author	M. Contrary				
6	Dept	Garden				
7	Division	Outdoor				
8	Date Printed	30-Aug-89				
9						
10	Date modified	Who modified and what				
11	4 Nov 1561	M. Contrary added a row for pretty maids				
12	23 Sep 1561	M. Contrary added a column for cockel shells				

This modification format allows the reader to read the history of changes to the original spreadsheet. You can see that Mary most recently added a row for pretty maids and before that a column of cockle shells. If the spreadsheet starts to misbehave when you use it, you have some strong hints where to begin looking for recently introduced errors. When the modification history grows unwieldy, you should write a new version of the spreadsheet and revise the entire introduction.

Rule 3: Declare the Model's Purpose

The model's purpose should be immediately available to the reader. He needs to know that his purposes and the spreadsheet's are similar. After the reader knows what the model intends to achieve, he needs to have some idea how the model will achieve it. This does not require a lengthy description, just a clear one. The model's intentions should be honorable and clearly stated.

Weak   *Strong*

	A	B	C	D	E	F	G
3	Description			Description			
4		Set of accounts on the			The purpose of this model		
5		King's travels.			is to maintain a set of accounts		
6					on the King's travels.		
7	Description			Description			
8		Accounts receivable.			Manage accounts receivable by		
9					recording transactions and		
10					printing summary reports.		
11	Description			Description			
12		Expense reports.			This spreadsheet will print		
13					the Queen's travel expense reports.		

One hallmark of a strong description is a telling verb, an action word that conveys the activity of the model. The right verb animates the description and quickly conveys the model's purpose. The phrase "The purpose of this model is" leaves no question in the reader's mind about the model's goal.

Weak

	A	B	C	D	E
4	Description				
5		Add all the tasks' means and variances			
6		and compute the project's mean			
7		and variance.			

Strong

	A	B	C	D	E
9	Description				
10		Estimate the length of a project that			
11		consists of several tasks.			
12					
13		Add all the tasks' means and variances			
14		and compute the project's mean			
15		and variance.			

First describe the goal, then how to achieve it. Only if the reader wants to estimate a project's length is he interested in the method. The weak version makes a good second line in the strong version. Answer "What?" before "How?" Be sure everyone has agreed on the mountain before you set out to climb it.

Strong

	A	B	C	D	E	F
1	**SMALLNEW**		17 July 1386	Mother Goose		
2	(C) Copyright 1985 by John M. Nevison					
3	27-Aug-89 : Date printed					
5	**Description**					
6			Provide a framework with which to begin building models.			
8	**To use**					
9			1. Call it up.			
10			2. Change its name.			
11			3. Save it with its new name.			
12			4. Edit to your purpose.			
15	**Initial data**					
16			Go here			
19	**Model**					
20			Goes here			

Here you see a model devoid of content, yet with a description that serves a purpose. The description succinctly tells what SMALLNEW's purpose is: to provide a framework with which to begin building models. This is a start-up model that you can use to make other models. This simple template saves your having to think about how to organize your work. It allows you to begin by editing rather than writing.

Rule 4: Give Clear Instructions

Just as the initial description bridges the gap between the model and the outside world, clear instructions can bridge the gap between the reader of the model and its user. Some who work with a model will only read a paper copy. Others will see it in operation on a computer screen. The description may satisfy the reader, but often the user needs instructions. A step-by-step numbered list is an excellent way to give clear instructions.

Weak

	A	B	C	D	E	F
5	Directions. Correct the status of the sheep. Group all the lost sheep together.					
6	Revise the COUNT and SUM functions in the model. Call up the pie					
7	chart entitled SHEEP'S PIE.					

Strong

	A	B	C	D	E	F
18	**Directions**					
19	1. Correct the "lost" and "found" status of the sheep in the initial data.					
20	2. Sort the initial data to group all the lost sheep together.					
21	3. Revise the COUNT functions under "Number" in the model to count					
22	the two groups of lost and found.					
23	4. Revise the SUM functions under "Value" in the model to sum					
24	the value of the two groups lost and found.					
25	5. Call up pie chart entitled SHEEP'S pie.					

The weak and strong examples differ in two important aspects. The obvious aspect is that the strong version is a numbered list. The numbers explicitly order the steps and make it easy for a user to check off each step as it is completed. The subtle aspect is that the weak version is not as clear as it should be. The weak version is a first draft. After you write instructions, be sure to let someone else try to follow them. Such a trial will show you whether the directions are adequate and, if not, how they can be improved. The strong version is a revised draft that was written after readers had trouble following the weak version.

Here is another set of directions taken completely out of context:

Strong

	A	B	C	D	E	F
18	**Directions**					
19	In the initial data area:					
20	1. State the decision and the desired result.					
21	2. Put in choices and make comments.					
22	3. Enter "must" objectives--things that must be satisfied.					
23	4. Enter "want" objectives--things that you would like to have.					
24	5. Weight the importance of the "want" objectives and comment.					
25	6. Rate or rank the choices against each objective.					
26	For example, rate the best choice (of four) as 4 and let the others have 3,					
27	2, or 1. You may have ties if you wish. You may rate a choice 0 if you wish.					
28	In the decision model					
29	7. Examine the model's results and graph.					
30	8. Revise and reexamine the importance of objectives, the rank of choices,					
31	and other features to be sure of your choice.					
32	9. List the adverse consequences of the best choice to see if it will work.					

Notice that these instructions can stand by themselves. Even without their model they make a certain amount of sense. They are broken into pieces that make it easier for the user to locate where to do which steps. The directions are further clarified in the actual model by a working example that illustrates where within the area to do each step.

A long list of instructions raises the question of where to place it. Frequently, just before the initial data area is a convenient spot. Sometimes, however, the user's needs are best served by including instructions nearer the point where they will be used. In a large model with many pieces, this means that the directions will be moved from the top of the model out to the part of the model where the user will be working. (See discussion of sub-models in Chapter 5.) If significant instructions have been moved, leave a note to that effect in the description at the top.

Strong

	A	B	C	D	E	F	G
17	Instructions on how to use the Monte Carlo portion of the model appear there.						

The user can quickly see that the additional support will be available on the Monte Carlo method near its use in the model.

Beyond instructions for the user, more detailed explanation about the ideas behind the model are sometimes necessary to ensure a full understanding of the extent and limitations of the model.

Rule 5: Reference Critical Ideas

Reference in the strong sense. Provide a full, accurate guide to the journal, book, or professional communication where the idea originated. Santayana cautioned, "Those who cannot remember the past are condemned to repeat it." Many ideas in a model are original and some borrowed ideas are too simple to bear mention, but an important idea should reveal its past. If it is incorrect, the reader must be given a chance to discover the source of the error. Sometimes an enterprising reader will spot an idea, follow the reference back to the source, and work forward to compose a model tailored to his or her special needs. Do not deny the reader this link to the past.

Strong

	A	B	C	D	E	F
19	References					
20		The Real Mother Goose, Chicago, IL: Rand McNally, 1916.				
21						
22		Thomas, Katherine Elwes, The Real Personages of Mother				
23		Goose, Boston, MA: Lothrop, Lee & Shepard Co, 1930.				
24						
25		Kepner, Charles H., and Tregoe, Benjamin B., The New				
26		Rational Manager, Princeton, NJ: Princeton Research				
27		Press, 1981.				
28						
29		Nevison, John M., The Little Book of BASIC Style: How to				
30		Write a Program You Can Read, Reading, MA:				
31		Addison-Wesley, 1978.				
32						
33		See Materials Handling Procedure Manual, Document				
34		Number A34.77, Rev. 3.6, pp. 64-68.				
35						
36						
37		If you have any questions, call Bo Peep at extension 3456.				

A reference need not be only to a book. A knowledgeable individual, a file with the related information, or a standard form the organization has been using for years can each be an appropriate reference in certain circumstances.

Rule 6: Map the Contents

The underlying organization of a spreadsheet is spatial. Geography is all. To let the reader know where things are requires a map. One of the most convenient maps is a table of contents. If the sections of your model are kept to the left and stacked vertically, the table of contents can be an accurate map to the location of each part of the model.

A table of contents is the last part of the Introduction in all but the smallest spreadsheets. As soon as the spreadsheet slips off the screen and escapes your visual span of control you will need a table of contents to see where you are.

Strong

	A	B	C	D	E	F
1	**NINPENCE (Ninepence)**			10 December 1536	King Henry	
2						
3	Description					
4		To show how income is distributed in the kingdom				
5						
6	Contents					
7		Introduction: Title, description, contents				
8		Initial data and beginning assumptions				
9		Income distribution model				
10		Report on kingdom's spending for the year				
11		Report on distribution of royal burden				
12		Data for pie chart of burden				

Strong

	A	B	C
40	Contents		
41		Initial Data	
42		Finance Model	
43		Quarterly Sales Report	
44		Pie Chart Data	
47	**Initial Data**		
48	.		
49	.		
50	.		
52	**Finance Model**		
53	.		
54	.		
55	.		
57	**Quarterly Sales Report**		
58	.		
59	.		
60	.		
62	**Pie Chart Data**		
63	.		
64	.		
65	.		

A table of contents is a powerful organizer for a reader. If the reader is only concerned with the spending report, she can focus her attention on it at once. But if she wishes to know more about the data that led to the graphs, she knows where to look.

The name in the table of contents should correspond to the name in that area of the spreadsheet.

You can name the areas of the spreadsheet with the Define Name and Create Name commands and note the fact in the table of contents. After you have defined a name for each area, you may jump to any area with very few keystrokes (use the Goto command and select the area from the list of names).

Strong

	A	B	C	D	E	F
1	**TENPENCE**		10 December 1536	King Henry		
2	27-Aug-89 : Date Printed					
4	**Description**					
5			To show how income is distributed in the kingdom			
7	**Contents (each area is named)**					
8		Introduction: title, description, contents				
9		Initial data				
10		Income distribution model				
11		Report on kingdom's spending for the year				
12		Report on distribution of royal burden				
13		Data for pie chart of burden				

TENPENCE gives the user an extra reason to be interested in the table of contents: By naming the areas, the user can jump to the right place in the spreadsheet. By naming areas you also avoid the annoying problem of using cell locations that must be changed every time the spreadsheet is rearranged. The reader of a printed version of the model welcomes the extra information about the organization of the spreadsheet.

Naming the areas of a spreadsheet is such a good idea that **all** of the rest of the spreadsheets in this book have had their areas named. Because the practice is assumed, no mention of it occurs in the contents.

Strong

	A	B	C	D	E	F
1	**NEW**	17 July 1386	Mother Goose			
2	(C) Copyright 1985 by John M. Nevison					
3	27-Aug-89 : Date printed					
5	Description					
6		Provide a framework with which to begin building models				
8	To use					
9		1. Call it up.				
10		2. Change its name.				
11		3. Save it with its new name.				
12		4. Edit to your purpose.				
14	Contents					
15		Introduction: title, description, contents				
16		Initial data				
17		Model				
18		Other sections as necessary				
21	Initial data					
22		Go here				
25	Model					
26		Goes here				

This template, NEW, extends the template SMALLNEW by including a table of contents. NEW is the common starting place for most of the spreadsheets in this book. The already named ranges give the user a head start with the work.

Sometimes a model's geography has horizontal spread as well as vertical depth. If so, include a map beneath the table of contents.

Weak

	A	B	C
7	Contents		
8		North America	
9		Europe	
10		Asia	
11		South America	
12		Africa	
13		Australia	
14		Antartica	

Strong

	A	B	C	D	E
16	Contents				
17		North America			
18		Europe			
19		Asia			
20		South America			
21		Africa			
22		Australia			
23		Antartica			
25	Map				
26		North America	Europe	Asia	
27		South America	Africa		
28					
29				Australia	
30		Antartica			

Weak

	A	B	C
33	Contents		
34		raw material purchases	
35		payables	
36		finished product orders	
37		receivables	
38		general ledger	
39		payroll	

Strong

	A	B	C	D	E
41	Contents				
42		raw material purchases			
43		payables			
44		finished product orders			
45		receivables			
46		general ledger			
47		payroll			
49	Map				
50	raw material purchases		finished product orders		
51	payables		receivables		
52		general ledger			
53		payroll			

With the continents mapped, the user knows which way to travel with his cursor, and the reader knows which way to travel with his eye. The reader knows when to go down and when to go sideways. The raw materials and finished products are arranged in parallel. They feed the general ledger, which is below them. The payroll is a separate function below the general ledger.

The map tells the user where to safely insert rows and columns. The Australia section can have rows inserted in it without hitting Africa. The user knows at once where the lower right corner of the model is: below Antarctica and to the right of Australia or below payroll and to the right of receivables.

Experienced users testify that a map is a powerful way to reclaim control over a spreadsheet that has gotten out of hand. The map organizes and informs. Sometimes it will even point out how to reorganize your model. It will always make your model easier to comprehend, to grasp as a whole. A map restores your visual span of control over even the largest spreadsheets.

Beyond a sharp title, a clear purpose, good directions, helpful references, and a simple map, the Introduction may include additional information. What you should add to the description depends on the function of the model, the knowledge of the reader, the skill of the user, and the framework of the organization within which the model will be used. (See Chapter 8 for more discussion of the organization.) Err on the side of overinforming your reader. He may not be stupid, but he is probably more ignorant than you suspect. Avoid unnecessary jargon. The Introduction should include everything necessary to make a successful bridge from the model itself to the world in which it will be used.

After the spreadsheet has been thoroughly introduced, it must set to work to achieve its purpose. Good spreadsheet form is more architecture than interior design. The next rules define the second and third parts, the major architectural elements, of the basic form: the Initial Data Area and the Model Area. The spreadsheet's goal is to arrive clearly at the desired results. Each part serves this goal in its own way. The Initial Data Area stores the beginning material of the model, the raw data, and the initial assumptions. The Model Area is where formulas manufacture consequences from the raw material. Here complex formulas are explained, intermediate terms appear, and final results are often displayed.

The Initial Data Area

Rule 7: Identify the Data

Data are the grist for the model's mill. They are the numbers you know when you write the model. They may be three key constants or three thousand items in a database. They belong in their own area, where they may be clearly labeled and conveniently arranged. Such an area makes it easy for both the reader and user to identify the data. Without an Initial Data Area, a weak model can be an unintended mystery.

Weak

	A	B	C	D	E	F	G
1	**INFLATEA**		1 January 1510	J. Horner			
2	(C) Copyright 1983 John M. Nevison						
3	28-Aug-89 Date printed						
4							
5	Description						
6		Find the profit margin in an inflationary world where raw material					
7		costs, labor costs, and prices each grow at a different rate.					
8							
9	Growth Rate	1.03	1.15		1.07		
10							
11	Year	Raw mat	Labor	Total cst	Price	Profit	Margin
13	1510	56.00	21.00	77.00	100.00	23.00	23.00%
14	1511	57.68	24.15	81.83	107.00	25.17	23.52%
15	1512	59.41	27.77	87.18	114.49	27.31	23.85%
16	1513	61.19	31.94	93.13	122.50	29.37	23.98%
17	1514	63.03	36.73	99.76	131.08	31.32	23.90%
18	1515	64.92	42.24	107.16	140.26	33.10	23.60%

This weak example does not have an Initial Data Area. It is more puzzle than model. The model shows the profit of a product with different cost components growing at different rates. You see that a price increase of 7%—a 7% increase has a factor of 1.07—preserves profit margin. But you don't know with any certainty what the initial data are.

Strong

	A	B	C	D	E	F	G
1	**INFLATE B**		1 January 1510	J. Horner			
2	(C) Copyright 1984 by John M. Nevison						
3	28-Aug-89 :Date printed						
5	Description						
6		Test pricing in an inflationary world where different costs					
7		growing at different rates affect the margin (% profit). By					
8		varying the price growth rate the user can attempt to preserve					
9		a certain margin in some future year.					
11	Contents						
12		Introduction: title, description, and contents					
13		Initial data					
14		Model					
17	Initial data						
18			Beginning assumptions				
20		1510	Starting Year				
21							
22			Cost structure			Growth rates	
24		$56.00	Raw material cost		1.03	Raw material growth rate	
25		$21.00	Labor cost		1.15	Labor growth rate	
26		$100.00	Price		1.07	Price growth rate	
29	Model						
30		Year	Material	Labor	Total Cost	Price	Profit	Margin
32		1510	56.00	21.00	77.00	100.00	23.00	23.00%
33		1511	57.68	24.15	81.83	107.00	25.17	23.52%
34		1512	59.41	27.77	87.18	114.49	27.31	23.85%
35		1513	61.19	31.94	93.13	122.50	29.37	23.98%
36		1514	63.03	36.73	99.76	131.08	31.32	23.90%
37		1515	64.92	42.24	107.16	140.26	33.10	23.60%

In the strong example, the Initial Data Area lets you see what's going on. The starting year, the assumptions about the cost structure of the product, and the growth factors are all clearly identified.

Not only can you use the initial mode more quickly, you can modify it faster. (Suppose the user had a different product with an $83 price, a $40 labor cost, and a $10 raw material cost.)

Aristotle once observed, "Well begun is half done." The Initial Data Area sketches out the scope of the model before you actually encounter the Model

Area. When you have seen the initial values, you can guess at the information to be derived from them. By knowing which terms are the independent assumptions, you have a good idea how the model may be manipulated to achieve a variety of answers.

Storing the data in a separate Initial Data Area makes it easier to ask the "what if" questions that depend on varying the initial data. You can also update a whole set of initial data without getting ensnared in the thicket of formulas in the Model Area. Keeping the data separate from the model lowers the chance that you will accidentally alter a formula.

Strong

	A	B	C	D	E	F	G	H	I	J	K	L	M	N	O	P	Q
1	**ACTIVITY (Activity Tracking)**								3 January 1520			T. Tittlemouse					
2	(C) Copyright 1985 by John M. Nevison																
3	28-Aug-89 Date printed																
5	**Description**																
6				Track the number of assigned activities during a project.													
7				The project is to build a new catapult.													
9	**To use**																
10				1. Enter the new weekly data in the Initial Data													
11				2. Examine the model													
12				3. Print the graphs													
14	**Contents**																
15				Introduction: title, description, contents													
16				Initial data													
17				Quarterly model													
18				Graphing area													
19				Verify area													
22	**Initial data**																
23		Activities as they occurred															
24	Week number	1	2	3	4	5	6	7	8	9	10	11	12	13	14	15	...
25	Design activities																
26	Assigned	5	6	7	7	7	8	7	6	6	5	4	4	3	3	3	...
27	Completed	0	3	4	5	6	7	7	6	5	4	5	6	5	4	4	...
28	Build activities																
29	Assigned	0	0	0	0	0	0	3	4	5	4	4	5	6	7	5	...
30	Completed	0	0	0	0	0	0	0	2	4	5	4	5	5	6	6	...
31	Test activities																
32	Assigned	0	0	0	0	0	0	0	0	0	0	0	0	0	0	0	...
33	Completed	0	0	0	0	0	0	0	0	0	0	0	0	0	0	0	...

(continued)

	A	B	C	D	E	F	G	H	I	J	K	L	M	N	O	P	Q
36	**Quarterly model**																
37				THE CATAPULT PROJECT: activities completed in early autumn.													
38					1520												
39		Qtr 1		Otr 2		Otr 3		Qtr 4		Total			Date: 3 January 1521				
40	Design activities																
41	Assigned	75		11		0		0		86							
42	Completed	63		23		0		0		86							
43	Build activities																
44	Assigned	31		79		14		0		124							
45	Completed	25		71		28		0		124							
46	Test activities																
47	Assigned	0		29		33		1		63							
48	Completed	0		17		35		11		63							
49																	
50	Total activities																
51	Assigned	106		119		47		1		273							
52	Completed	88		111		63		11		273							

You see again how much easier it is to use a model that extricates the raw numbers from the model itself. ACTIVITY clearly separates raw data from the quarterly model. The user can easily add weekly data without intruding into the Model Area. ACTIVITY labels the initial data so the reader sees that the data are collected weekly to be used in a quarterly fashion. (In fact, data this numerous cry out to be graphed; the full model contains a rather elaborate graphing area to support the spreadsheet's graphs. See Chapter 4 for more details.) A model with unidentified data can turn the reader into a detective.

Weak

	A	B	C	D	E	F	G	H
1	**PLANA**	22 Aug 1485		Humpty Dumpty				
2		4-Nov-89	Date printed					
4	**Description**							
5		Make a five-year income statement projection. Begin with						
6		sales, subtract costs that are a percentage of sales or are						
7		constant, find net income.						

(continued)

	A	B	C	D	E	F	G	H
10	Model	($ in Millions)						
11			1486	1487	1488	1489	1490	
12	Sales		100.00	108.00	116.64	125.97	136.05	
13	Cost of goods sold		42.50	45.90	49.57	53.54	57.82	
14	Gross profit		57.50	62.10	67.07	72.43	78.23	
15								
16	S G & A		33.00	35.64	38.49	41.57	44.90	
17	Depreciation		7.00	7.00	7.00	7.00	7.00	
18	Fixed expenses		40.00	42.64	45.49	48.57	51.90	
19								
20	Interest		2.25	2.25	2.25	2.25	2.25	
21								
22	Profit before tax		15.25	17.21	19.33	21.61	24.08	
23	Tax		6.10	6.88	7.73	8.65	9.63	
24	Net Income		9.15	10.33	11.60	12.97	14.45	

Strong

	A	B	C	D	E	F	G	H
1	**PLANB**	22 August 1485		Humpty Dumpty				
2		4-Nov-89	Date printed					
4	**Description**							
5			Make a five-year income statement projection. Begin with					
6			sales, subtract costs that are a percentage of sales or are					
7			constant, find net income.					
9	**Contents**							
10			Introduction: title, description, contents					
11			Initial data					
12			Income statement projection					
15	**Initial data**							
16			Beginning assumptions					
17		1486	Starting year					
18		100.00	Sales for starting year ($ M)					
19		7.00	Depreciation					
20		2.25	Interest					

(continued)

	A	B	C	D	E	F	G	H
23	Income statement projection				($ in Millions)			
25			1486	1487	1488	1489	1490	
27	Sales		100.00	108.00	116.64	125.97	136.05	
28	Cost of goods sold		42.50	45.90	49.57	53.54	57.82	
29	Gross profit		57.50	62.10	67.07	72.43	78.23	
30								
31	S G & A		33.00	35.64	38.49	41.57	44.90	
32	Depreciation		7.00	7.00	7.00	7.00	7.00	
33	Fixed expenses		40.00	42.64	45.49	48.57	51.90	
34								
35	Interest		2.25	2.25	2.25	2.25	2.25	
36								
37	Profit before tax		15.25	17.21	19.33	21.61	24.08	
38	Tax		6.10	6.88	7.73	8.65	9.63	
39	Net Income		9.15	10.33	11.60	12.97	14.45	

PLAN B tells you more than PLAN A. You can understand for the first time what the raw data of this model are: the starting year of 1490, the starting sales of $100 M, the constant $7 M depreciation, and the constant $2.25 M interest. You feel you have some of the answers to the mystery. Yet for all its improvement over PLAN A, PLAN B is not complete. The witness is still holding back: The spreadsheet still hides assumptions from the reader.

Rule 8: Surface and Label Every Assumption

One of the most serious errors of spreadsheet modeling is burying an assumption. A raw number—a constant, a factor, or a rate—can lurk submerged in a formula in the model. Such an assumption must be forced to the surface and clearly labeled. It should be placed before the model in the Initial Data Area.

Surfacing an assumption gives you an opportunity to label it. This label can go a long way toward explaining the true nature of the model.

Strong

	A	B	C	D	E	F	G	H
1	**PLAN C**	22 August 1485		Humpty Dumpty				
2		4-Nov-89	:Date printed					
4	**Description**							
5		Make a five-year income statement projection. Begin with sales,						
6		subtract costs that are a percentage of sales or are constant, and						
7		find net income.						
9	**Contents**							
10		Introduction: title, description, and contents						
11		Initial data						
12		Income statement projection						
15	**Initial data**							
16		Beginning assumptions						
18	1486	Starting year						
19	100.00	Sales for starting year ($ M)						
20	8.0%	Annual sales growth rate						
21	42.5%	Cost of goods sold as a percentage of sales (COGS_pct)						
22	33.0%	Selling, general, and administrative costs as						
23		a percentage of sales (SGA_pct)						
24	15.0%	Interest rate						
25	40.0%	Tax rate						
26								
27		1486	1487	1488	1489	1490		
29	Depreciation	7.00	7.00	7.00	7.00	7.00		
30	Debt	15.00	15.00	15.00	15.00	15.00		
33	**Income statement projection**		($ in Millions)					
34		1486	1487	1488	1489	1490		
36	Sales	100.00	108.00	116.64	125.97	136.05		
37	Cost of goods sold	42.50	45.90	49.57	53.54	57.82		
38	Gross profit	57.50	62.10	67.07	72.43	78.23		
39								
40	S G & A	33.00	35.64	38.49	41.57	44.90		
41	Depreciation	7.00	7.00	7.00	7.00	7.00		
42	Fixed expenses	40.00	42.64	45.49	48.57	51.90		
43								
44	Interest	2.25	2.25	2.25	2.25	2.25		
45								
46	Profit before tax	15.25	17.21	19.33	21.61	24.08		
47	Tax	6.10	6.88	7.73	8.65	9.63		
48	Net Income	9.15	10.33	11.60	12.97	14.45		

Finally you see the hidden detail of PLAN. The buried assumptions are 1) the 8% annual growth rate; 2) the 42.5% cost of goods sold as a percentage of sales; 3) the 33% selling-general-and-administrative costs as a percentage of sales; 4) the 15% interest rate; and 5) the 40% tax rate. You also see that depreciation and debt are assumed to be constant over the five-year period. Because the constants are spread out in the initial data, the reader may infer that the author thought that it was likely that the user might like to change a value in any year.

By using the Create Names and Apply Names commands (see details in Appendix A) you can insert the names of all these assumptions in the actual formulas in the rest of the spreadsheet. When a name gets long and it would take up too much room in a formula, a shortened name can be adopted. For example, "Cost of goods sold as a percentage of sales" has been abbreviated as "COGS_pct" and is indicated at the end of the line. Unless noted, **all** constants in the spreadsheets in this book have the name as listed.

Sometimes a spreadsheet identifies the data, but combines the Initial Data Area with another area. This possibility is explored later in this chapter in the section entitled "Common Sense and Spreadsheet Partitioning."

The Model Area

Rule 9: Model to Explain

A model is a web of relations woven with formulas. If you have assiduously separated out raw data and initial assumptions, then the model itself should be pure formulas.

The formulas of the model are themselves assumptions. The first responsibility of the Model Area is to explain clearly what assumptions are embedded in the formulas. The Model Area should provide three levels of explanation:

1. The values that appear in the model.

2. The written explanation of any tricky formula.

3. The complete printout of all the formulas in the model.

The Model Area's first level of explanation is the values that appear in the cells. If a formula produces results that are not entirely clear, it is a good idea to break the formula into its component pieces, where each step can be viewed.

Weak

	A	B	C
56	1402.08	Total expense	
57	674.08	Total adjustment	

Strong

	A	B	C
59	1402.08	Total expense	
60	250.00	Cash advance	
61	478.00	Other prepaid	
62	674.08	Total adjustment	

Here you see how the total travel expenses were reduced by cash advances and prepaid charges (such as conference registrations) to arrive at the total adjustment. In the weak example the intermediate numbers are hidden in a formula; in the strong example they are presented as intermediate results.

How much to explain depends on the reader's and the user's backgrounds. When you are in doubt, err on the side of overexplaining. Six months later, oversimplified steps will be a welcome relief as you struggle to read your own model. If someone else uses the model, the steps will increase his or her confidence in its accuracy.

A formula should be easy to read aloud. If a formula gets so complicated that it is hard to read aloud, it probably should be broken into two formulas. If you break a formula into pieces and the intermediate values in the extra cells intrude on the layout of the report you were preparing, create a separate region below the model for making the report.

The Model Area's second level of explanation is a written summary of a tricky formula. The next model changes the independent variable from sales to net income. As a result, the Model Area must explain some tricky formulas.

Strong

	A	B	C	D	E	F	G	H	I
1	**PLAND**	22 February 1486 Tom Tucker							
2		From an original model done 22 August 1485 by Humpty Dumpty							
3		4-Nov-89 Date printed							
4									
5	**Description**								
6		Make a five-year income statement projection based on net							
7		income growth. Begin with net income, add costs that are a							
8		percentage of net income or are constant, find sales.							
9									
10	**Contents**								
11		Introduction: title, description, contents							
12		Initial data							
13		Income statement projection							
16	**Initial data**								
17			Beginning assumptions						
18		1486	Starting year						
19		9.15	Net income starting year ($ M)						
20		10.0%	Annual net income growth rate						
21		464.5%	Cost of goods sold as a percentage of net income (COGS_pct_net)						
22		360.7%	Selling, general, and administrative costs as						
23			a percentage of net income (SGA_pct_net)						
24		15.0%	Interest rate						
25		40.0%	Tax rate						
26			1486	1487	1488	1489	1490		
27	Depreciation		7.00	7.00	7.00	7.00	7.00		
28	Debt		15.00	15.00	15.00	15.00	15.00		
31	**Income statement projection**								
32									
33	Tricky formulas below include:								
34		Tax from net = (net/(1-tax rate))*tax rate							
35		SG&A = (SG&A %)*Net							
36		Cost of goods sold = (COGS %)*net							
37		($ in Millions)							
38			1486	1487	1488	1489	1490		
40	Net Income		9.15	10.07	11.07	12.18	13.40		
41	Tax		6.10	6.71	7.38	8.12	8.93		
42	Profit before tax		15.25	16.78	18.45	20.30	22.33		
43									

(continued)

	A	B	C	D	E	F	G	H	I
44	Interest		2.25	2.25	2.25	2.25	2.25		
45	S G & A		33.00	36.30	39.93	43.92	48.32		
46	Depreciation		7.00	7.00	7.00	7.00	7.00		
47	Fixed expenses		40.00	43.30	46.93	50.92	55.32		
48									
49	Cost of goods sold		42.50	46.75	51.43	56.57	62.22		
50	Gross profit		33.00	36.30	39.93	43.92	48.32		
51	Sales		75.50	83.05	91.36	100.49	110.54		

You need help with the formulas in this model because PLAN D turns PLAN C on its head. PLAN C began with sales and ended with net income; PLAN D does the reverse. In the inverted model, a few formulas get tricky; they have been explained near where they occur. PLAN D also reverses the order of the lines in the model to make the top-to-bottom flow of the reader correspond to the top-to-bottom flow of the calculation. The Model Area is trying above all to explain how the calculations are performed. In order to get an easy-to-read report, a Report Area can be added (see Chapter 4 for details).

The Model Area's third level of explanation of the calculations is a printed copy of all the formulas in the model. In the case of PLAN D they might look like this:

First three years of model (detail):

	A	B	C	D	E
37			($ in Millions)		
38			1486	1487	1488
40	Net Income		9.15	10.07	11.07
41	Tax		6.10	6.71	7.38
42	Profit before tax		15.25	16.78	18.45
43					
44	Interest		2.25	2.25	2.25
45	S G & A		33.00	36.30	39.93
46	Depreciation		7.00	7.00	7.00
47	Fixed expenses		40.00	43.30	46.93
48					
49	Cost of goods sold		42.50	46.75	51.43
50	Gross profit		33.00	36.30	39.93
51	Sales		75.50	83.05	91.36

First three years of model as formulas (detail):

	A	B	C	D	E
37				($ in Millions)	
38			=B18	=C38+1	=D38+1
40	Net Income		=$B$19	=C40*(1+$B$20)	=D40*(1+$B$20)
41	Tax		=C40/(1-$B$25)*$B$25	=D40/(1-$B$25)*$B$25	=E40/(1-$B$25)*$B$25
42	Profit before tax		=C40+C41	=D40+D41	=E40+E41
43					
44	Interest		=$B$24*C28	=$B$24*D28	=$B$24*E28
45	S G & A		=$B$22*C40	=$B$22*D40	=$B$22*E40
46	Depreciation		=C27	=D27	=E27
47	Fixed expenses		=C45+C46	=D45+D46	=E45+E46
48					
49	Cost of goods sold		=$B$21*C40	=$B$21*D40	=$B$21*E40
50	Gross profit		=C43+C45+C48	=D43+D45+D48	=E43+E45+E48
51	Sales		=C50+C49	=D50+D49	=E50+E49

Be sure when you print a paper copy of the finished model for the reader that you print a second copy with the model's formulas. In order to help the formulas fit, they are shown here **before** the constant names are applied to them. (See Chapter 8 for more on this idea.) Details on how to print formulas are in the appendices.

Formulas may well appear in other parts of the spreadsheet besides the Model Area. A frequent use of a formula in the Initial Data Area is to be sure that one piece of data implies another. For example, if you wish to divide something between two players using a percentage, the results might look like this:

Weak

	A	B
5	0.14	Player A
6	0.86	Player B

Strong (formula)

	A	B
5	0.14	Player A
6	=(1-$A$5)	Player B

Strong (values)

	A	B
5	14%	Player A
6	86%	Player B

The strong version uses a formula to avoid an entry error. One entry gets two correct results.

Formulas may occur in other regions as well. Wherever a formula appears, its function should be apparent and should support the particular area's purpose (see Chapter 4 for more on other areas).

Rule 10: Point to the Right Source

As you build your formulas, you will have occasion to refer to an earlier cell for a value. Whenever you do this, be sure you are referring to the right occurrence of the value. That is, be sure you point to the value that makes it easiest for the reader and user to understand the formula.

If the best source is another cell in the body of the model, it will be nearby and will have the context of the model to help explain it. If the best source is in the initial data, it will probably have some explanatory text near it. The right source is the one that speeds the reader's comprehension of the formula.

For example, consider the following three lines from the body of the model in Plan C.

Strong

	A	B	C
40	S G & A	=$A$22*B36	=$A$22*C36
41	Depreciation	=B29	=C29
42	Fixed expenses	=B40+B41	=C40+C41

The formula for selling, general, and administrative costs (S G & A) uses the fixed percentage found in the initial area at $A$22. Initial data items that appear as single values are often used as "absolute" cells in model formulas. In this case, pointing to the original source is the method that best illustrates what the formula means.

In line 42, however, you see a different solution to the problem. The good formula C42=C40+C41 says "add the two lines above." Fixed expenses equals S G & A plus depreciation. Any other form would make more work for the reader. The poor alternative C42=C40+C29 embroils the reader in an unnecessary search for what's going on up in row 29.

When a line, a column, or a row of initial data such as Depreciation is repeated in the model itself, the best course is usually to refer to the nearby line in the model. The nearby line is easier to find.

An isolated single value, however, is almost always better referred to the original source. If you make it a habit to refer to the original source, the reader of the paper version can make sense out of the model more quickly, and the user of the model can handle the model with greater certainty. Both people know that if they change the model in the Initial Data Area they are changing the unique reference point that feeds formulas all over the model.

One way of making an Excel formula even easier to read, as was suggested earlier, is to name the constant and apply the name to all the formulas in the spreadsheet. The result of this application (from PLAN C) is pictured below:

Strong

	A	B	C
40	S G & A	=SGA_pct*B36	=SGA_pct*C36
41	Depreciation	=B29	=C29
42	Fixed expenses	=B40+B41	=C40+C41

With this information, the reader can deduce that S G & A is computed by multiplying a fixed percentage times an earlier term.

The Dual Role of the Model Area

In the basic form, the Model Area plays two roles—as the area that explains the calculations and as the area that displays the results. Because many spreadsheets can be built with the Model Area also serving the purpose of the Report Area, the discussion of the Report Area is deferred to Chapter 4. If a conflict arises between being clear about the calculation and displaying the results, a Report Area should be added.

The basic form is the essential first step of good spreadsheet design. The Introduction, the Initial Data Area, and the Model Area form a powerful triumvirate, the fundamental triad of a good design. The 10 basic rules in this chapter will help you build models that can be used and reused with confidence.

Using the Basic Form

Even with the Report Area discussion deferred, serious questions remain about the relationship between the Initial Data Area and the Model Area. At first, the idea of a separate Initial Data Area may appear to violate the fundamental simplicity of spreadsheets. But remember that the rule is not "Set up an Initial Data Area," the rule is "Identify the data."

The mystery spreadsheet below focuses the issue. What do you call it?

	A	B	C	D
1	**Mystery spreadsheet**			
2			Column of row sums	
3	Mass of raw		.	
4	numbers in		.	
5		a large table.	.	
6				
7	Row of column sums . . .		Grand total	

Is this an Initial Data Area with a few extra formulas? A Model Area without an Initial Data Area? Or a Report Area without an Initial Data Area or a Model Area?

To answer these questions, remind yourself that the Initial Data Area identifies the raw data, the Model Area explains the calculation, and the Report Area prints the results for a particular reader. If you can make one area display the raw data, explain the calculation, and print out clear results, then call it an Initial Data Area. The first requirement is the greatest requirement: You must always identify the data.

If the mystery spreadsheet is an Initial Data Area with a few added formulas and you add more formulas to the first few, at what point should the spreadsheet spawn a Model Area?

First form

	A	B	C	D
10	**Initial Data**			
11			Column of row sums	
12	Mass of raw		.	
13	INTERMEDIATE ROW OF FORMULAS		.	
14	numbers in		.	
15	INTERMEDIATE ROW OF FORMULAS			
16		a large table.		
17				
18	Row of column sums . . .		Grand total	

When should you split this into two areas?

- When you become uncomfortable thinking that identifying the data is the primary purpose of the spreadsheet;

- When the calculations become confused or obscure; or

- When you need room to rearrange the model to make it easier to read.

Any one of these reasons is sufficient cause for a Model Area.

Second form

	A	B	C	D
21	**Initial Data**			
22				
23	Mass of raw			
24	numbers in			
25	a large table.			
26	(with explanations.)			
29	**Model**			
30			Column of row sums	
31	Mass of raw		.	
32	INTERMEDIATE ROW OF FORMULAS		.	
33	numbers in		.	
34	INTERMEDIATE ROW OF FORMULAS			
35	a large table.			
36				
37	Row of column sums . . .		Grand total	

When you break the spreadsheet into two areas you may be bothered by seeing a big block of numbers twice, but you will find compensatory freedoms. You will be able to label the Initial Data clearly without intruding on your model's format. You will also be able to shape the model to reveal what the calculations are and to convince the reader that these calculations are correct.

If separating the Initial Data Area and the Model Area makes you feel stupid at first, do it anyway. If, after a few months of going out of your way to apply these rules, your models are not substantially better, back off from this practice until you find a balance that is right for you and for the users of your spreadsheets. (See Building the Initial Data Area and the Model Area in Appendix A.) Your overriding concern should be for ease of use over ease of construction, for clarity of expression over speed of writing.

Spreadsheets That Do Not Have Model Areas

Some spreadsheets are exceptions to the basic rules. Rules should aid your common sense, not replace it. Some spreadsheets honestly do not need a Model Area. Here's one example:

Strong

	A	B	C	D	E	F	G	H	I
1	**TRAVEL**		15 June 1588		Queen Elizabeth				
3	Description								
4			Print the Queen's travel expenses.						
6	To use								
7			1. Call up program and save with a new name.						
8			2. Enter trip information in the appropriate places.						
9			3. Collect all the prepaid expenses as a formula in the						
10			"prepaid expenses" cell.						
11			4. Include appropriate notes.						
12			5. Print a copy for your personal records and a copy for the Treasury.						
15	Initial data, beginning assumptions, and travel report.								
16									
17			TRAVEL EXPENSES OF QUEEN ELIZABETH						
18									
19	Date:		23-28 September 1588						
20	Name:		Queen Elizabeth						
21	Place:		Visit to Banbury Cross						
22	Purpose:		To talk with the lords and visit the people						
23									
24									
25			SUN	MON	TUE	WED	THR	FRI	SAT	TOTAL
26	Travel			96.00	96.00	110.00	80.00	96.00		478.00
27	Local trans									0.00
28	Stable			24.00	32.00	38.00	44.00	23.00		161.00
29	Inn		104.85	97.97	103.77	100.42	95.57			502.58
30	Meals									
31	Breakfast			8.00	8.00		35.00	5.00		56.00
32	Lunch			5.00		5.00	45.00		55.00
33	Dinner		15.50	25.00	45.00	27.00		10.00		122.50
34	Entertainment			3.00	4.00	2.00	4.00	3.00		16.00
35	Miscellaneous			3.00		8.00				11.00
36									
37	Total		120.35	256.97	293.77	285.42	263.57	182.00	0.00	1,402.08

(continued)

	A	B	C	D	E	F	G	H	I
38									
39	1402.08	:Total expense Signed: _____							
40	250.00	:Treasury advance							
41	478.00	:Other (prepaid) Date: _____							
42	674.08	:Total adjustment							
43									
44	0.00	:Due treasury							
45	674.08	:Due Queen							
46									
47									
48	**Notes:**	1. Tuesday dinner with mayor							
49		2. Thursday breakfast with castle force							
50		3. Friday lunch with the General							

TRAVEL is a spreadsheet that does not need a Model Area. It has only a very few simple equations. Its purpose is to identify the initial data and present it clearly, so the author calls it an Initial Data Area with a few totals. We do not have a Model Area at all. What we print out is the Initial Data Area.

Databases are another case where the Initial Data Area overwhelms the Model Area. Often, however, databases trail summary reports that are Model Areas.

Strong

	A	B	C	D	E	F	G
1	**SHEEP**	15 April 1566 Bo Peep					
2	5-Nov-89	Date printed					
3							
4	**Description**						
5		Maintain a database on the sheep herd. Track the number and value					
6		of the lost and found sheep. Revise it periodically to keep it current.					
8	**Contents**						
9		Introduction: title, description, contents					
10		Initial data					
11		Sheep count model					
12		Sheep pie chart data					
14	**Directions**						
15		1. Correct the "lost" and "found" status of the sheep in the initial data.					
16		2. Check the results in the model.					
17		3. Call up pie chart entitled SHEEP'S PIE.					

(continued)

	A	B	C	D	E	F	G
20	**Initial data**						
21							
22	NAME	STATUS	COLOR	VALUE			
23	Agnus	Lost	White	200			
24	Alistair	Lost	White	100			
25	Angus	Found	Black	300			
26	Brian	Found	White	100			
27	Hugh	Lost	Red	300			
28	Ian	Found	White	200			
29	Janet	Lost	White	400			
30	Margaret	Found	Plaid	200			
31	Mary	Lost	White	100			
34	**Sheep count model**						
35	Tricky formulas						
36			The numbers and values are done using "array" formulas				
37			For examples, <number found> = SUM(IF(LEFT(Status)="F",1,0))				
38			<value found> = SUM(IF(LEFT(Status)="F",Value,0))				
39							
40		Number	Percent	Value			
41	Lost	5	56%	1100			
42	Found	4	44%	800			
43	Total	9	100%	1900			
46	**Sheep pie chart data**						
47			Value	Percent value			
48		Lost	1100	58%			
49		Found	800	42%			

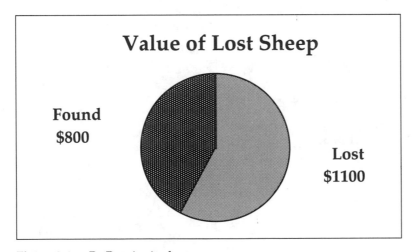

Figure 2-1.   Bo Peep's pie chart.

Sheep is a collection of data with a modest model wagging along behind. There are no major assumptions, just a collection of data. The model area provides space to note tricky features of the formulas. Notice that the model has spun off a graphics area (more on that in Chapter 4). A major reason for dividing a spreadsheet into areas is that it makes later modification easier.

With a very large database you might want to rearrange the contents to have two different areas for data: an area for the "what if" initial assumptions and a database for the bulk of the raw data.

Data in a database may be so large and changing that you want to keep it below the rest of the model. This practice has the advantage that the location of your reports remains stable since it is above the point where rows are inserted and deleted because of the constantly varing size of the database. If the sheep herd had numbered in the hundreds, Bo Peep might have structured her model with the data at the bottom.

Strong

	A	B	C	D	E	F
5	Contents					
6		Introduction: title, description, contents, directions				
7		Initial data				
8		Sheep count model				
9		Sheep pie chart data				
10		Database of sheep data				

3

The Mind's Eye: Design

MULTIPLICATION IS VEXATION
Multiplication is vexation,
    Division is as bad;
The Rule of Three doth puzzle me,
    And Practice drives me mad.

The problem of design is one of working out ideas in advance and of testing completed structures. Design also encompasses an abiding concern for the overall appearance of things. The next four procedural rules help you apply the first ten. They suggest what to do and when: They are rules for the mind's eye.

Rule 11: First Design on Paper

Do your first thinking with pencil and paper. Design can encompass many things, but one thing is certain: Your first idea will not be your last and only rarely will it be your best. Ideas demand editing. You will need to react to your initial impulse, to brood over your vision, to rearrange, to revise, to rethink. All of this is much easier done on paper. If you resist the intemperate urge to type on the computer and instead deliberate over your initial design on paper, you will complete your whole project faster.

If you cannot resist the urge to leap to your computer and begin typing, please think of your first efforts as being "paper" efforts. Use nonsense collections of letters such as "xxx yyy xxx" to simulate text and rows or columns of 99999.99 to simulate blocks of numbers. Move blocks around until you have a good feel for the gross arrangement of the whole model. In short, tell yourself that your first efforts are to sketch a preliminary design and to mull over basic ideas.

When beginning an absolutely new model, some find it helpful to write a one-sentence statement of purpose that begins, "The purpose of this spreadsheet is.... " This sentence can be followed by a paragraph that begins, "How the spreadsheet achieves this purpose is.... " For people who think best with words, these two phrases can cut a clear path through a lot of fuzzy thinking.

For those who prefer pictures, sketches on a large piece of paper can be a big help. You can lay out each region as a block. Within a region, columns and rows can appear as subblocks. Areas for text can be outlined to see how the general shape and size will appear. The blocks can be arranged so that they relate to each other in the best way. Blocks that create information can be placed ahead of blocks that use the information.

Your model will be easier to read if you group areas that work together. A tricky formula is easier to explore if its constituent elements lie nearby. Grouping allows nearby references to be quickly checked.

Design from the major idea to the minor. Start with the area of central importance—the model or the database—and work out to the minor regions—back to the initial data and description, forward to submodels that compute pieces of data, and over to collateral models that develop parallel figures. Sometimes the area of central importance will be a report, sometimes a graph.

Don't be surprised if the region of central importance shifts. Sometimes you may begin thinking your model's report is the central idea only to discover that the real heart of the matter is a graph. Stay clear in your own mind about what the major idea is. This clarity of purpose will allow you to design faster and better.

If your current idea is not a totally new idea, sometimes an old design can serve as a template for your new project. By using a template you are less likely to overlook a necessary part and more likely to cast your final ideas in a form familiar to your eye. Be sure that you don't let the old idea unnecessarily restrict you. Be prepared to break the mold and move on to a new and better approach if your idea requires it.

If you have been doing your initial "paper" design on the computer, remember that you can systematically extract regions from the rough draft and move them to a brand-new spreadsheet (or insert them into a preexisting template). Extracting a few good regions is sometimes faster than editing many bad regions. When you extract, you will lose special definitions of column width and special formats for cells.

Design your spreadsheet once so that it can be used many times. One hard test for a good design is ease of reuse. If a model is easy to reuse, it is probably designed in a straightforward manner. If you think about how the model could be used a year from now, you will probably design it better. Design it to last five years.

Rule 12: Test and Edit

A correct model requires testing just as clear English requires editing. As you work on your model in solitude, do both: Test your spreadsheet by varying the initial parameters and seeing if the appropriate conclusions are altered in the expected ways; edit your comments to make sure they stay current with the model as you build and revise it.

You may more fully test a model by using a known example to be sure the answer agrees with the known correct answer. You may use 0s and 1s for a quick practice, but you should avoid them when providing sample data to verify formally that the final model is correct.

Weak

	A	B	C	D	E	F	G	H	I
51	Model								
53	Tricky formulas:								
54	Expected = (low + 4*likely + high)/6								
55	Standard deviation = (high - low)/6								
56	Variance = (standard deviation)^2								
57	Project standard deviation = square root(project variance)								
59	Task name	Low	Likely	High	Expected	Variance			
61	Activity 1	0	3	6	3.0	1.0			
62	Activity 2	0	3	6	3.0	1.0			
63	Activity 3	0	3	6	3.0	1.0			
64	Activity 4	0	3	6	3.0	1.0			
65	Activity 5	0	3	6	3.0	1.0			
66	Activity 6	0	3	6	3.0	1.0			
67	Activity 7	0	3	6	3.0	1.0			
68	Activity 8	0	3	6	3.0	1.0			
69	Activity 9	0	3	6	3.0	1.0			
70							Standard deviation		
71	Project totals				27.0	9.0	3.0		
72	Check sums	0	27	54	27.0				

Strong

	A	B	C	D	E	F	G	H	I
51	**Model**								
53	Tricky formulas:								
54	Expected = (low + 4*likely + high)/6								
55	Standard deviation = (high - low)/6								
56	Variance = (standard deviation)^2								
57	Project standard deviation = square root(project variance)								
59	Task name	Low	Likely	High	Expected	Variance			
61	Activity 1	2	5	14	6.0	4.0			
62	Activity 2	2	5	14	6.0	4.0			
63	Activity 3	2	5	14	6.0	4.0			
64	Activity 4	2	5	14	6.0	4.0			
65	Activity 5	2	5	14	6.0	4.0			
66	Activity 6	2	5	14	6.0	4.0			
67	Activity 7	2	5	14	6.0	4.0			
68	Activity 8	2	5	14	6.0	4.0			
69	Activity 9	2	5	14	6.0	4.0			
70							Standard deviation		
71	Project totals				54.0	36.0	6.0		
72	Check sums	18	45	126	54.0				

The test data should try to avoid 0s and 1s because they do special things that might mask errors. For example, 1^2 is 1 while 2^2 is 4. If there were a mistake in squaring the standard deviation to compute the variance, it would not be visible if the standard deviation was 1. In test data, use numbers that change things. A number added to 0 or multiplied by 1, does not.

A strong set of test data can be checked by hand. This model has four tricky equations that can be verified by inspection when a strong set of initial data is applied. The numbers 2 and 14 are the smallest positive whole numbers (larger than one) that yield a standard deviation that is a whole number bigger than 1. A 5 is the smallest whole number between 2 and 14 that yields a whole number for the expected value. A 9 is the smallest number of tasks that yields a project standard deviation different from the task standard deviation.

If you write your introduction as you write your model, you will have an extra check on your thinking and you will be able to start your editing early. As you continue your work, you should pause and edit. Rewrite your words when they need it—don't put off the rewriting until the last minute.

Never release a spreadsheet for use until you have read the whole thing on paper. Paper is quiet. Paper is large. Paper allows your eye to range over the entirety of the model. Paper gives your common sense a chance to engage the model's results in a dialogue.

After you feel you have completed your model, allow someone else to test it and to proofread it. Listen to his or her responses and revise your work accordingly. Your final model will be better for it.

Rule 13: Keep It Visible

A finished model must be written for the reader of the printed version. Since the decision to use the model is often based on the printed version, it is critically important that the model make all the facts available to the reader. The model must keep the information visible.

Spreadsheets allow a number of things to be hidden. Formulas and formats lurk behind numbers. Constants can hide in formulas. Named ranges can lie waiting in the framework and never be explained. Graphs can hang on models and not be revealed to the reader. For the on-line user of a simple spreadsheet, these hidden concerns may be only an annoyance. But for the off-line reader of a completed model all these concerns matter a great deal.

As you work on your model, ask yourself, "How will the reader (not the user) know this?" Answer the question by making the idea visible. Tricky formulas can be explained. Unusual formats can be described. Some created names can be included in the table of contents and others can be collected in an alphabetical index. Graphs can be listed at the beginning of the graphing section.

Excel's ability to include notes can extend the help you offer an on-line reader. Notes have two disadvantages: The reader must locate them by row and column address, and they are not visible on the spreadsheet. If information is critical to the understanding of your spreadsheet, place it on the spreadsheet itself, not in a note. If you include notes in your spreadsheet, be sure to print them out and keep them with the final copy of the spreadsheet.

If you seriously try to create a model whose printed version you can read and understand, you will succeed in keeping your ideas visible. A great many models fail because their authors wrote for the user of the model and not for the reader of the model. The user is important and you are not forgetting him or her when you write for the reader. In fact, quite the contrary: If you write for the reader, you will help the user as well. The user is also a reader and any time saved by reading the facts rather than discovering them embedded in the model will speed the model's productive use.

Rule 14: Space the Spreadsheet for Easy Reading

Smooth the path for the reader's eye. Make it easy for him or her to peruse your model. Space paragraphs. Wherever possible, use space between rows or columns rather than lines. Use initial capital letters followed by lower-case letters in most titles. When you use lines or double lines to separate items, make the ink a symbol of something important: The models in this book use a single line to border the bottom of an area, and a double line to border the bottom of a spreadsheet (or a submodel).

Strong

	A	B	C	D	E
15	Model				
16					
17					
18				(Bottom of area)	
21	Report				
22					
23					
24					
25				(Bottom of spreadsheet)	
28					

An area begins with a boldfaced title in the upper left-hand corner, sometimes includes blank rows (5 points high in Excel 2.2 on the Macintosh), and concludes with a single line between two blank rows (again, each 5 points high).

In general, keep models to the left side of the page where the reader expects to begin a new area or a new paragraph. Most of the models in this book are arranged vertically so that the next section of a model appears below the current one. This vertical arrangement makes it easier to conclude a paragraph with a blank line and an area with a single line.

A note of caution about spacing: Spacing within the body of a block of numbers in the model area should be included late in the model's development. When you revise a model and try to copy a formula down an interrupted column or try to connect a graphing area to a model with an interrupted row you will notice the inconvenience of the inserted spaces.

If you do insert spaces into the body of a block of numbers—say at every fifth line to make the numbers easier to read—do it just before you put the model to bed.

Weak (easy to work with)

	A	B	C	D	E
1	123	456	789	111	222
2	987	654	321	999	333
3	888	777	666	999	444
4	222	444	666	888	111
5	432	543	654	765	876
6	123	345	234	234	543
7	765	345	987	234	765
8	234	123	544	235	654
9	123	456	123	554	342
10	453	765	675	876	786
11	987	786	654	543	432
12	234	432	543	666	777
13	888	999			

Strong (easy to read)

	A	B	C	D	E
1	123	456	789	111	222
2	987	654	321	999	333
3	888	777	666	999	444
4	222	444	666	888	111
5					
6	432	543	654	765	876
7	123	345	234	234	543
8	765	345	987	234	765
9	234	123	544	235	654
10	123	456	123	554	342
11					
12	453	765	675	876	786
13	987	786	654	543	432
14	234	432	543	666	777
15	888	999			

The inserted lines literally give the eye a much needed break. The lines also allow the reader to count the data quickly. The strong example reveals that the numbers are arrayed in 13 lines.

When you wake the model up for a different day's work:

1. Remove the blank lines to reestablish the contiguous blocks of numbers.

2. Do your work—inserting new rows, deleting old columns, and copying formulas across and down.

3. Reinsert blank lines at the end of the session.

Your Own Reader

More than all but the most hardened user, you will be the reader of your own spreadsheets. If you begin with a careful design and test your results, and if you keep your ideas visible and are kind to the reader's eye, you will greatly speed your own work. This speed is the consequence of being kind to yourself, to your own mind's eye.

4

Other Functions, Other Forms

THREE WISE MEN OF GOTHAM
Three wise men of Gotham
Went to sea in a bowl;
If the bowl had been stronger
My song had been longer.

The basic three-part spreadsheet—Introduction, Initial Data Area, and Model Area—can only go so far. As you work with spreadsheets, a variety of quite complex tasks will require different actions and additional areas on your spreadsheets. You will need other forms for other functions.

Rule 15: Give a New Function a New Area

The esthetic of larger spreadsheets is that distinct activities deserve distinct areas on the spreadsheet. This does not always happen because some people do not know how to keep a large number of regions under control with a table of contents and a map. Others think it is too much extra work to put into a "simple" spreadsheet. Most still do not understand how important it is to make a model easy to modify later.

As soon as someone suggests that a model should be easy to modify, giving a new function a new area becomes a reasonable idea. If modification means a change in some function, then the part to change is easy to locate: It is the area where the current function is done. When you want to alter a report, you go to the report area. When you wish to change a graph, you modify the graph and perhaps the graphing area in the spreadsheet. When you want to alter a macro, you go to a macro sheet and then revise the macro area on the spreadsheet. Giving a new function a new area is a simple way to let form follow function.

When this idea was applied to computer programs in the early 1970s, experience showed that the programs could be modified in half the time. Because modifying programs accounted for 80 percent of the cost of programming, cutting this cost in half represented an overall saving of 40 percent of the effort in working with a computer program! Applying this lesson to your spreadsheets will save you a great deal of time and effort.

A table of contents from a project management spreadsheet shows how powerful this idea can be in practice.

Strong

	A	B	C	D	E
5	Contents				
7	Introduction Input area				
8	Initial data				
9	Report area				
10	Report on budgeted project by task				
11	Report on budgeted project by week				
12	Report on budgeted project by worker				
13	Report on actual project to date by task				
14	Report on actual project to date by week				
15	Report on actual project to date by worker				
16	Report of budget versus actual, by week, worker, and task				
17	Graphing Area				
18	Project budgeted versus actual				
19	Bar chart of workers actual				
20	Macro Sheet and Area				
21	Queries on the database				
22	Choosing a report to print				
23	Project database				

You can see from the contents alone where new functions grow in new areas. These areas address two kinds of functions. First, the generic behavior of the spreadsheet leads to areas such as database, graphics, and macros. Second, within these areas, the requirements of business require special places for a particular report or a special graph. The table of contents shows that the project database is at the bottom of the spreadsheet. The information in the database is collected in a series of reports. The Graphing Area collects those items that need to be graphed. The Macro Sheet and Area lists those macros contained on an accompanying macro sheet.

If someone needs a different report on workers and their actual accomplishments, you know right where to go to begin your work: the "Report on actual project to date by worker." (If the Report Area fully documents its ties to other areas, you will also know if you must explore the Graphing Area and the Macro Sheet and Area for related details.)

If the need arises to revise one of the charts or graphs that this spreadsheet produces, you will know to look in the Graphing Area. If a new week's data arrives, you know where to go to enter it in the database. Because the spreadsheet grew new business functions (the reports) in new areas, when the business need changes, the spreadsheet will change in the appropriate area.

A final note on major and minor function. The dominating assumption in the foregoing discussion is that the whole spreadsheet was devoted to one major business function. If, in the course of combining activities in one physical spreadsheet, you find two or more distinct business functions, subordinate spreadsheet function to business function.

Weak   *Strong*

	A	B	C	D	E	F
25	Contents			Contents		
27	Introduction			Introduction		
28	Verify area			Verify area		
29	Initial data			Submodel for business function 1		
30	Data for business function 1			Initial data		
31	Data for business function 2			Model area		
32	Model area			Report A		
33	Model of business function 1			Graphing area		
34	Model of business function 2			Chart A		
35	Report area			Chart B		
36	Report A on business function 1			Macro A		
37	Report B on business function 2					
38	Report C on business function 2			Submodel for business function 2		
39	Graphing area			Initial data		
40	Chart A on business function 1			Model area		
41	Chart B on business function 1			Report area		
42	Chart C on business function 2			Report B		
43	Chart D on business function 2			Report C		
44	Macro area			Graphing Area		
45	Macro A on business function 1			Chart C		
46	Macro B on business function 2			Chart D		
47				Macro B		

Business function is more important than spreadsheet function because changes in business function drive changes in your spreadsheets. (Only rarely will changes in spreadsheets drive changes in business.) To modify a spreadsheet quickly, it should be organized to respond to changes in business function.

Remember that Excel will allow you to link spreadsheets. You may use these spreadsheets to give a new function not just a new area, but a new sheet. (Macros must always appear on a separate macro sheet.)

NOTE: Because cell references do not dynamically adjust between spreadsheets, using cell references across sheets should be avoided. References that have **names**, however, are dynamically adjusted between sheets. So if you use more than one spreadsheet, **always use names for cells on other spreadsheets**. Later, if you insert or delete a row or a column, the references on the other sheet will adjust automatically and continue to point to the correct section. (See Chapter 5, The Submodel, for more details on how to construct robust, independent subsections of spreadsheets.)

Rule 16: Report to Your Reader

The purpose of a report is to communicate as clearly and concisely as possible with a particular reader. Think about your reader as you fashion the report. If he or she is interested in your report, you may put the important points last; if not, put them first. If a reader likes to know when the report was made, include the date and time. If the reader is already familiar with a certain style, or layout, present the information in that style. Remember that if the reader does not read the report, he or she won't receive the information you wish to convey. Your report should arrest the eye, engage the attention, and win the conviction of your reader.

If you allow yourself a region for each report, you will give yourself the elbow room you need to fashion crisp, appropriate, compelling reports. If you try to format one basic model to please all your readers, you may end up pleasing none.

What you say and how you say it will vary with whom you wish to say it to. Nevertheless, here are two short lists to help you remember some essentials.

Report style:

1. Lay it out in a familiar style: Conform to department practices.

2. Lay it out in an appealing style.

3. Use typographic variation for emphasis.

4. Group numbers that must be compared.

5. Abbreviate numbers to their useful level of significance.

6. Go from row causes to column effects.

7. Work from left to right—the way the reader reads.

8. Have a reader proofread the report for content and format before it becomes official.

Report information:

1. Give a full, accurate title.

2. Include the date and, sometimes, the time.

3. Include where appropriate:

- The name of the company;

- The name of the work group within the company;

- An introduction in plain English;

- References to related graphs, macros, and models; and

- How to contact the author.

Strong

	A	B	C	D	E	F	G	H
1	OUR DEPARTMENT'S QUARTERLY PERFORMANCE							
2	12-Jun-60		*Progress report for MAY (Month 2 of Quarter 2)*					
3			Quarter to date			Until end of quarter		
4		Plan	Actual	Rate		Plan	To go	Rate
5	Sales	58	54.0	93%		79.0	25.0	68%
6	Costs	40.6	39.5	97%		57.8	18.3	68%
7	Profits	17.4	14.5	83%		21.2	6.7	68%
8								
9	We are close to being on target. Let's keep up the good work!							
10	The third month will be a big one. We can make our sales target if we continue							
11	at the level of the last two months. Let's go for it!							
12								

Here's a straightforward report. It is laid out in the style familiar to the department for which it was written. It uses capital and lowercase letters to emphasize the title. In real life it would contain the name of the actual department where it says "OUR DEPARTMENT" now. It has a full, accurate title and it contains the date it was printed. It contains a few words of interpretation and encouragement. The numbers that are being compared are close together and clearly labeled. The numbers have been abbreviated to their useful level of significance.

Most reports are printed without their spreadsheet borders. Here is the first report without its border.

Strong

OUR DEPARTMENT'S QUARTERLY PERFORMANCE						
12-Jun-60		*Progress report for MAY (Month 2 of Quarter 2)*				
		Quarter to date			Until end of quarter	
	Plan	Actual	Rate	Plan	To go	Rate
Sales	58	54.0	93%	79.0	25.0	68%
Costs	40.6	39.5	97%	57.8	18.3	68%
Profits	17.4	14.5	83%	21.2	6.7	68%
We are close to being on target. Let's keep up the good work!						
The third month will be a big one. We can make our sales target if we continue						
at the level of the last two months. Let's go for it!						

The same basic report might appear in different wrapping in different departments. Here are two alternatives (without borders):

Strong

NURSERY KINGDOM   * CONFIDENTIAL INFORMATION ***

Spreadsheet name:	DEPT-BUDG
Last revised:	3 June 1560
Last revised by:	M. Contrary
Date:	12 June 1560
Division:	Outdoor
Dept:	Garden

GARDEN DEPARTMENT'S QUARTERLY PERFORMANCE
PROGRESS FOR MAY (Month 2 of Quarter 2)

	Quarter to date				Until end of quarter		
	Plan	Actual	Rate		Plan	To go	Rate
Sales	58	54.0	93%		79.0	25.0	68%
Costs	40.6	39.5	97%		57.8	18.3	68%
Profits	17.4	14.5	83%		21.2	6.7	68%

The first of these alternatives has a definite form that identifies the company, division, and department who is currently responsible for the results and when the relevant work was performed.

Strong

Outdoor division, Garden Department   **NURSURY KINGDOM**

Printed on:	12 June 1560	DEPT-BUDG	:**Source spreadsheet**
		M. Contrary	:**Last modified by**
		OG5-375566.1	:**Document number**
		Unclassified	:**Classification**

GARDEN DEPARTMENT'S QUARTERLY PERFORMANCE
FOR MONTH OF MAY (Month 2 of Quarter 2)

	Quarter to date				Until end of quarter		
	Plan	Actual	Rate		Plan	To go	Rate
Sales	58	54.0	93%		79.0	25.0	68%
Costs	40.6	39.5	97%		57.8	18.3	68%
Profits	17.4	14.5	83%		21.2	6.7	68%

The second alternative is a form that might be familiar to the reader employed by a federal, state, or local government. Note that this version includes a document number and an explicit location for the classification of the document (unclassified, classified, secret, etc.).

When you work with two-dimensional tables, remember that a person reads **from row causes to column results**. Consider the following table and two possible reports.

Strong

	A	B	C	D	E	F	G	H
24	Model							
25	Observed cell counts							
26			Elves	Fairies	Goblins	Trolls	Total	
27		Unicorns	9	7	2	0	18	
28		Griffins	3	6	9	2	20	
29		Dragons	1	2	5	8	16	
30		Total	13	15	16	10	54	
31								

The model itself betrays a prejudice that mythical beasts pick their mythical masters. When the report from this model is prepared it could look like this:

Strong

18-Nov-90	**PETS CHOOSE THEIR MASTERS**				
	Elves	Fairies	Goblins	Trolls	Total
Unicorns	50%	39%	11%	0%	100%
Griffins	15%	30%	45%	10%	100%
Dragons	6%	13%	31%	50%	100%

Notice that the title of the report asserts the row cause affects the column results, "Pets choose their masters." The percentages are across the page so that the reader can compare the actors, the pets.

The initial information allows an alternative interpretation. Masters could choose their pets. You could assert this by arranging the same data in a different way.

Strong

18-Nov-90	MASTERS CHOOSE THEIR PETS			
	Unicorns	Griffins	Dragons	Total
Elves	69%	23%	8%	100%
Fairies	47%	40%	13%	100%
Goblins	13%	56%	31%	100%
Trolls	0%	20%	80%	100%

Here the reverse assertion is made in the title and supported by the row-cause, column-effect arrangement of the report. Elves greatly prefer unicorns, trolls greatly prefer dragons, fairies are more evenly divided, and goblins have a slight preference for griffins.

Again, the percentages across make it easy to compare between the actors. Here it is clear that Elves will grab unicorns almost as fast as Trolls will choose dragons. Goblins gravitate strongest to griffins. If you wanted to compare effects, you would run percentages down the columns.

Sometimes a report can stand a little help. Here is a report on the current year-to-date selling efficiency that refers to a graph that provides the background of the last 12 month's behavior.

Strong

	A	B	C	D	E	F	G	H
48	12-Jun-90	SALES AND SELLING COSTS						
49		MONTH OF MAY						
51		January	February	March	April	May	June	July
52	Sales	16.00	20.00	21.00	27.00	27.00	0.00	0.00
53	Costs	5.50	5.50	5.50	6.00	6.00	0.00	0.00
54	Costs as % of sales	34%	28%	26%	22%	22%	0%	0%
55	Smoothed(5 mth)*							
56	Sales	21.4	22	22.2	25	27	0	0
57	Costs as % of sales	26%	25%	25%	24%	22%	0%	0%
58								
59	*Next to last month is smoothed over 3 months, last month is unsmoothed.							
60								
61	Note: This report is supported by the graph "Selling costs (%) down slightly in							
62	the last six months"							

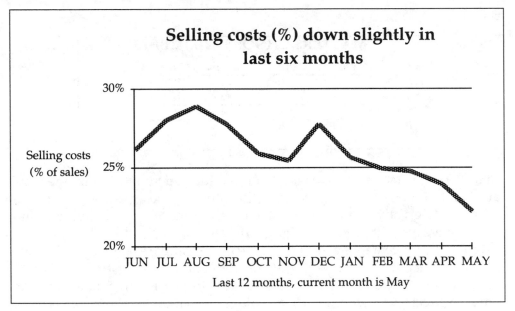

Figure 4-1.

Sometimes a small detail can add a lot to a report. Notice the use of asterisks in the next two examples, the same report in June and again in August.

Strong

10-Jul-35	**PERFORMANCE THROUGH MONTH OF JUNE**							
	Quarterly performance				Half performance		Year	
	***	***	+++	+++	******	++++++	******++++++	
	Qtr 1	Qtr 2	Qtr 3	Qtr 4	Half 1	Half 2	To date	To end
Planned	44	46	54	72	90	126	90	216
Actual	47	44	0	0	91	0	91	91
	---------	---------	---------	---------	---------	---------	---------	---------
Ahead (behind)	3	(2)	--	--	1	--	1	(125)
% of plan	107%	96%	0%	0%	101%	0%	101%	42%

Strong

10-Sep-35	**PERFORMANCE THROUGH MONTH OF AUGUST**							
	Quarterly performance				Half performance		Year	
	***	***	**+	+++	******	**++++	********++++	
	Qtr 1	Qtr 2	Qtr 3	Qtr 4	Half 1	Half 2	To date	To end
Planned	44	46	54	72	90	126	129	216
Actual	47	44	41	0	91	41	132	132
	---------	---------	---------	---------	---------	---------	---------	---------
Ahead (behind)	3	(2)	(13)	--	1	(85)	3	(84)
% of plan	107%	96%	76%	0%	101%	33%	102%	61%

The asterisks reinforce visually how much data are being reported. In June, data for all of the second quarter and the first half (six months) of the year are reported. In August, data for two-thirds of a quarter and two-sixths of the second half (eight months) of the year are reported. The asterisks illustrate what has been completed for the year: through June in the first example and through August in the second example.

A report helps the reader when it provides no more numerical accuracy than is warranted.

Strong

26-Nov-40	**ESTIMATED PROJECT COMPLETION TIME**					
	(Working Days)					
6	Number of activities on the project critical path					
137.5	Project mean completion time (50-50 chance)					
28.0	Project completion time standard deviation					
	PROJECT COMPLETION TIMETABLE					
Time:	54	102	114	123	131	138
Probability:	~0%	10%	20%	30%	40%	50%
Time:	138	144	152	161	173	221
Probability:	50%	60%	70%	80%	90%	~100%

The report includes one decimal place when showing the project mean and standard deviation, but, when it gets to the table of days, the numbers are rounded off to realistic whole days. In a 138-day project, it would be silly to talk about tenths of a day. The extra accuracy in the mean and standard

deviation allows the reader, by consulting a table of normal distribution figures, to verify independently that the calculations in the timetable are correct. The table itself allows the user to see quickly that the job will be done in
138 days, plus or minus 28 days. If the person doing the estimate is new, then
the reader can assume the project will probably run long.

When a report draws on data in more than one submodel, the report area
can become a submodel in its own right. The last submodel in the spreadsheet NEWBUD is a report. (See the discussion in Chapter 5 for a full explanation of the next example.)

Strong

	20-Jan-91
Corporate Financial Ratios	
Asset turnover	1.15
Profit as a % of sales	9.6%
Return on assets	11.0%
Return on equity	16.2%

The report itself is terse. It will be included in an annual report where the
surrounding text will explain the importance of the ratios. Knowing the
context of a report affects what goes into it.

Rule 17: Graph to Illuminate

A graph seeks to shed light on fundamental ideas. Some graphs brilliantly
summarize enormous amounts of data. Some pictorially represent a few
simple numbers for an important reader who must be made aware of the
numbers' importance. Most are concerned with the pattern of things, sales
over time, markets over regions, variables causing other variables to do
something, parts of the whole, or the general line in the cloud of particular
points. A picture, however, is not always worth a thousand words. In fact,
some pictures require a thousand words before they make sense. If you
would have your pictures speak for you, be clear about what you want them
to say.

Your job is to be sure you are presenting the pattern in a way that elicits
the proper response from your reader. An effective graph achieves the appropriate reaction from the reader. A graph is a special kind of report; a short
checklist can help you to remember the essentials:

1. Lay it out in a familiar style: Conform to department practices.

2. Lay it out in an appealing style: Seduce the viewer's eye.

3. Put your major conclusion in your title.

4. Have a reader proofread the graph for content and format before it becomes official.

Because computer graphing allows heretofore difficult graphing to be done quickly and easily, you will find you are pioneering with new forms when you do some of your graphs. If you are breaking new ground, be careful to do a good job with your graphs. Well-received graphs have a way of becoming the standard, and you will help everyone if your candidates for standards are the best possible pictures.

The foundation of a good graph is the appropriate data in the proper arrangement. In order to ensure this arrangement, you should establish a graphing area in your spreadsheets and base your charts and graphs on this area. The effort you expend to set up the area will be repaid in the freedom you achieve to draw the right graph.

Strong

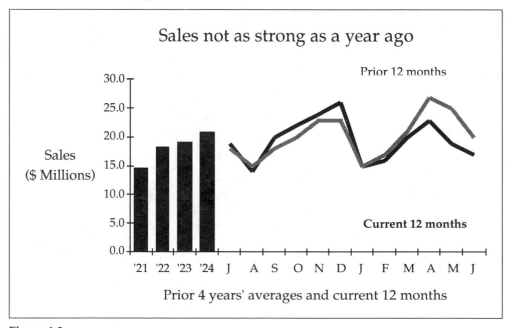

Figure 4-2.

Here's a graph that conveys a large amount of information in a small area. It shows what the most recent 12 months of data are: cyclic in nature with highs in December and April. The long-term trend can be inferred from the past years' bars: Sales are up over several years (1621–1624). A recent problem is highlighted by the comparison with the prior 12-months' data: Recent sales are off. The main point the author wants to make is explicitly stated in the title of the graph: "Sales are not as strong as a year ago."

Strong

	A	B	C	D	E	F	G	H	I	J	K	L	M	N	O	P	Q	R
1	**SALES**		21 July 1625		S. Simon													
2	7-Nov-89	Date printed																
3	® 1989 John M. Nevison																	
5	**Description**																	
6			Sales figures for Simon Corporation				($ Millions)											
8	**To add a new month:**																	
9			1. Add the figure to the raw data for 1625.															
10			2. Erase the left-hand end of the rolling twelve-month table															
11			in the graphing section.															
12			3. Shift the graphing variables to the left one month.															
13			4. Add the new month at the right-hand end of the rolling															
14			twelve-month table.															
15			5. Be sure the graphs are still well defined.															
16			6. Plot the graphs.															
18	**Contents**																	
19			Introduction: title, description, and contents															
20			Initial data															
21			Graphing area															
24	**Initial data**						Months											
25			J	F	M	A	M	J	J	A	S	O	N	D				
27		1621	10	14	16	18	20	16	15	13	11	13	14	15				
28		1622	10	15	19	20	21	20	19	15	17	20	22	21				
29		1623	12	17	19	23	22	19	18	15	18	20	23	23				
30		1624	15	17	21	27	25	20	19	14	20	22	24	26				
31		1625	15	16	20	23	19	17										
34	**Graphing area**																	
35	1. Sales 12 months: last 12, prior 12, and back years' sales figures.																	
36							1st Mth										12th Mth	
37			'21	'22	'23	'24	J	A	S	O	N	D	J	F	M	A	M	J
38	Curr						19	14	20	22	24	26	15	16	20	23	19	17
39	Prior						18	15	18	20	23	23	15	17	21	27	25	20
40			14.6	18.3	19.1	20.8												

By establishing a graphing section, SALES gives you the freedom to do several things. First, you can make a row of labels for the x-axis that appears just the way you want it to. You could alter the labels to be the full names of the months that begin the year's quarters, January, April, July, and October. Because you are working in the graphing section, you know you are not messing up a printed report when you fiddle with the month names.

Second, you can maintain a rolling 12-month graph without disturbing the convenient format of the raw data. A rolling 12-month graph could be a major inconvenience to a person who was maintaining a graph drawn on the raw data. By establishing a graphing area, you allow the data to be manipulated in a convenient way from month to month, so that the spreadsheet can continue being useful after it has been turned over to someone else to use.

Third, you can assemble the information for the average annual bars in exactly the right format for our graphing routine. These average annual bars illustrate how a demanding format for a final graph can be accommodated if you allow yourself the freedom of a separate graphing area. Without the separate graphing area you might not even believe it possible to construct this graph. The separate area allows you to push on the limits of the graphing tools at your disposal.

The next example illustrates that the graphing area may be the home of special calculations necessary to produce the right picture.

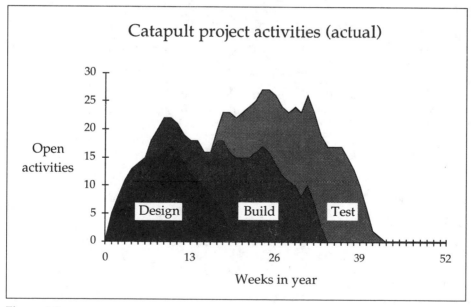

Figure 4-3.

The graph tells a story about building a catapult. Activities were classified as design, build, or test activities. The total number of activities open at any one time was never greater than 27. When the project began, everyone was designing the catapult. In the 6th week, some building activity started. By the 17th week, building was going full swing, a little late design was being finished up, and a little early testing of some components was beginning. Testing and building went on together, with testing becoming the dominant activity by the 33rd week. The last weeks were exclusively given over to completing the testing, which occurred during the 43rd week.

The graph depends on the number of open activities. This number depends in turn upon the difference between the cumulative number of activities opened and closed. The graphing area looks like this:

Strong

	A	B	C	D	E	F	G	H	I	J	K	L	M	N	O	P
55	Graphing area	Graphs supported include:														
56		1. "Open activity"														
57		2. "Total activity"														
58																
59		Cumulative counts														
60	Week number	1	2	3	4	5	6	7	8	9	10	11	12	13	14	15
61	Design activities															
62	Assigned	5	11	18	25	32	40	47	53	59	64	68	72	75	78	81
63	Completed	0	3	7	12	18	25	32	38	43	47	52	58	63	67	71
64	Build activities															
65	Assigned	0	0	0	0	0	0	3	7	12	16	20	25	31	38	43
66	Completed	0	0	0	0	0	0	0	2	6	11	15	20	25	31	37
67	Test activities															
68	Assigned	0	0	0	0	0	0	0	0	0	0	0	0	0	0	0
69	Completed	0	0	0	0	0	0	0	0	0	0	0	0	0	0	0
70	Total activities															
71	Assigned	5	11	18	25	32	40	50	60	71	80	88	97	106	116	124
72	Completed	0	3	7	12	18	25	32	40	49	58	67	78	88	98	108
73																
74																
75	Open activities															
76	Design	5	8	11	13	14	15	15	15	16	17	16	14	12	11	10
77	Build	0	0	0	0	0	0	3	5	6	5	5	5	6	7	6
78	Test	0	0	0	0	0	0	0	0	0	0	0	0	0	0	0
79																
80	Total (check)	5	8	11	13	14	15	18	20	22	22	21	19	18	18	16
81	Week axis label	1												13		

Again, you see how the separate graphing area provides the necessary freedom to arrange the information in an appropriate manner for the proper pictures. The graph names are listed at the beginning of the Graphing Area. Notice that some simple formulas lurk behind the figures in the Graphing Area. The cumulative figure is the prior cumulative figure plus the current week's value. Open activities are the difference between cumulative assigned and cumulative completed. At some point, if the number and complexity of the formulas increased, they might be separated into a Model Area where they could be arranged so they would be easier to understand.

The next graph discloses an underlying pattern not obvious in the raw numbers.

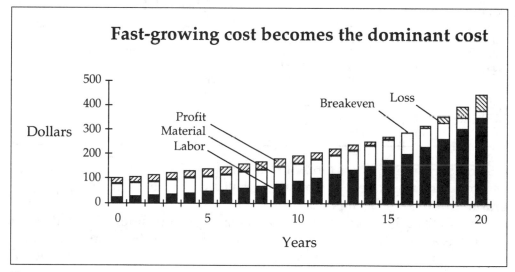

Figure 4-4.

This chart from the model INFLATE shows how the initially small cost—labor—grows to dominate the cost structure of the product. In order to maintain a profit, the price must follow the high growth cost component more closely as it becomes the dominant cost. In the above example, a 6.8 percent price growth rate leads to losses beginning in the seventeenth year. The point of the graph is spelled out in its title, "Fast-growing cost becomes the dominant cost." The pattern that is clear in the graph is hidden in the table of numbers.

	A	B	C	D	E	F	G
85	Graphing Section						
86							
87	YEAR	MATERIAL	LABOR	TOTL COST	PRICE	PROFIT	MARGIN
88	0	56	21	77	100	23	23.0%
89		58	24	82	107	25	23.4%
90		59	28	87	114	27	23.6%
91		61	32	93	122	29	23.6%
92		63	37	100	130	31	23.4%
93	5	65	42	107	139	32	23.0%
94		67	49	115	149	33	22.4%
95		69	56	125	159	34	21.5%
96		71	64	135	170	35	20.3%
97		73	74	147	181	34	18.9%
98	10	75	85	160	194	33	17.3%
99		78	98	175	207	32	15.3%
100		80	112	192	221	29	13.1%
101		82	129	211	236	25	10.5%
102		85	149	233	252	19	7.5%
103	15	87	171	258	270	11	4.2%
104		90	197	286	288	2	0.5%
105		93	226	319	308	-11	-3.6%
106		95	260	355	329	-27	-8.1%
107		98	299	397	351	-46	-13.1%
108	20	101	344	445	375	-70	-18.6%

A reader looking at this table of numbers would stare at it for several days before seeing the pattern of labor costs that leaps to the eye in the graph. The graph illuminates the important idea.

Sometimes a very simple chart can help explain position. The following chart tells a department how things are going two months through the quarter. This information is very interesting to people whose bonuses ride on making the goals.

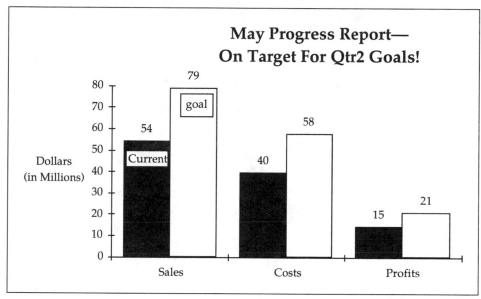

Figure 4-5.

Some readers find it easier to look at legends than to look at labels on the graph. You should choose whichever form suits your reader.

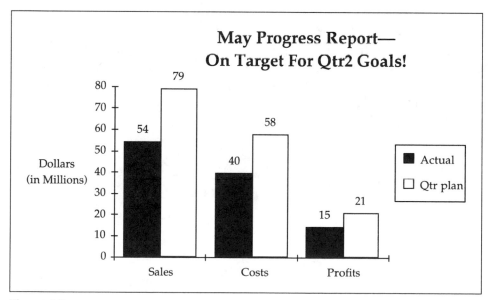

Figure 4-6.

The next example shows how a graph can present a great deal in a small space.

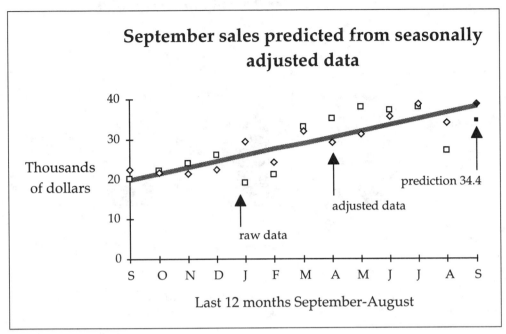

Figure 4-7.

This chart shows the raw data of the last 12 months, the seasonally adjusted data of the same period, the best-fit line to the seasonally adjusted data, the projected value for the next month, and the predicted raw value. It is a good graph because it condenses lots of information into a compact, meaningful whole.

The portion of the graphing area on which the graph was based looks like this:

Strong

	A	B	C	D	E	F	G	H	I	J	K
107	Graph area										
108	1. "Next month's sales"										
109	2. "Seasonal factors"										
110	Next month's sales							Seasonal factors			
111	x-label	x(i)	y(i)	s(i)	Line	s(13)	y(13)	x-label			
113	S	1	20	22.3	20.1			J	0.65	1	
114	O	2	22	21.5	21.6			F	0.87	1	
115	N	3	24	21.2	23.1			M	1.04	1	
116	D	4	26	22.5	24.6			A	1.21	1	
117	J	5	19	29.4	26.2			M	1.22	1	
118	F	6	21	24.1	27.7			J	1.04	1	
119	M	7	33	31.9	29.2			J	0.98	1	
120	A	8	35	29.0	30.7			A	0.79	1	
121	M	9	38	31.2	32.3			S	0.90	1	
122	J	10	37	35.7	33.8			O	1.02	1	
123	J	11	38	38.7	35.3			N	1.13	1	
124	A	12	27	34.1	36.8			D	1.16	1	
125	S	13			38.4	38.4	34.4				

Again you see a list of the graphs by name and a column of labels set up to help the graph. Notice also that the area uses a whole column to get s(13) and y(13) on the graph exactly the way it wants.

Sometimes a large amount of data can be reduced to a series of graphs that tells a story. The next three graphs summarize a model with over 330 equations. The model lets three firms compete for a growing market for ten years. Firm A wants to capture a large share of the market, Firm B wants to preserve its initial one-third of the market, and Firm C is willing to give up share in exchange for a few year's of high prices. All three firms begin at the same place.

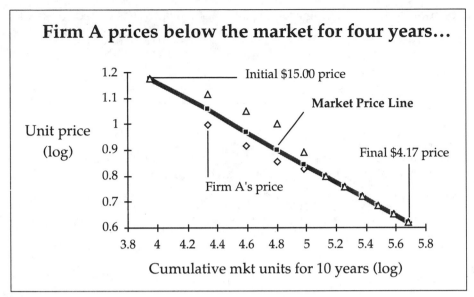

Figure 4-8.

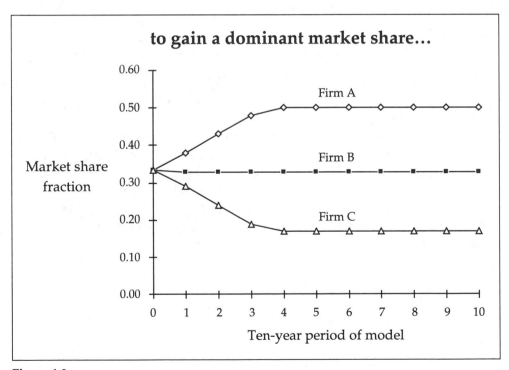

Figure 4-9.

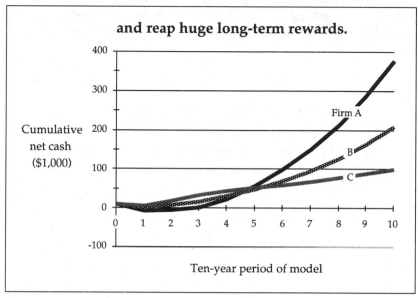

Figure 4-10.

Notice that the first plot uses the logarithms of some data in order to show the price decline as a straight-line function of the cumulative market volume. The place where the logarithms are computed is in the graphing area. If data that you graph can be more clearly revealed if you transform it, the graphing area will give you a place to do your transformations.

Strong

	A	B	C	D	E	F	G	H	I
81	**Graphing area**								
82	1. "Firm A prices below the market" -- three firms' prices over 10 years								
83	2. "To gain a dominant market share" -- three firms' market share over 10 years								
84	3. "And reap huge long-term rewards" -- three firms' 10-year net cash								
85			Price			log(price)		Cumulative	
86		Year	Firm A	Firm B	Firm C	Firm A	Firm B	Firm C	Market	Log(mkt)
87		0	15.00	15.00	15.00	1.18	1.18	1.18	9,000	3.95
88		1	9.93	11.43	13.01	1.00	1.06	1.11	21,600	4.33
89		2	8.25	9.34	11.28	0.92	0.97	1.05	39,240	4.59
90		3	7.21	8.05	10.17	0.86	0.91	1.01	62,172	4.79
91		4	6.87	7.16	8.00	0.84	0.85	0.90	89,690	4.95
92		5	6.47	6.47	6.47	0.81	0.81	0.81	122,712	5.09
93		6	5.91	5.91	5.91	0.77	0.77	0.77	162,339	5.21
94		7	5.44	5.44	5.44	0.74	0.74	0.74	209,891	5.32
95		8	5.04	5.04	5.04	0.70	0.70	0.70	266,953	5.43
96		9	4.68	4.68	4.68	0.67	0.67	0.67	335,428	5.53
97		10	4.36	4.36	4.36	0.64	0.64	0.64	417,597	5.62

The next graph is a summary of information contained in a report shown earlier. The graph of project completion time shows much more about when the project will end.

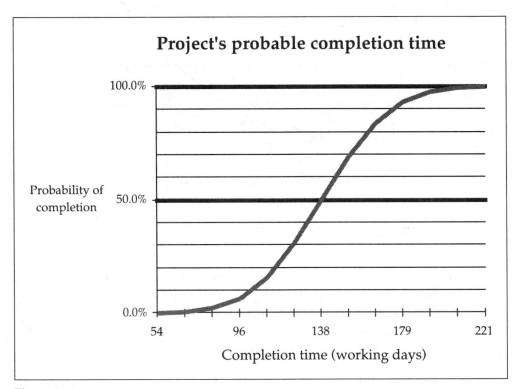

Figure 4-11.

You can see at a glance that if you say you will be done in 179 days, you have more than a 90 percent chance of being right.

Because graphs make extraordinary first impressions, be sure to try out your graph on a real reader. Ask him or her to tell you what the point of the graph is. Revise your graph until it makes a first impression that is both powerful and correct.

Rule 18: Import with Care

When you move data between spreadsheets you are sometimes faced with the dilemma of importing a block of unknown size. A good way to import such a block is to land it on your spreadsheet to the right of your working model. Work imported in this location can be longer and wider than you anticipated and it will not damage your preexisting work. After you have landed the data safely, you may move it to its final resting place in your spreadsheet.

Even if your spreadsheet regularly receives a fixed block of information, set it down in your import area before moving it to its final location. This cautious practice will protect you against an unannounced change in size and give you a chance to catch someone else's oversight before it affects your work.

Because the import area is a temporary staging area for information destined to be moved elsewhere on your spreadsheet, it usually consists of two cells.

Strong

	G	H
1	Import area	
2		
3	XXXXXXXXXX	

The XX cell is where you anchor the upper-left corner of the block. After you have moved the new information to its final resting place, erase any leftovers and reenter the XXs before you knock off work for the day. Leave the area as clean as you found it.

Rule 19: Verify Critical Work

When you build large models, you will want to prove to yourself that everything is functioning properly. To be sure of your spreadsheet, you must verify critical work. A good way to guard against error is to build the model defensively by incorporating checks wherever possible.

A second reason to verify critical work is that you will want to be sure that any change you make in your program—changing a formula in the fifth column, erasing the fourth row, adding a new constant to the initial data—does not alter the important work of the model.

Verifying critical work springs from an attitude that has its roots in fourteenth century Italian traders who invented double-entry bookkeeping to be sure their accounts were in order. A modern-day accountant continues to ask whether the figures double-check. Did you add the correct number of items? Was the sum correct? Did the row totals agree with the column totals? Was any number out of bounds by being either too large or too small?

In a spreadsheet model you can ask these questions by employing a defensive formula like this:

(If everything is okay, Print the answer, Otherwise print "error")

This expression can take many forms.

Weak   **Strong**

	A	B
200		
201	Postive number	Postive number
202	=A67	=IF(A67>=0,A67,"ERR")
203		
204	Monthly salary	Monthly salary
205	=B20	=IF(AND(B20>=1000,B20<=30000),B20,"ERR")
206		
207	Grand total of A1..S99	Grand Total of A1..S99
208	=SUM(A1:S99)	=IF(SUM(T1:T98)=SUM(A100:S100),SUM(A1:S99),"ERR")
209		
210		
211	Sum of 100 Entries	Sum of 100 Entries
212	where the value 100 is in cell A5	where the value 100 is in cell A5
213	=SUM(A55:A207)	=IF(COUNT(A55:A207)=A5,SUM(A55:A207),"ERR")
214		

You may think of these defensive formulas as warning lights. The positive number warning turns to error when the number goes negative. The monthly salary warning goes off when someone makes less than $12,000 a year or more than $360,000 a year. The grand total warning is triggered if the column of row totals does not cross-check with the row of column totals. The sum of a fixed number (100) of entries is wrong if there are not exactly the right number of entries. (The fixed number is an initial datum stored in A5.)

Be careful with checks of equality and cross-checked sums in particular. Sometimes two sums will not be equal because of computer round-off error. The two totals will differ by a tiny amount that you will only see if you subtract the one quantity from the other. The difference may be as small as .00000000001. The safe way to ask if two numbers are equal is to ask if they differ by an insignificant amount. Because you won't know which is the bigger number, you should ask about the absolute value of the difference. If the absolute value of the difference is less than a tiny number, the numbers are "equal." The way to say that in a spreadsheet formula is:

If (absolute value(sum − check sum) < .000001,

  print sum, print "error")

Strong

	T
100	=IF(ABS(SUM(T1:T98)-SUM(A100:S100))<0.000001,SUM(A1:S99),"ERR")
101	Grand Total of A1:S99

The strong formula works in all cases where the difference is less than one part in a million. You may need to experiment to determine what small number is appropriate to your spreadsheet. If you are at all unsure what to use, ask someone who knows about computer round-off errors to help you.

You may be interested in only the relative error between two numbers. The formula for making sure the error is less that a tenth of a percent is:

If (absolute value(1 – (sum/check sum)) < .001,

 print sum, print "error")

In a large model, after you have established your warning lights, you may find it convenient to collect some of the critical lights into a "control panel" that will let you know quickly whether or not any of your warning lights have been set off. You may do this by establishing a Verify Area.

Strong

	A	B	C	D	E	F
14	Verify area					
15						
16	34470496 The model verification sum					
17						
18	If an error appears here, check below and then the appropriate area of the model.					
19	(Be sure you have recalculated the whole model.)					
20						
21	347000 The raw data cross-check					
22	666352 The model cross-check					
23	344 The number of items in the report					
24	33456777 The sum of all the checked values in the database					
25	23 The number of graphed periods					

This Verify Area collects several warning lights in one place. If a cross-check fails, an "error" appears in the individual listing and in the model verification sum. The verification sum is a nonsense number that uses the sum function as a quick way to detect if any item in the sum has gone bad.

Strong

	A	B	C	D	E	F
14	Verify area					
15						
16	#REF! The model verification sum					
17						
18	If an error appears here, check below and then the appropriate area of the model.					
19	(Be sure you have recalculated the whole model.)					
20						
21	347000 The raw data cross-check					
22	666352 The model cross-check					
23	#REF! The number of items in the report					
24	33456777 The sum of all the checked values in the database					
25	23 The number of graphed periods					

In the above example, the verify sum model check is flashing "error." The individual item is from the report area. When you go to the Report Area, you will see the "error" warning there and you may correct the problem. Notice that the directions for the Verify Area include a reminder to recalculate the model before assuming that the warning lights are valid.

If you know of other corrective actions for your model, include them in the Verify Area.

Rule 20: Control All Macros

A macro can be a source of convenient help or a burden of confusing clutter. It is intended to help save typing time by allowing you to abbreviate several keystrokes to a single keystroke. A macro also allows the author of a model to simplify things for the eventual user. (If you do not understand macros, consult the Excel Reference Manual or the on-line help.)

How much you engage in writing macros is directly related to who will be using the spreadsheet and how you want them to use it. On the one hand, a macro can make possible an application that might otherwise be too time consuming. On the other hand, a macro must be expressed in a sloppy programming language that is fraught with perils. A macro will be useful only if you keep it under strict control.

The first level of control you should exhibit over macros is when to write one. Write as few macros as necessary. If you have a choice of making the spreadsheet clearer for the reader by documenting a feature or automating it with a macro, document it. Macros are hard to read; documentation is easy. The likelihood that the model will be reusable is much higher if you are clearly communicating with your reader.

The second level of control is to collect the macros you write in an area devoted to macros. Excel takes care of this by insisting that your macros be written on a separate macro sheet. Because they appear on their own sheet, you have plenty of room to surround your macros with appropriate comment.

The third level of control is the documentation you bring to the macro. Macros are a frightfully terse form of expression. This imbues them with great power, but also with great mystery. Understanding your own work and explaining what you did to a second reader, requires careful attention to the detail of your comment.

In the examples below, the word "statement" is intended to be a place-holder for real macro statements that the author of a full macro could insert at those points. The macro itself illustrates the logical structure you should employ when dealing with an "If...Then...Else" structure.

Weak

	A	B
3		IfTrial
4		=ARGUMENT("Var")
5		=ARGUMENT("Hur")
6		Not over the hurdle
7		=IF((NOT(Var>Hur)),GOTO(B12))
8		statement
9		=SET.VALUE(B6,"Over the hurdle")
10		statement
11		=GOTO(B16)
12		statement
13		statement
14		=SET.VALUE(B6,"Not over the hurdle")
15		statement
16		statement
17		=RETURN(B6)

Strong

	A	B
19	IfTrial	• This macro demonstrates an "If...Then...Else" structure
20		• It asks the question "Is the variable bigger than the hurdle?"
21		=ARGUMENT("Var")
22		=ARGUMENT("Hur")
23	Result3	Not over the hurdle
24	Iff1	=IF((NOT(Var>Hur)),GOTO(Else1))
25		statement
26		=SET.VALUE(Result3,"Over the hurdle")
27		statement
28		=GOTO(Endif1)
29	Else1	•
30		statement
31		=SET.VALUE(Result3,"Not over the hurdle")
32		statement
33	Endif1	•
34	IfTrialEnd	=RETURN(Result3)

The documentation here consists of both name labels in column A and embedded comments in the actual macro. Every name in the first column labels the cell to its immediate right in the B column. For example, B19 has the name IfTrial. **Always** put the cell name label in the cell to the left of the one that is named. Because you need left-hand name labels, the macro itself usually goes down column B. In addition to the name labels, explanatory comments can be placed in column B. When an extended remark is necessary, it can be placed on several lines in the B column, or in Column C.

The weak and strong examples also show why it is a good idea to refer to other locations by name, not by location. In the strong example, the names gives a strong indication of purpose and, because they are clearly displayed in column A, they make locating things easy for the reader. In the weak example, the reader is left to figure out the obscure purpose of B6 on his or her own; in the strong example, it is labeled Result3 (the 3 will be explained below).

The strong example also illustrates the fourth, fifth, and sixth levels of control. It keeps each line of macros short to aid both comprehension and editing. There is only one command on each line. The example distinguishes commands (UPPERCASE) from areas acted upon (lowercase). You should use names for all areas on the sheet, both other locations and (not shown here) to refer to the parent spreadsheet. Names preserve your freedom to move areas on the spreadsheet because names move dynamically while cell references do not.

A seventh level of control is to keep the macro area under lock and key. The consequences of the inadvertent alteration of a single cell in this region can be calamitous. Always keep your macro sheets protected.

The weak versus strong in the next example shows the cumulative effect of the above rules. Both versions do exactly the same thing. Only the strong version could be used by a second user, or conveniently modified for extended reuse.

Weak

	A	B
1		**EXPT.Macro**
3		IfTrial
4		=ARGUMENT("Var")
5		=ARGUMENT("Hur")
6		Not over the hurdle
7		=IF((NOT(Var>Hur)),GOTO(B12))
8		statement
9		=SET.VALUE(B6,"Over than hurdle")
10		statement
11		=GOTO(B16)
12		statement
13		statement
14		=SET.VALUE(B6,"Not over the hurdle")
15		statement
16		statement
17		=RETURN(B6)
20		ForLoopTrial
21		=ARGUMENT("Lim")
22		12
23		=SET.VALUE(B27,0)
24		=FOR("LoopVariable",1,Lim,1)
25		statement
26		statement
27		=B27+1
28		statement
29		statement
30		=NEXT()
31		=SET.VALUE(B22,B27)
32		=RETURN(B22)

(continued)

	A	B
35		WhileLoopTrial
36		=ARGUMENT("Lim")
37		12
38		=SET.VALUE(B44,0)
39		=SET.VALUE(B46,Lim)
40		=WHILE(B46>0)
41		statement
42		statement
43		statement
44		=B44+1
45		statement
46		=B46-1
47		=NEXT()
48		=SET.VALUE(B37,B44)
49		=RETURN(B37)
52		Subroutine1
53		statement
54		statement
55		statement
56		=RETURN()

Strong

	A	B
1		**EXPT.Macro**
2		6 September 1989 John M. Nevison
3		(C) Copyright 1989 by John M. Nevison
4		
5		**Description**
6		Hold in one place all the macros that the spreadsheet EXPT uses.
7		
8		**Reference**
9		For further directions, see the spreadsheet EXPT.
10		
11		**Contents**
12		Macro Names (with arguments) Keystroke for command
14		IfTrial (Variable, Hurdle) -none-
15		ForLoopTrial (Limit) -none-
16		WhileLoopTrial (Limit) -none-

(continued)

	A	B
19	IfTrial	• This macro demonstrates an "If...Then...Else" structure
20		• It asks the question "Is the variable bigger than the hurdle?"
21		=ARGUMENT("Var")
22		=ARGUMENT("Hur")
23	Result3	Not over the hurdle
24	Iff1	=IF((NOT(Var>Hur)),GOTO(Else1))
25		statement
26		=SET.VALUE(Result3,"Over than hurdle")
27		statement
28		=GOTO(Endif1)
29	Else1	•
30		statement
31		=SET.VALUE(Result3,"Not over the hurdle")
32		statement
33	Endif1	•
34	IfTrialEnd	=RETURN(Result3)
37	ForLoopTrial	• Count every time the "For" loop is passed through
38		=ARGUMENT("Lim")
39	Result1	12
40		=SET.VALUE(PassCount,0)
41	For1	=FOR("LoopVariable",1,Lim,1)
42		statement
43		statement
44	PassCount	=PassCount+1
45		statement
46		statement
47	Fnext1	=NEXT()
48		=SET.VALUE(Result1,PassCount)
49	ForTrialEnd	=RETURN(Result1)
52	WhileLoopTrial	• Count every time the "While" loop is passed through
53		=ARGUMENT("Lim")
54	Result2	12
55		=SET.VALUE(PassCount1,0)
56		=SET.VALUE(WhileCount,Lim)
57	While1	=WHILE(WhileCount>0)
58		statement
59		statement
60		statement
61	PassCount1	=PassCount1+1
62		statement
63	WhileCount	=WhileCount-1
64	Wnext1	=NEXT()
65		=SET.VALUE(Result2,PassCount1)
66	WhileLpTrialEnd	=RETURN(Result2)

(continued)

	A	B
69	Subroutine1	• This macro illustrates a blank subroutine
70		statement
71		statement
72		statement
73	Subend1	=RETURN()

Notice that both the macro sheet and the Macro Area on the spreadsheet (see example below) contain a table of contents. If you add a new macro to your model every day, these twin tables of contents help you find the correct macro.

Macros and Computer Programming

A fundamental result of computer science is that you can write every computer program with three logical forms: sequence, decision, and repetition. Every macro proceeds down the spreadsheet until it encounters a blank line which forces it to stop (sequence). The above example, by illustrating the programming structures IF...THEN...ELSE (decision) and DO...WHILE (repetition), demonstrates that you can write regular computer programs with macro instructions.

The name "If" was changed to "Iff" to avoid conflicting with the Excel function "IF."

By relying on Excel macro functions, you can reduce the chances for careless mistakes. Repetition structures should let the language do the counting by using a FOR loop. Should you need a loop to go on for a long time until some condition is met, use a WHILE loop.

The strong examples all illustrate another feature of good programming: Each logical form has a single beginning cell and a single ending cell. This enables these forms to appear in a sequence, do their work, and return to the sequence when they are done. The sequence could be inside a repetition or inside a branch of a decision. These forms can be embedded inside one another to create larger forms. Decisions can occur inside loops, and loops can occur inside branches of a decision. If you were to make repeated use of an IF structure, the first set of names could be Iff1, Else1, and Endif1. The second structure could begin Iff2, and so on. Note that similar result cells are named "Result1," "Result2," and "Result3."

In the strong examples, the names that have to do with programming structures are on the **left** side of the A column; the simple names of cells, are on the right. This custom allows the experienced user to follow indentation schemes for program structure that are familiar to all experienced computer programmers. The example illustrates how indentation is used to indicate the nested control of the logical flow.

The strong example uses function arguments to pass information and to keep the macro independent of the spreadsheet. These sample functions could be put in a toolkit that many spreadsheets could draw upon. Many spreadsheets will probably refer to two macro sheets: the one with generic functions and commands, the other with functions and commands especially built for the particular spreadsheet.

The actual spreadsheet that uses the macros looks like this.

Strong

	A	B	C	D	E	F	G	H
1	**EXPT (Experiment)**		6 September 1989 John M. Nevison					
2	(C) Copyright 1989 by John M. Nevison							
3	11-Sep-89	Date printed						
5	Description							
6		EXPT is an experiment designed to show off a						
7		sound logical form for macros.						
9	References							
10		Macro Sheet EXPT.Macro						
11								
12		John M. Nevison, Excel Spreadsheet Design,						
13		New York, NY: Brady Books, 1990.						
15	To use							
16		While studying a copy of EXPT.Macro, vary the values of						
17		the variables in the initial data below and watch the						
18		values of the macro functions change.						
20	Contents							
21		Introduction: title, description, contents						
22		Initial data						
23		Model						
24		Macro area						

(continued)

	A	B	C	D	E	F	G	H
27	Initial data							
28			Variables (alphabetical order)					
29		10	Hurdle					
30		12	Limit					
31		6	Variable					
34	Model							
35								
36	The "If...then...else" trial							
37	The function version of the macro		=EXPT.Macro!IfTrial(Variable,Hurdle)					
38	The value of the macro		Not over the hurdle					
39	The "For" loop trial							
40	The function version of the macro		=EXPT.Macro!ForLoopTrial(Limit)					
41	The value of the macro		12.00					
42	The "While" loop trial							
43	The function version of the macro		=EXPT.Macro!WhileLoopTrial(Limit)					
44	The value of the macro		12.00					
47	Macro area							
49	Macro Sheets	Macro Names (with arguments)			Keystroke for command			
51	EXPT.Macro							
52		IfTrial (Variable, Hurdle)			-none-			
53		ForLoopTrial (Limit)			-none-			
54		WhileLoopTrial (Limit)			-none-			

The spreadsheet uses these macros as functions in the model area, but takes the space in the Macro Area to document them completely.

If you must write a lot of macros, be sure to consult a good book on Excel macros (see References at the back of this book). You should extend your control over macros by learning as much as you can about what computer programmers call structured programming and be able to apply it to writing your macros. If you find yourself writing many large macros, see a professional programmer for help.

With macros you can also construct your own custom menus and dialog boxes. Because menus give you a way to write documentation that is familiar to the user, an eighth level of control over macros is to place the macros themselves on a menu. The first choice in the above example might be "IfTrial;" the second choice, "ForLoopTrial;" the third, "WhileLoopTrial." Consult your Excel Reference Manual for further details.

Should you find yourself this deeply involved in writing macros, seriously consider hiring a professional to help you with this part of your spreadsheet. Carefully distinguish between those macros you need and those you wish you needed. Always, always control your macros.

Rule 21: Focus the Model's Activity

Sometimes a model is written so that a user can systematically vary one of the initial variables and observe the effects on a critical result that is at the far end of the spreadsheet. To look at both numbers easily, the spreadsheet may be split into two windows. If, however, several widely dispersed results must be examined, the window solution becomes inconvenient. The way to resolve this problem is to define a new area, the Active Area. Treat the Active Area like an animated report that focuses the model's activity.

The Active Area is a dynamic area that collects in one place both the initial data to be manipulated and the final results to be watched. It should be attractively formatted to be easy to use.

Before beginning the day's activity, the author (or the user) can move the original initial data to the Active Area and leave behind formulas in the Initial Data Area that point to the Active Area. The user may then go to the Active Area, vary the initial variables to his or her heart's content, print out appropriate findings (the Active Area has been set up like a Report Area so the results are printable), and think about his or her findings. When the user is done, he or she restores the initial data to the original Initial Data Area (or throws away the active version of the spreadsheet) and quits for the day.

Strong

	A	B	C	D	E	F
195	Active area					
196						
197	MANPOWER COVERAGE OF SCHEDULED WORK FOR NEXT FOUR QUARTERS					
198		3 July 1586				
199		23 Manpower available at end of current quarter				
200		2 Current quarter number				
201						
202	Scheduled work covered by current manpower					
203	Quarter	Work covered (%)				
204	3	87				
205	4	65				
206	5	110				
207	6	120				

Here the user changes the number of people available and the quarter when they are available to see what percentage of the upcoming scheduled work will be covered. The user might decide to get more people and want to see what effect it has on the project:

Strong

	A	B	C	D	E	F
210	Active area					
211	MANPOWER COVERAGE OF SCHEDULED WORK FOR NEXT FOUR QUARTERS					
212	3 July 1586					
213	25 Manpower available at end of current quarter					
214	2 Current quarter number					
215						
216	Scheduled work covered by current manpower					
217	Quarter	Work covered (%)				
218	3	92				
219	4	75				
220	5	130				
221	6	150				

Strong

	A	B	C	D	E	F
224	Active area					
225	MANPOWER COVERAGE OF SCHEDULED WORK FOR NEXT FOUR QUARTERS					
226	3 July 1586					
227	30 Manpower available at end of current quarter					
228	2 Current quarter number					
229						
230	Scheduled work covered by current manpower					
231	Quarter	Work covered (%)				
232	3	102				
233	4	90				
234	5	160				
235	6	175				

From these trials the user chooses the last as a reasonable alternative. Note that this active area probably depends on a large, elaborately scheduled model that integrates all the projects the group is working on.

As a general rule, the model should be saved with the initial data in the Initial Data Area. If, however, a particular spreadsheet only exists to perform an Active Area chore, then the spreadsheet might be profitably rearranged with the Active Area at the top:

Strong

	A	B	C	D
5	Contents			
6		Introduction		
7		Active area		
8		Initial data		
9		Supporting model		
10		Occasional report		
11		Rarely used graphing area		

This arrangement provides the user with the convenience of quickly getting to the Work Area. The Active Area might also be saved in its active state. (But a note to warn the user should also be included in the Initial Data Area. For example, "WARNING: Some of the initial data are controlled from the Active Area.")

Strong

	A	B	C	D	E	F
33	**Active area**					
34						
35	GNP Growth, Unemployment, and Inflation as a Function					
36	of Monetary Growth(M1) and Fiscal Control(Natl. Debt).				15 Sept 1986	
37						
38		Year 1	Year 2	Year 3	Year 4	Year 5
39	M1 growth	10.0%	15.0%	13.0%	11.0%	8.0%
40	Natl. Debt ($B)	240	160	90	60	0
41						
42	GNP growth	4.6%	7.6%	5.1%	3.2%	0.0%
43	Unemployment	6.7%	4.9%	4.3%	4.8%	6.8%
44	Inflation	4.6%	5.2%	7.5%	6.1%	4.5%

This is an Active Area that a policy maker can use to manipulate different assumptions about the monetary (M1) growth rate and the national debt to see the effects on gross national product (GNP), unemployment, and inflation. The supporting spreadsheet may well contain pages of calculations, several different kinds of reports, and many charts and graphs. But what the policy maker needs to see, and occasionally needs to print out, are two key assumptions and three critical results. The Active Area provides just what is needed.

The impulse behind the Active Area is to give a casual user an easy way to manipulate the spreadsheet. If you pursue this impulse very far, you will find yourself using macros to prepare for the user, to guide the user through certain tasks, and to help the user end the session gracefully. You should consult a book on writing and using macros for help and guidance. If you combine the macro methods you learn there with well-structured spreadsheets, you will provide the casual user with an industrial strength spreadsheet that will withstand heavy use.

Conclusion

Beyond the basic spreadsheet model, giving new functions new forms leads to an expanded set of areas. This chapter has discussed the most common forms, but you should not stop here. Create your own when you need to. The concluding example in this chapter, FULL RULE, contains all the areas and lists all the rules in each area.

Strong

	A	B	C	D	E	F	G	H	I
1	**FULL RULE**		17 July 1383	Mother Goose			**Import area**		
2	(C) Copyright 1989 by John M. Nevison						(move right before use)		
3			TITLE TO TELL				XXXXXXX		
4		10-Sep-89	: Date printed				IMPORT WITH CARE		
5			MAKE A FORMAL INTRODUCTION						
7	Description		DECLARE THE MODEL'S PURPOSE						
8			Provide a framework with which to begin building models.						
10	To use		GIVE CLEAR INSTRUCTIONS						
11			Call it up,						
12			change its name,						
13			save it with its new name,						
14			and edit to your purpose.						
16	Reference		REFERENCE CRITICAL IDEAS						
17			John M. Nevison, Excel Spreadsheet Design,						
18			New York, NY: Brady Books, 1990.						

(continued)

	A	B	C	D	E	F	G	H	I
20	Contents	MAP THE CONTENTS							
21		Introduction: title, description, contents					Import Area		
22		Initial data							
23		Model							
24		Report area							
25		Graph area							
26		Verify area							
27		Active area							
28		Macro area							
29		Sample submodel							
32	Initial data								
33		IDENTIFY THE DATA							
34		SURFACE AND LABEL EVERY ASSUMPTION							
37	Model								
38		MODEL TO EXPLAIN							
39		POINT TO THE RIGHT SOURCE							
42		FIRST DESIGN ON PAPER							
43		TEST AND EDIT							
44		KEEP IT VISIBLE							
45		SPACE SO THE SPREADSHEET MAY BE EASILY READ							
46		GIVE A NEW FUNCTION A NEW AREA							
49	Report area								
50		REPORT TO YOUR READER							
53	Graph area								
54		GRAPH TO ILLUMINATE							
57	Verify area								
58		VERIFY CRITICAL WORK							
61	Active area								
62		FOCUS THE MODEL'S ACTIVITY							
65	Macro area								
66		CONTROL ALL MACROS							
69	Sample submodel								
70		ENTER CAREFULLY							
71	Initial data								
72	Data entering from another submodel								
75									
76	Submodel								

If you chose to begin your spreadsheets with FULL RULE, you may avoid many sins of omission. Because you will be throwing away the areas you don't need you will not forget those you do need. The template also places a quick reminder of the rules in front of you. Beginning with good rules and appropriate areas will increase the speed and strength of your spreadsheet construction.

5

The Submodel

A CANDLE
Little Nanny Etticoat
In a white petticoat
And a red nose;
The longer she stands
The shorter she grows.

Sometimes a large spreadsheet gets out of control. Several areas of a large model can depend on each other in such complex ways that the model becomes hard to understand and difficult to modify. Sometimes the activities associated with one part of a model evolve more rapidly than the activities associated with the rest. Sometimes one part gets used in several different spreadsheets. Sometimes two or more old spreadsheets combine to make one effective new one. Sometimes a spreadsheet gets used by several individuals, each of whom wants to control a part of the spreadsheet. Any one of these events could require the creation of a sound submodel.

With Excel, you have the ability to divide your spreadsheet into a collection of spreadsheets. A properly constructed submodel will allow you to exploit this ability to create a family of related spreadsheets and to form individual members that you can conveniently use and reuse.

Consider for a moment what you might do to break up a large, complex model into submodels. Converting such a model is a little like doing a condominium conversion on an apartment house—when you are finished you will have the same basic material, but each piece will have a certain independence from the others.

Before   *After*

	A	B	C	D	E	F	G
8	Contents			Contents			
9		Introduction			Introduction		
10		Initial data			Submodel 1		
11		Data for part 1			Initial and entering data		
12		Data for part 2			Model		
13		Data for part 3			Report A		
14		Model			Submodel 2		
15		Part 1			Initial and entering data		
16		Part 2			Model		
17		Part 3			Submodel 3		
18		Report A using Part 1			Initial and entering data		
19		Report B using Parts 2 & 3			Model		
20		Report C using 3			Report C		
21					Submodel 4		
22					Entering data		
23					Report B (using Submodels 2 & 3)		

Notice that each independent submodel was created with an Initial and Entering Data Area. This new area is one of the results of the fundamental rule of the spreadsheet submodel.

Rule 22: Enter Carefully

Any cell of a spreadsheet can be used in a formula somewhere else. Because any cell can appear in a remote formula at any time, every spreadsheet area and submodel is completely vulnerable to unannounced exits. Because you cannot control a submodel's exits, you must control its entrances. You can do this by being sure that everything enters a submodel through its Initial and Entering Data Area.

Entering data can be controlled in a familiar way. Every basic spreadsheet controls data with its Initial Data Area, and a submodel does the same. The reason entrances should be controlled is that they are of immediate interest to you, the author of the submodel. In order to see what the submodel depends on, you must establish an Initial and Entering Data Area. Without this, you cannot independently test the submodel and prove to yourself that it works. When you build a submodel, you must enter carefully.

The logic of spreadsheets asserts that exiting data is inherently unstable. Figure 5-1 depicts the outflow from Part 1 of a model. Even if you wished to control these exits by moving them to an Exit Area at the bottom of Part 1, the next undisciplined author who added a Part 4 could tap into your Part 1 at any point. The open nature of a spreadsheet renders exiting data impossible to control.

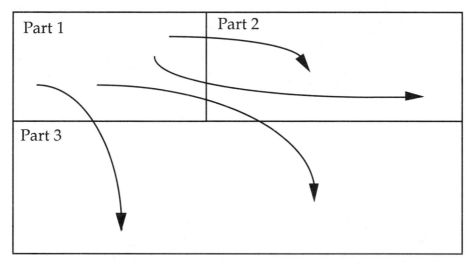

Figure 5-1.   Uncontrolled exits from Part 1 occur when foreign formulas refer to cells in Part 1.

Notice that a spreadsheet gets larger when it is broken into submodels because all the entering data are labeled in a separate place for the first time. Submodels also disperse the control from one central location to several locations. In the next example, a kingdom's spreadsheet will be divided up among three castles.

	A	B	C	D	E	F	G
1	THREE CASTLE KINGDOM—Step #1						
2	Initial data						
3		King's flag					
4		Stone					
5		Wood					
6		Red paint					
7		Yellow paint					
8		Black paint					
9	Castle Red						
10		Red walls = stone + red paint					
11		Red tower = yellow tower copy + stone + red paint					
12		Red drawbridge = black drawbridge copy + wood + red paint					
13		Red castle = red walls + red drawbridge + red tower + King's flag					
14	Castle Yellow						
15		Yellow walls = red wall copy + stone + yellow paint					
16		Yellow tower = stone + yellow paint					
17		Yellow drawbridge = black drawbridge copy + wood + yellow paint					
18		Yellow castle = yellow walls + yellow drawbridge + yellow tower + King's flag					
19	Castle Black						
20		Black walls = stone + black paint					
21		Black tower = yellow tower copy + stone + black paint					
22		Black drawbridge = wood + black paint					
23		Black castle = black walls + black drawbridge + black tower + King's flag					

In THREE CASTLE KINGDOM—Step #1, you see some of the model's data flows: from the initial data to the model (stone and wood); from one location in the initial data to many parts of the model (King's flag); from one part of the model to another (Red wall copy); from one part of the model to many other parts (Black drawbridge copy); and from many parts of the model to one part (Red castle formula).

Step 2 will show the evolution of a large model into three submodels.

	A	B	C	D	E	F	G
1	THREE CASTLE KINGDOM—Step #2						
2	Castle Red						
3	Initial data						
4		King's flag					
5		Red paint					
6	Model						
7		Red walls = stone + red paint					
8		Red tower = yellow tower copy + stone + red paint					
9		Red drawbridge = black drawbridge copy + wood + red paint					
10		Red castle = red walls + red drawbridge + red tower + King's flag					
11	Castle Yellow						
12	Initial data						
13		Stone					
14		Yellow paint					
15	Model						
16		Yellow walls = red wall copy + stone + yellow paint					
17		Yellow tower = stone + yellow paint					
18		Yellow drawbridge = black drawbridge copy + wood + yellow paint					
19		Yellow castle = yellow walls + yellow drawbridge + yellow tower + King's flag					
20	Castle Black						
21	Initial data						
22		Wood					
23		Black paint					
24	Model						
25		Black walls = stone + black paint					
26		Black tower = yellow tower copy + stone + black paint					
27		Black drawbridge = wood + black paint					
28		Black castle = black walls + black drawbridge + black tower + King's flag					

Step 2 shows the intermediate partitioning of the model. Notice that here we have a problem with terms in formulas that come from other submodels (the copies of the drawbridge, stone, and King's flag). These terms could be nearby or far away. They are not visible locally if you wanted to modify them. If you tried to extract one submodel from the spreadsheet, and remembered to freeze the values in the Initial Data Area, you would still find mysterious errors in the submodel's Model Area. For example, an extracted Castle Yellow would look like this:

Weak

	A	B	C	D	E	F	G
1	Castle Yellow (extracted from THREE CASTLE KINGDOM—Step #2)						
2	Initial data						
3		Stone					
4		Yellow paint					
5	Model						
6		Yellow walls = #REF! + stone + yellow paint					
7		Yellow tower = stone + yellow paint					
8		Yellow drawbridge = #REF! + #REF! + yellow paint					
9		Yellow castle = #REF! + #REF! + yellow tower + #REF!					

When a submodel is correctly extracted from a large spreadsheet, no error should occur. But when Castle Yellow's extracted submodel contains errors in the Model Area, the submodel partitioning has serious problems. The last step resolves these problems.

	A	B	C	D	E	F	G
1	THREE CASTLE KINGDOM—Step #3						
2	Castle Red						
3	Initial and entering data						
4		King's flag					
5		Red paint					
6	From Castle Yellow						
7		Stone					
8		Yellow tower design					
9	From Castle Black						
10		Wood					
11		Black drawbridge design					
12	Model						
13		Red walls = stone + red paint					
14		Red tower = yellow tower copy + stone + red paint					
15		Red drawbridge = black drawbridge copy + wood + red paint					
16		Red castle = red walls + red drawbridge + red tower + King's flag					
17	Castle Yellow						
18	Initial and entering data						
19		Stone					
20		Yellow paint					
21	From Castle Red						
22		King's flag					
23		Red wall design					
24	From Castle Black						
25		Wood					
26		Black drawbridge design					

(continued)

	A	B	C	D	E	F	G
27	Model						
28			Yellow walls = red wall copy + stone + yellow paint				
29			Yellow tower = stone + yellow paint				
30			Yellow drawbridge = black drawbridge copy + wood + yellow paint				
31			Yellow castle = yellow walls + yellow drawbridge + yellow tower + King's flag				
32	Castle Black						
33		Initial and entering data					
34			Wood				
35			Black paint				
36		From Castle Red					
37			King's flag				
38		From Castle Yellow					
39			Stone				
40			Yellow tower design				
41		Model					
42			Black walls = stone + black paint				
43			Black tower = yellow tower copy + stone + black paint				
44			Black drawbridge = wood + black paint				
45			Black castle = black walls + black drawbridge + black tower + King's flag				

In the final step, the Initial and Entering Data Area distinguishes between new data that first appear in the submodel and old data that come from another submodel. For example, Castle Yellow has its own stone, but it depends on Castle Red for the King's flag and on Castle Black for its wood.

The general form of the Initial and Entering Data Area is:

Initial and entering data area
    Raw initial data necessary for this submodel
    Data from another Submodel
    Data from yet another Submodel

While Step 3 continues to have complex data flows, it has established control over them by entering carefully. In every submodel, you can see that stone is quarried near Castle Yellow and that wood is lumbered near Castle Black. You know for sure where the design for each part of a castle comes from.

Because all exterior data enters a submodel at the top, references in the body of a submodel stay within the submodel or refer to the Initial and Entering Data Area. The data are visible locally if you wish to modify them locally. If Castle Yellow wanted to modify the "Red wall design," it would:

- Move the value from "From Castle Red" to "Initial Data" and

- Relabel the value "New wall design."

When data enter the submodel from other submodels, they should continue to be connected to the original source. An initial piece of data should exist in only one submodel's "raw initial data" area and be referred to by every other submodel in its "Entering from ..." area (for example, the King's flag). If the entering piece of data comes from the body of another submodel, of course you point to the cell where it first appears. (In Castle Yellow's Initial and Entering Data Area, the red wall design points to Castle Red's wall.)

Because every formula in the body of a submodel goes through the Initial and Entering Data Area on its way to the original source, the risk of intermediate error is introduced into the spreadsheet. Castle Black could mistakenly modify the design of the Yellow tower and not realize that it was no longer using the design from Castle Yellow. This risk of intermediate error is a high, but reasonable, price to pay for a clear division of the spreadsheet and a firm control of every submodel.

Submodel: The Reuse of Tools

Submodels provide you with a larger and more versatile library of tools to use in future models. Because the pieces are set up to become technically independent, you can use them in another context more quickly.

A user can "freeze" the numbers and labels in the Initial and Entering Data Area and cut the submodel out of the large model for independent use. A cut-out submodel can be added to another model, connected where it needs to be, and used with the conviction that it works.

With THREE CASTLE KINGDOM—Step #3, you can extract one submodel and use it on its own. An extracted Castle Yellow might look like this:

Strong

	A	B	C	D	E	F	G
1	Castle Yellow (extracted from THREE CASTLE KINGDOM—Step #3)						
2	Initial (and entering?) data						
3		Stone					
4		Yellow paint					
5		King's flag					
6		Red wall design					
7		Wood					
8		Black drawbridge design					
9	From ??						
10	From ??						
11	Model						
12		Yellow walls = red wall copy + stone + yellow paint					
13		Yellow tower = stone + yellow paint					
14		Yellow drawbridge = black drawbridge copy + wood + yellow paint					
15		Yellow castle = yellow walls + yellow drawbridge + yellow tower + King's flag					

In its independent form, all of Castle Yellow's initial and entering data become initial data. Before Castle Yellow is successfully inserted in a new spreadsheet, data that come from submodels in the new spreadsheet would be broken out in "From ??" areas.

A large model broken into submodels differs from a large integrated model because you can reassert full control over each submodel. First, you have intellectual control: Each model explains itself to the reader in a way the reader is likely to comprehend and remember. Second, you have physical control: If you want to temporarily exercise just one submodel, you can do that by varying the values in the submodel's Initial and Entering Data Area. (This local variation may cut the submodel's ties to other submodels; the temporary version should be thrown away after use.) Third, you have evolutionary control: By breaking the model into pieces that correspond to business function (see the earlier discussion in Chapter 4 under the rule "Give a New Function a New Area") you give the future user a better chance to accurately modify the current spreadsheet to a future need. The model is more likely to evolve smoothly with the business it is intended to serve.

Below you see a family budget spreadsheet as it might evolve over time. The budget allows each member of the family to earn money. The family has fixed expenses that vary little from month to month. The family also has a few policies: The parents each get an allowance based on their monthly income; the father holds the family's entertainment budget, which is a percentage of the parent's joint earnings; the mother controls the clothing budget for the husband and son; the daughter may spend up to 33 percent of her earnings on clothes; the son must save 50 percent of his special earnings; and both children get a fixed allowance in addition to whatever they earn on their own.

Weak

	A	B	C	D	E	F	G
1	FAMILYFIN (Family Finance) 30 June 1600 B. Bunting						
2	(C) Copyright 1986 by John M. Nevison						
3							
4	Show the family's finances						
5							
6	Contents: (each section is a named range)						
7	INTRO		Introduction: Title, description, contents, and map.				
8	INITIAL		Initial data and beginning assumptions				
9	MODEL		Model				
12	Initial data and beginning assumptions						
13	5%	Percent of income permitted as parent allowance					
14	3%	Percent of joint parent income for entertainment					
15	33%	Percent of Daughter's earnings that may be spent on clothes					
16	50%	Percent of Son's earnings he must save					
17							
18		Springtime					
19		April	May	June			
20	Father						
21	Income	1000	900	1050			
22	House	450	450	450			
23	Fuel	200	0	0			
24	Insurance	0	0	250			
25	Mother						
26	Income	1000	1100	1200			
27	Health ins	300	300	300			
28	Car expenses	200	250	275			
29	Food	200	200	200			
30	Clothing	100	100	100			
31	Son						
32	Income	0	0	18			
33	Allowance	5	5	5			
34	Daughter						
35	Income	100	74	130			
36	Allowance	15	15	15			

(continued)

	A	B	C	D	E	F	G
39	Model						
40		Springtime					
41		April	May	June	Total		
42	Father						
43	Income	1000	900	1050	2950		
44	House	450	450	450	1350		
45	Fuel	200	0	0	200		
46	Insurance	0	0	250	250		
47	Entertainment at %	60	60	68	188		
48	Allowance at %	50	45	53	148		
49							
50	Total family income	2100	2074	2398	6572		
51	Total family spending	1663	1504	1827	4994		
52	Total family saving	437	570	571	1578		
53							
54	Mother						
55	Income	1000	1100	1200	3300		
56	Health ins	300	300	300	900		
57	Car expenses	200	250	275	725		
58	Food	200	200	200	600		
59	Clothing	100	100	100	300		
60	Son	50	55	60	165		
61	Income	53	44	72	169		
62							
63	Son						
64	Income	0	0	18	18		
65	Allowance	5	5	5	15		
66	Extra spending	0	0	9	9		
67							
68	Daughter						
69	Income	100	74	130	304		
70	Allowance	15	15	15	45		
71	Clothing allowance	33	24	43	100		

This model, while relatively small, has quite a few complex dependencies. The mother sums spending from the children and includes the teenage daughter's clothing allowance and the young son's extra spending. The father sums incomes from everyone, and expenses from the mother and himself.

The individual members of the family all wanted to have their own spreadsheets so they could control their own parts. The family agreed to split up the entertainment into equal parts, to divide the clothing allowance unevenly between the mother, father, and son, and establish individual submodels for each person.

Strong

	A	B	C	D	E	F	G
1	**FAMILY (Family Individual Finance)**				15 July 1600	B. Bunting	
2	(C) Copyright 1986 by John M. Nevison						
3							
4	**Description**						
5		Give each member of the family a submodel for each					
6		individual's budget.					
7							
8	**Contents**						
9		Introduction: Title, description, contents, and map.					
10		Initial data and beginning assumptions					
11		Son's submodel					
12		Daughter's submodel					
13		Mother's submodel					
14		Father's submodel					
15		Family's summary submodel					
16		Verify area					
20	**Son's submodel**						
21	SON'S INITIAL AND ENTERING DATA						
22	20%	Son's portion of clothing allowance					
23		(daughter excluded from allowance)					
24	50%	Percent of Son's earnings he must save					
25		Springtime					
26		April	May	June			
27	Outside income	0	0	18			
28	Allowance	5	5	5			
29	SON'S ENTERING DATA (FROM FATHER)						
30	Entertainment budget	15	15	17			
31	SON'S ENTERING DATA (FROM MOTHER)						
32	Clothing budget	100	100	100			

(continued)

	A	B	C	D	E	F	G
35	SON'S BUDGET	Springtime					
36		April	May	June	Totals		
37	Outside income	0	0	18	18		
38	Spending						
39	Entertainment	15	15	17	47		
40	Allowance	5	5	5	15		
41	Clothing allowance	20	20	20	60		
42	Extra spending	0	0	9	9		
43	Total	40	40	51	131		
44							
45	Saving	0	0	9	9		
49	**Daughter's submodel**						
50	DAUGHTER'S INITIAL AND ENTERING DATA						
51	33% Percent of Daughter's earnings that may be spent on clothes						
52		Springtime					
53		April	May	June			
54	Outside income	100	74	130			
55	Allowance	15	15	15			
56	DAUGHTER'S ENTERING DATA (FROM FATHER)						
57	Entertainment budget	15	15	17			
60	DAUGHTER'S BUDGET	Springtime					
61		April	May	June	Totals		
62	Outside income	100	74	130	304		
63	Spending						
64	Entertainment	15	15	17	47		
65	Allowance	15	15	15	45		
66	Clothing allowance	33	24	43	100		
67	Total	63	54	75	192		
68							
69	Saving	67	50	87	204		

(continued)

	A	B	C	D	E	F	G
73	**Mother's submodel**						
74	MOTHER'S INITIAL AND ENTERING DATA						
75	45%	Mother's portion of clothing allowance					
76	5%	Percent of income permitted as parent allowance					
77		Springtime					
78		April	May	June			
79	Outside income	1000	1100	1200			
80	Health ins	300	300	300			
81	Car expenses	200	250	275			
82	Food	200	200	200			
83	Family clothing budget	100	100	100			
84	MOTHER'S ENTERING DATA (FROM FATHER)						
85	Entertainment	15	15	17			
86	MOTHER'S ENTERING DATA (FROM SON)						
87	Total spending	40	40	51			
88	MOTHER'S ENTERING DATA (FROM DAUGHTER)						
89	Total spending	63	54	75			
92	MOTHER'S BUDGET	Springtime					
93		April	May	June	Total		
94	Outside income	1000	1100	1200	3300		
95	Spending						
96	Health ins	300	300	300	900		
97	Car expenses	200	250	275	725		
98	Food	200	200	200	600		
99	Clothing allowance	45	45	45	135		
100	Allowance at %	50	55	60	165		
101	Entertainment	15	15	17	47		
102	Total	810	865	897	2572		
103							
104	Saving	190	235	303	728		
105	Other						
106	Children's spending	103	94	126	323		

(continued)

	A	B	C	D	E	F	G
110	**Father's submodel**						
111	FATHER'S INITIAL AND ENTERING DATA						
112	35% Father's portion of clothing allowance						
113	3% Percent of joint parent income for entertainment						
114	4 Number of individuals sharing the entertainment budget						
115	5% Percent of income permitted as parent allowance						
116	Springtime						
117		April	May	June			
118	Outside income	1000	900	1050			
119	House	450	450	450			
120	Fuel	200	0	0			
121	Insurance	0	0	250			
122	FATHER'S ENTERING DATA (FROM MOTHER)						
123	Income	1000	1100	1200			
124	Clothing	100	100	100			
127	FATHER'S BUDGET	Springtime					
128		April	May	June	Total		
129	Family entertainment	60	60	68	188		
130							
131	Outside income	1000	900	1050	2950		
132	Spending						
133	House	450	450	450	1350		
134	Fuel	200	0	0	200		
135	Insurance	0	0	250	250		
136	Allowance	50	45	53	148		
137	Entertainment	15	15	17	47		
138	Clothing allowance	35	35	35	105		
139	Total	750	545	804	2099		
140							
141	Saving	250	355	246	851		

(continued)

	A	B	C	D	E	F	G
145	Family's summary submodel						
146	Springtime						
147		April	May	June			
148	FAMILY'S ENTERING DATA (FROM SON)						
149	Income	0	0	18			
150	Spending	40	40	51			
151	FAMILY'S ENTERING DATA (FROM DAUGHTER)						
152	Income	100	74	130			
153	Spending	63	54	75			
154	FAMILY'S ENTERING DATA (FROM MOTHER)						
155	Income	1000	1100	1200			
156	Spending	810	865	897			
157	FAMILY'S ENTERING DATA (FROM FATHER)						
158	Income	1000	900	1050			
159	Spending	750	545	804			
162	FAMILY SUMMARY BUDGET		Springtime				
163		April	May	June	Total		
164	Total family income	2100	2074	2398	6572		
165	Total family spending	1663	1504	1827	4994		
166	Total family saving	437	570	571	1578		
170	Verify Area						
171		3478.43	Model verification sum				
172							
173		18	Son's outside income total				
174		304	Daughter's outside income total				
175		728.125	Mother's total saving				
176		850.625	Father's total savings				
177		1577.68	Total family saving				

While both of these examples basically do the same thing, the spreadsheet broken into submodels is clearly easier to use in pieces. The individual submodels allow each member of the family to control his or her own portion of the model. Note that whenever any one member corrects or changes his or her submodel, the other members of the family benefit from this change—everyone's submodel is revised to reflect the latest information.

The individual family members are here a metaphor for any organization that has divided its work into different, semi-autonomous tasks. Such tasks need to be handled one piece at a time. The corrections in one portion should be shared by all and can be if each task is a submodel. The organization's results will be the integrated combination of all the pieces.

In the next strong example, any of NEWBUD's submodels could be broken out and turned over to the appropriate manager to work with. The President would get the executive budget; the Vice President of Manufacturing, the factory budget; the Vice President of Sales, the sales budget; the Vice President of Finance, the cash budget; the Chairman of the Board, the income statement and balance sheet. After they had each worked over their individual initial and entering data they could contribute their best estimate of their initial (but not entering) data to NEWBUD to see how the pieces fit together.

The Submodel Focuses Attention

Different tasks imply different focuses of attention. Even if one person is responsible for all the tasks in a spreadsheet, the submodel breakdown allows that individual to focus on one area at a time. This narrowing of focus increases understanding, speeds revision, and lowers the likelihood of introducing errors in a large model. (You only have to solve that portion of the problem you are interested in. You may leave the rest neatly alone and know that it is still okay.)

Such is not the case with a large integrated model—when you change one part, you must recheck it all to assure its integrity. Consider trying to understand the following model composed of six major parts. The basic idea is that four operating budgets (executive, factory, sales, and cash) coordinate with each other and then feed two accounting statements (the income statement and the balance sheet). (See Figure 5-2.)

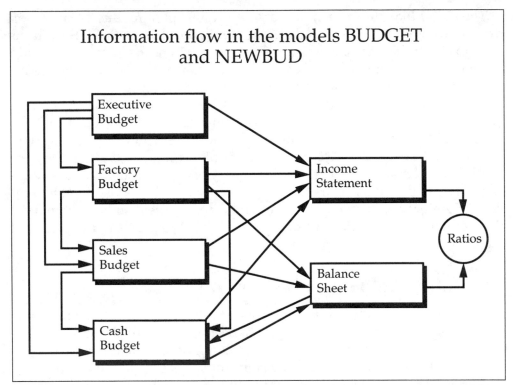

Figure 5-2.   The complex information flows in the spreadsheets BUDGET and NEWBUD.

Contrast the terse, undocumented, large, complexly interrelated, and weak example called BUDGET with the same ideas broken up in manageable pieces in the strong example called NEWBUD. Ask yourself which example you would choose if your job required you to understand, use, and revise this model.

Weak

	A	B	C	D	E	F	G	H
1	BUDGET 1 January 1500 Peter Piper							
2								
3	(C) Copyright 1983,1989 John M. Nevison							
4								
5	Show how three operating budgets for executive office, factory,							
6	and sales office are combined to produce the operating							
7	cash budget and the annual accounting statements.							
8								
9	Assumptions:							
10			50%	Percent exec. budget allocated to factory				
11			50%	Percent exec. budget allocated to sales				
12			$0.20	Mnfg labor $/unit				
13			$0.37	Raw material $/unit				
14			45	Average age of receivables (calendar days)				
15			90	Average age of payables (calendar days)				
16			14.5%	Annual interest rate				
17			*	Assumption somewhere in marked budget line				
18								
19		EXECUTIVE BUDGET	Qtr 1	Qtr 2	Qtr 3	Qtr 4	Year	
20								
21	*	Total	1,160	1,165	1,164	1,170	4,659	
22								
23								
24								
25		FACTORY DATA	Qtr 1	Qtr 2	Qtr 3	Qtr 4	Year	
26								
27	*	Units	22,361	22,600	22,500	22,600	90,061	
28								
29		FACTORY BUDGET						
30								
31		Direct costs						
32		Mnfg labor	4,472	4,520	4,500	4,520	18,012	
33		Raw materials	8,334	8,423	8,386	8,423	33,568	
34	*	Power, heat, light	22	22	23	23	90	
35		Total direct costs	12,829	12,965	12,909	12,966	51,670	
36								
37		Period costs						
38	*	Supervision	310	325	365	300	1,300	
39	*	Insurance	23	23	25	24	95	
40	*	Depreciation	875	875	875	875	3,500	
41	*	Management	1,800	1,850	1,900	1,780	7,330	
42		Allocated corp. overhead	580	583	582	585	2,330	
43		Total period costs	3,588	3,656	3,747	3,564	14,555	
44								
45		Total costs	16,417	16,621	16,656	16,530	66,224	

(continued)

	A	B	C	D	E	F	G	H
46								
47								
48		SALES DATA	Qtr 1	Qtr 2	Qtr 3	Qtr 4	Year	
49								
50	*	Units	23,817	23,600	24,600	25,200	97,217	
51	*	Price	1.15	1.18	1.19	1.21		
52								
53		SALES BUDGET						
54								
55		Revenue	27,390	27,848	29,274	30,492	115,004	
56								
57		Factory costs	16,417	16,621	16,656	16,530	66,224	
58	*	Delivery	80	83	86	84	333	
59		Gross margin	10,893	11,144	12,532	13,878	48,446	
60								
61	*	Sales support	1,350	1,400	1,430	1,487	5,667	
62	*	Advertising	90	100	110	100	400	
63								
64	*	Selling and management	4,740	4,745	4,752	4,763	19,000	
65		Allocated corp. overhead	580	583	582	585	2,330	
66								
67		Contribution	20,550	20,938	22,314	23,473	87,274	
68								
69								
70		CASH BUDGET DATA						
71			Qtr 0	Qtr 1	Qtr 2	Qtr 3	Qtr 4	Year
72								
73	*	Units mfd	24,770	22,361	22,600	22,500	22,600	90,061
74	*	Units sold	23,000	23,817	23,600	24,600	25,200	97,217
75		Inventory change	1,770	-1,456	-1,000	-2,100	-2,600	-7,156
76	*	Sales on credit	24,150	27,390	27,848	29,274	30,492	115,004
77	*	Purchases on credit	8,424	8,334	8,423	8,386	8,423	33,568
78								
79		CASH BUDGET						
80								
81		Receipts	Qtr 0	Qtr 1	Qtr 2	Qtr 3	Qtr 4	Year
82		Collected receivables		25,770	27,619	28,561	29,883	111,833
83		Total receipts		25,770	27,619	28,561	29,883	111,833
84								

(continued)

	A	B	C	D	E	F	G	H
85		Disbursements						
86		Disbursed payables		8,424	8,334	8,423	8,386	33,568
87		Production payroll		4,472	4,520	4,500	4,520	18,012
88		Mnfing expenses		2,155	2,220	2,313	2,127	8,815
89		Selling expenses		6,260	6,328	6,378	6,434	25,400
90		Corp overhead		1,160	1,165	1,164	1,170	4,659
91		Interest		1,183	1,168	1,092	993	4,436
92	*	Taxes		1,200	1,300	1,450	1,650	5,600
93		Total disbursements		24,854	25,035	25,321	25,280	100,490
94								
95		Net cash		916	2,584	3,240	4,603	11,342
96								
97		Cumulative cash						
98		Beginning balance		32,000	32,500	33,000	33,500	32,000
99		Net cash		916	2,584	3,240	4,603	11,342
100	*	Minimum balance needed		500	500	500	500	2,000
101		Debt reduction (increase)		416	2,084	2,740	4,103	9,342
102		Ending balance	32,000	32,500	33,000	33,500	34,000	34,000
103		Debt	32,632	32,216	30,133	27,393	23,290	23,290
104								
105								
106								
107		ANNUAL STATEMENTS						
108								
109		INCOME STATEMENT	$					
110								
111		Sales	115,004					
112		Cost of goods	60,395					
113		Gross profit	54,608					
114								
115		Depreciation	3,500					
116		Selling genl. & admin.	30,059					
117								
118		Interest	4,436					
119								
120		Profit before taxes	16,613					
121		Tax	5,600					
122		Net income	11,013					
123								

(continued)

	A	B	C	D	E	F	G	H
124		BALANCE SHEET						
125			Last year	Change	This year			
126		Assets						
127								
128		Current assets						
129	*	Cash	32,000		34,000			
130		Accounts receivable	12,075		15,246			
131	*	Raw materials	2,500		2,500			
132	*	Finished goods	8,000	-4,098	3,902			
133		Total current assets	54,575		55,648			
134								
135		Fixed assets						
136	*	Land	2,222		2,222			
137	*	Plant and equipment	55,555		55,555			
138	*	Accumulated depreciation	11,111	3,500	14,611			
139		Net plant and equipment	44,444		40,944			
140		Total fixed assets	46,666		43,166			
141								
142	*	Other assets	999		999			
143								
144		Total assets	102,240		99,813			
145								
146		Liabilities and net worth						
147								
148		Current liabilities						
149		Accounts payable	8,424		8,423			
150	*	Notes payable	12,632	-9,342	3,290			
151		Total current liabilities	21,056		11,713			
152								
153	*	Long-term liabilities	20,000		20,000			
154								
155		Common stock	35,629		40,544			
156	*	Retained earnings	25,555	2,000	27,555			
157								
158		Total liabilities and net worth	102,240		99,813			
159								
160								
161		RATIOS						
162								
163		Asset turnover	1.15					
164		Profit as a % of sales	9.6%					
165		Return on assets	11.0%					
166		Return on equity	16.2%					

Strong

	A	B	C	D	E	F	G
1	**NEWBUD**	2 January 1500	Peter Piper				
2	® Copyright 1985,1989 John M. Nevison						
3		12-Sep-89 Date printed					
5	Description						
6	Combine three operating budgets for executive office, factory,						
7	and sales office to produce the operating cash budget,						
8	the income statement, and the balance sheet.						
10	This spreadsheet illustrates a cooperating network of models.						
12	Reference						
13	For a detailed explanation of the model see Chapter Two of the						
14	following reference:						
15	Nevison, John M., "Executive Computing: How to Get It Done						
16	With Spreadsheets and Graphs," Atlanta: GA, Association for						
17	Media-Based Continuing Education for Engineers, 1986.						
19	Contents						
20	Title, intro., contents, and references.						
21	Verify area						
22	Executive Office Budget (and initial data)						
23	Factory Budget (and initial data)						
24	Sales Budget (and initial data)						
25	Cash Budget (and initial data)						
26	Income Statement (and initial data)						
27	Balance Sheet (and initial data)						
28	Financial Ratios (report)						
31	**Verify area**						
32	232,732 Verification sum						
33							
34	If an error appears here, check below and then the appropriate area of the model.						
35	(Be sure you have recalculated the whole model.)						
36							
37	66,224 Factory budget, total yearly costs						
38	21,050 Sales budget, total yearly contribution						
39	11,342 Cash budget, yearly net cash						
40	23,290 Cash budget, end of year debt						
41	11,014 Income statement, net income						
42	99,813 Balance sheet, this year's total liabilities						
43	and net worth						
47	**EXECUTIVE BUDGET INITIAL DATA**						
48		Qtr 1	Qtr 2	Qtr 3	Qtr 4		
49	Totals	1,160	1,165	1,164	1,170		

(continued)

	A	B	C	D	E	F	G
52	**EXECUTIVE BUDGET**						
53		Qtr 1	Qtr 2	Qtr 3	Qtr 4	Year	
54	Total	1,160	1,165	1,164	1,170	4,659	
58	**FACTORY BUDGET INITIAL DATA**						
59		50%	Percent exec. budget allocated to factory				
60		$0.20	Mnfg labor $/unit				
61		$0.37	Raw material $/unit				
62		Qtr 1	Qtr 2	Qtr 3	Qtr 4		
63	Units mfd	22,361	22,600	22,500	22,600		
64	Power, heat, light	22	22	23	23		
65	Supervision	310	325	365	300		
66	Insurance	23	23	25	24		
67	Depreciation	875	875	875	875		
68	Management	1,800	1,850	1,900	1,780		
69							
70	FACTORY BUDGET ASSUMPTIONS (From executive budget)						
71	Total executive budget	1,160	1,165	1,164	1,170		
74	**FACTORY BUDGET**						
75		Qtr 1	Qtr 2	Qtr 3	Qtr 4	Year	
76	Direct costs						
77	Mnfg labor	4,472	4,520	4,500	4,520	18,012	
78	Raw materials	8,334	8,423	8,386	8,423	33,568	
79	Power, heat, light	22	22	23	23	90	
80	Total direct costs	12,829	12,965	12,909	12,966	51,670	
81							
82	Period costs						
83	Supervision	310	325	365	300	1,300	
84	Insurance	23	23	25	24	95	
85	Depreciation	875	875	875	875	3,500	
86	Management	1,800	1,850	1,900	1,780	7,330	
87	Allocated corp. overhead	580	583	582	585	2,330	
88	Total period costs	3,588	3,656	3,747	3,564	14,555	
89							
90	Total costs	16,417	16,621	16,656	16,530	66,224	

(continued)

	A	B	C	D	E	F	G
94	**SALES DATA INITIAL DATA**						
95		50%	Percent exec. budget allocated to sales				
96		Qtr 1	Qtr 2	Qtr 3	Qtr 4		
97	Units sold	23,817	23,600	24,600	25,200		
98	Price	1	1	1	1		
99	Delivery	80	83	86	84		
100	Sales support	1,350	1,400	1,430	1,487		
101	Advertising	90	100	110	100		
102	Selling and management	4,740	4,745	4,752	4,763		
103							
104	SALES DATA ASSUMPTIONS (From executive budget)						
105	Total executive budget	1,160	1,165	1,164	1,170		
106							
107	SALES DATA ASSUMPTIONS (From factory budget)						
108	Total factory costs	16,417	16,621	16,656	16,530		
111	**SALES BUDGET**	Qtr 1	Qtr 2	Qtr 3	Qtr 4	Year	
112							
113	Revenue	27,390	27,848	29,274	30,492	115,004	
114							
115	Factory costs	16,417	16,621	16,656	16,530	66,224	
116	Delivery	80	83	86	84	333	
117	Gross margin	10,893	11,144	12,532	13,878	48,446	
118							
119	Sales support	1,350	1,400	1,430	1,487	5,667	
120	Advertising	90	100	110	100	400	
121							
122	Selling and management	4,740	4,745	4,752	4,763	19,000	
123	Allocated corp. overhead	580	583	582	585	2,330	
124							
125	Contribution	4,133	4,317	5,658	6,943	21,050	
129	**CASH BUDGET INITIAL DATA**						
130		45	Average age of receivables (calendar days)				
131		90	Average age of payables (calendar days)				
132		14.5%	Annual interest rate				
133		Qtr 0	Qtr 1	Qtr 2	Qtr 3	Qtr 4	
134	Units mfd	24,770					
135	Units sold	23,000					
136	Sales on credit	24,150					
137	Purchases on credit	8,424					
138	Taxes		1,200	1,300	1,450	1,650	
139	Minimum balance needed		500	500	500	500	
140							

(continued)

	A	B	C	D	E	F	G
141	CASH BUDGET ASSUMPTIONS (From executive budget)						
142	Total exec budget		1,160	1,165	1,164	1,170	
143							
144	CASH BUDGET ASSUMPTIONS (From factory budget)						
145			Qtr 1	Qtr 2	Qtr 3	Qtr 4	
146	Units mfd		22,361	22,600	22,500	22,600	
147	Purchases on credit		8,334	8,423	8,386	8,423	
148	Mnfg labor		4,472	4,520	4,500	4,520	
149	Power, heat, light		22	22	23	23	
150	Supervision		310	325	365	300	
151	Insurance		23	23	25	24	
152	Management		1,800	1,850	1,900	1,780	
153							
154	CASH BUDGET ASSUMPTIONS (From sales budget)						
155	Units sold		23,817	23,600	24,600	25,200	
156	Sales on credit		27,390	27,848	29,274	30,492	
157	Delivery		80	83	86	84	
158	Sales support		1,350	1,400	1,430	1,487	
159	Advertising		90	100	110	100	
160	Selling and management		4,740	4,745	4,752	4,763	
161							
162	CASH BUDGET ASSUMPTIONS (From last year's balance sheet)						
163	Cash	32,000					
164	Notes payable	12,632					
165	Long-term liabilities	20,000					
168	**CASH BUDGET**						
169	Tricky formulas:						
170	Collected receivables = (Avg age of rec./90) * last qtr sales +						
171	(90 - Avg age of rec.)/90 * curr qtr sales						
172	Dispersed payables = (Avg age of pay./90) * last qtr sales +						
173	(90 - Avg age of pay.)/90 * curr qtr sales						
174	Mnfing expenses = Power heat and light + supervision + insurance + management						
175	Selling expenses = Delivery + sales support + advertising + selling and mgt						
176	Interest = Annual int rate/4 * prior qtr's debt						
177	Cash ending balance = Beginning balance + net cash - debt reduction						
178	Debt = Prior qtr's debt - debt reduction						
179							
180		Qtr 0	Qtr 1	Qtr 2	Qtr 3	Qtr 4	Year
181	Inventory change--units	1,770	-1,456	-1,000	-2,100	-2,600	-7,156
182							
183	Receipts						
184	Collected receivables		25,770	27,619	28,561	29,883	111,833
185	Total receipts		25,770	27,619	28,561	29,883	111,833
186							

(continued)

	A	B	C	D	E	F	G
187	Disbursements						
188	Disbursed payables		8,424	8,334	8,423	8,386	33,568
189	Production payroll		4,472	4,520	4,500	4,520	18,012
190	Mnfing expenses		2,155	2,220	2,313	2,127	8,815
191	Selling expenses		6,260	6,328	6,378	6,434	25,400
192	Corp overhead		1,160	1,165	1,164	1,170	4,659
193	Interest		1,183	1,168	1,092	993	4,436
194	Taxes		1,200	1,300	1,450	1,650	5,600
195	Total disbursements		24,854	25,035	25,321	25,280	100,490
196							
197	Net cash		916	2,584	3,240	4,603	11,342
198							
199	Cumulative cash						
200	Beginning balance		32,000	32,500	33,000	33,500	32,000
201	Net cash		916	2,584	3,240	4,603	11,342
202	Minimum balance needed		500	500	500	500	2,000
203	Debt reduction (increase)		416	2,084	2,740	4,103	9,342
204	Ending balance	32,000	32,500	33,000	33,500	34,000	34,000
205	Debt	32,632	32,216	30,133	27,393	23,290	23,290

209	**INCOME STATEMENT ASSUMPTIONS (From executive budget)**
210	4,659 Total executive budget (corporate overhead)
211	
212	INCOME STATEMENT ASSUMPTIONS (From factory budget)
213	3,500 Total depreciation
214	2,330 Total corp overhead allocated
215	66,224 Total costs
216	
217	INCOME STATEMENT ASSUMPTIONS (From sales budget)
218	115,004 Total revenue
219	333 Total delivery costs
220	5,667 Total sales support costs
221	400 Total advertising costs
222	19,000 Total selling and management costs
223	
224	INCOME STATEMENT ASSUMPTIONS (From cash budget)
225	4,436 Total interest
226	5,600 Total tax

(continued)

	A	B	C	D	E	F	G
229	INCOME STATEMENT						
230	Tricky formulas:						
231	Cost of goods sold = Factory budget costs (less depreciation and corporate overhead)						
232	Selling, general, and administrative = All the sales budget costs and the executive budget						
233		$	% of Sales				
234	Sales	115,004	100%				
235	Cost of goods	60,395	53%				
236	Gross profit	54,609	47%				
237							
238	Depreciation	3,500	3%				
239	Selling genl. & admin.	30,059	26%				
240							
241	Interest	4,436	4%				
242							
243	Profit before taxes	16,614	14%				
244	Tax	5,600	5%				
245	Net income	11,014	10%				
249	BALANCE SHEET INITIAL DATA						
250		Last year					
251		32,000	Cash				
252		2,500	Raw materials				
253		8,000	Finished goods				
254		2,222	Land				
255		55,555	Plant and equipment				
256		11,111	Accumulated depreciation				
257		999	Other assets				
258		12,632	Notes payable				
259		20,000	Long-term liabilities				
260		25,555	Retained earnings				
261							
262		2,000	Increase (decrease) in retained earnings last				
263			year to this year				
264							
265	BALANCE SHEET ASSUMPTIONS (From factory budget)						
266		$0.20	Mnfg labor $/unit				
267		$0.37	Raw material $/unit				
268		8,423	Qtr 4 raw material (purchases on credit)				
269		3,500	Total depreciation				
270							
271	BALANCE SHEET ASSUMPTIONS (From sales budget)						
272		30,492	Qtr 4 revenue (sales on credit)				
273							

(continued)

	A	B	C	D	E	F	G
274	BALANCE SHEET ASSUMPTIONS (From cash budget)						
275	45	Average age of receivables (calendar days)					
276	90	Average age of payables (calendar days)					
277	8,424	Qtr 0 raw material (purchases on credit)					
278	24,150	Qtr 0 revenue (sales on credit)					
279	-7,156	Total inventory change--units					
280	9,342	Debt reduction (increase)					
281	34,000	Ending balance of cumulative cash					
284	**BALANCE SHEET**						
285	Tricky formulas:						
286	Cash (this year) = from accumulated cash budget						
287	Accounts receivable = Average age of receivables/90 * 0th or 4th qtr sales on credit						
288	Change in finished goods = change in inventory units from cash budget *						
289	(raw mat cost/unit + mfg labor cost/unit)						
290	Change in depreciation = from factory budget						
291	Accounts payable = Average age of payables/90 * 0th or 4th qtr purchases on credit						
292	Change in notes payable = from cash budget debt reduction						
293	Change in retained earnings = from assumptions						
294	Common stock (this year) = Total assets — short and long-term liabilities — retained earnings						
295							
296	BALANCE SHEET						
297	Assets	Last year	Change	This year			
298							
299	Current assets						
300	Cash	32,000		34,000			
301	Accounts receivable	12,075		15,246			
302	Raw materials	2,500		2,500			
303	Finished goods	8,000	-4,098	3,902			
304	Total current assets	54,575		55,648			
305							
306	Fixed assets						
307	Land	2,222		2,222			
308	Plant and equipment	55,555		55,555			
309	Accumulated depreciation	11,111	3,500	14,611			
310	Net plant and equipment	44,444		40,944			
311	Total fixed assets	46,666		43,166			
312							
313	Other assets	999		999			
314							
315	Total assets	102,240		99,813			
316							

(continued)

	A	B	C	D	E	F	G
317	Liabilities and net worth						
318							
319	Current liabilities						
320	Accounts payable	8,424		8,423			
321	Notes payable	12,632	-9,342	3,290			
322	Total current liabilities	21,056		11,713			
323							
324	Long-term liabilities	20,000		20,000			
325							
326	Common stock	35,629		40,544			
327	Retained earnings	25,555	2,000	27,555			
328							
329	Total liabilities and net worth	102,240		99,813			

	A	B	C	D	E	F	G
333	**RATIOS ASSUMPTIONS FROM INCOME STATEMENT**						
334	115,004 Sales						
335	11,014 Net income						
336	RATIOS ASSUMPTIONS FROM BALANCE SHEET						
337	99,813 Total assets						
338	40,544 Common stock						
339	27,555 Retained earnings						

	A	B	C	D	E	F	G
342	**RATIOS (Report from income statement and balance sheet)**						
343	20-Jan-91						
344	Corporate Financial Ratios			Formula is:			
345							
346	Asset turnover	1.15		Sales/total assets			
347	Profit as a % of sales	9.6%		Net income/Sales			
348	Return on assets	11.0%		Net income/total assets			
349	Return on equity	16.2%		Net income/			
350				(Common stock +retained earnings)			

The strong version of this model, NEWBUD, gives you, the reader, much more to work with. If you ever really wanted to understand what was going on in this model, you would study NEWBUD, not BUDGET. NEWBUD's biggest distinction is that it gives you a chance to learn one section at a time. You can understand and use one section without having mastered all of the other sections. Submodels give you intellectual control. NEWBUD also provides a Verify Area so you have some reassurance that all the submodels are operating correctly.

Collections of Spreadsheets

The cooperative effort, shown here on one spreadsheet, is also possible among several spreadsheets. The same Initial and Entering Data Area makes possible the coordinated use of several sheets. Because Excel only dynamically adjusts names, **make sure that all data entering from another spreadsheet are referred to by name, not location.**

As the number of spreadsheets grows, the need for organization and documentation grows faster. When several spreadsheets are involved, you need a piece of paper with a picture of the whole system and directions on how to use your portion of it. To the greatest extent possible, you should include the documentation in the cooperating models themselves. (These issues will be discussed further in the Chapter 6.)

Excel makes the use of submodels even more appealing because each submodel can be on a separate spreadsheet. If your large spreadsheet is broken up into a family of spreadsheets that each correspond to a submodel, you will be able to develop a tool kit of submodels that you can use in several models.

So, when your work group has a team activity where the division of labor dictates that each member knows part of the data best, you may find that the helpful spreadsheet is really a collection of submodels. Each member of the team can use his or her submodel secure in the knowledge that the pieces will work together because each submodel always makes sure that its data enters carefully.

6

Two Worked Examples

PAIRS OR PEARS
Twelve pairs hanging high,
Twelve knights riding by,
Each knight took a pear,
And yet left a dozen there.

The proof of the rules is in their use. The first question to answer is "How do the rules feel when you use them to build a new spreadsheet?" The second question is "How do the rules feel when you use them to modify an old spreadsheet?" To see how the rules work in practice, we will work through two examples, one from initial idea to final spreadsheet and one from slightly styled to fully restyled. We will make notes as we go, trying to see how the rules feel in practice, how long things really take to do, and how the rules can speed the development of a structured spreadsheet.

Building a New Spreadsheet: PROGRESS

The beginning of this spreadsheet is the template FULL RULE. We choose this template because it contains all the rules and we want them to remind us to do the right thing.

The first thing we need is a temporary name for this model. What we want to do is develop a model that contains a practical layout of a departmental budget, so we decide to call this model DEPARTMENT. We save a copy of the template under this new name.

	A	B	C	D
1	**Department**	23 October 1986	John M. Nevison	

After the new name we say out loud what we have only half thought out: "The purpose of this model is...." We write down our answer, stare at the result for a few minutes, and decide that it is a full, but reasonable, order at this stage. We correct the spelling errors and erase the rules TITLE TO TELL (this title could probably be improved; let's keep alert to that possibility as we work), MAKE A FORMAL INTRODUCTION (that's ensured by the structure of the introduction area in the template), and DECLARE THE MODEL'S PURPOSE (just finished doing the first draft of that).

	A	B	C	D	E	F
3	Description					
4		The purpose of this model is to illustrate a well-made spreadsheet				
5		that provides a department manager with the tools he needs to				
6		manage his departmental budget. In particular:				
7		A twelve-month plan for the year				
8		A month by month list of the actual expenses as they occur				
9		Reports and graphs for the manager				
10		Reports and graphs to be posted for the department to see				
11		Reports and graphs for upper management				

This statement of purpose begs the issue of what the reports and graphs actually are, but does alert us to the necessity of getting a clear picture of what they should be before we invest a great deal of time entering data into this model. We decide to begin with a simple list of reports in the Report Area and graphs in the Graph Area. We hope that if we choose explicit titles for these reports, we can then sketch them on a piece of paper or sketch them into the spreadsheet. If we know what some (not necessarily all) of the results are, we can then work back to the initial data and be reasonably sure that we won't forget a major item. **We design backward, from desired results to necessary initial conditions**.

	A	B	C	D	E	F
14	**Report area**	REPORT TO YOUR READER				
15	Departmental Quarterly goals--public					
16	Departmental Totals Sales, Costs, Profits budget versus Actual--public					
17	Departmental Detailed costs, Budgeted versus Actual --Dept manager					
18	Sales and selling costs--Dept manager					
19	Departmental YTD Profit Performance, Budgeted, Actual, Forecast--upper					
20	management					
23	**Graph area**	GRAPH TO ILLUMINATE				
24	Departmental Quarterly Sales Goal progress to date line chart--public					
25	Departmental Totals. Sales, Costs, Profits Budgeted versus Actual--YTD each month					
26	bar chart					
27	Sales and selling costs --Dept manager					
28	Departmental YTD Profit Performance, Budgeted, Actual, Forecast--line chart on					
29	profit					

The intended reader is included with the title of the reports and graphs in order to sharpen the focus of what should be included. The effect of this list is that we feel we can go off and rough out some reports and sketch some graphs. At this point we're beginning to feel some discomfort because we want to have fun with the spreadsheet model itself. Our better half, however, tells us first to refine what we think we want in each report and graph. (FIRST DESIGN ON PAPER.)

The results of the reports take longer than we thought they would (about three hours). We find that we spend a great deal of time thinking through the best way to REPORT TO YOUR READER. We vary column widths. We change and rearrange rows (and columns). We format the column headings to the right side of the cells. We format the pseudonumbers and ask and re-ask if the current report is the best one for the reader. We quit working on the reports when we feel that we must know more about the actual values of the numbers to improve our thinking about the report formats.

	A	B	C	D	E	F	G
214	Department goals for the quarter						
215		OUR DEPARTMENT'S QUARTERLY PERFORMANCE					
216			FOR MONTH OF MAY (Month 2 of Quarter 2)				
217		Actual	Qtrly goal	Miles to go	Rate so far	Comment	
218	Sales	xxx.xxx	xxx.xxx	xxx.xxx	xx%	The the the	
219	Costs	xxx.xxx	xxx.xxx	xxx.xxx	xx%	The the the	
220	Profits	xxx.xxx	xxx.xxx	xxx.xxx	xx%	The the the	
221							
222	Department's year-to-date performance						
223		OUR DEPARTMENT'S YEAR-TO-DATE PERFORMANCE					
224			FOR MONTH OF MAY (Month 5 of 12)				
225		Actual	Budgeted	Rate so far	Forecast *	Rate so far	Remaining
226	Sales	xxx.xxx	xxx.xxx	xx%	xxx.xxx	xx%	xxx.xxx
227	Costs	xxx.xxx	xxx.xxx	xx%	xxx.xxx	xx%	xxx.xxx
228	Profits	xxx.xxx	xxx.xxx	xx%	xxx.xxx	xx%	xxx.xxx
229		*Forecast is Revison of Budget					
230							
231	Department cost analysis						
232	DEPARTMENTAL COST ANALYSIS						
233			FOR MONTH OF MAY (Month 2 of Quarter 2)				
234		Month	Budget/for	Difference	Qtr	Budget/for	Difference
235	Item	xxx.xxx	xxx.xxx	xxx.xxx	xxx.xxx	xxx.xxx	xxx.xxx
236	Item	xxx.xxx	xxx.xxx	xxx.xxx	xxx.xxx	xxx.xxx	xxx.xxx
237	Item	xxx.xxx	xxx.xxx	xxx.xxx	xxx.xxx	xxx.xxx	xxx.xxx
238	Item	xxx.xxx	xxx.xxx	xxx.xxx	xxx.xxx	xxx.xxx	xxx.xxx
239	Item	xxx.xxx	xxx.xxx	xxx.xxx	xxx.xxx	xxx.xxx	xxx.xxx
240							
241	Total	xxx.xxx	xxx.xxx	xxx.xxx	xxx.xxx	xxx.xxx	xxx.xxx
242							
243	Sales and selling costs						
244		SALES AND SELLING COSTS					
245		January	February	March	April	May	June
246	Sales	xxx.xxx	xxx.xxx	xxx.xxx	xxx.xxx	xxx.xxx	xxx.xxx
247	Costs	xxx.xxx	xxx.xxx	xxx.xxx	xxx.xxx	xxx.xxx	xxx.xxx
248	% of sales	xx%	xx%	xx%	xx%	xx%	xx%
249	Smoothed(5 mth)						
250	% of sales	xx%	xx%	xx%	xx%	xx%	xx%
251							
252	Department profit performance						
253		IDEAL DEPARTMENT YEAR-TO-DATE PROFIT PERFORMANCE					
254	12-Jun-86	YTD	YTD		Annual	Annual	
255		Budget	Actual	Rate	Budget	Forecast	Budget
256	Sales	xxx.xxx	xxx.xxx	xx%	xxx.xxx	xxx.xxx	xx%
257	Variable costs	xxx.xxx	xxx.xxx	xx%	xxx.xxx	xxx.xxx	xx%
258	Fixed costs	xxx.xxx	xxx.xxx	xx%	xxx.xxx	xxx.xxx	xx%
259							
260	Profit	xxx.xxx	xxx.xxx	xx%	xxx.xxx	xxx.xxx	xx%
261							

The worst thing about these reports is that we know that we may change their format later. We have, however, achieved what we came for: a sharpened sense of exactly what data we will need and what the main model will look like.

To be sure we know what the results look like on paper, we print a full copy of the reports. (TEST AND EDIT.) The printed versions reveal a few minor items that we want to add, but basically confirm that these are the desired reports.

After finishing the review of the paper copy of the reports, we sketch on paper what the graphs might look like and capture the outcome of that work with some notes in the Graph Area.

	A	B	C	D	E	F	G	H
262	Graph area							
263		GRAPH TO ILLUMINATE						
264	Departmental quarterly goals: sales, costs, profits. Public three pairs of bar charts.							
265	Sales and selling costs rough and smooth line chart. Last several years and last 12 months.							
266	Departmental profit performance, budgeted, actual, current forecast--line							
267	chart on profits--upper management							
268								

What we learn is that we need fewer graphs than we had thought. The selling efficiency graph, however, will require more data than only the current year: It will require 13 months of back data.

Now, a first draft of the outcomes of the spreadsheet has been completed. (Note that we have ambitions of serving several constituencies with one spreadsheet because we know one model can spawn several reports with several Report Areas.) We are ready to go back to the basic model and the departmental data we need to feed the model. Elapsed time at this point is four hours.

In the model itself we decide we want to see several measures at once: Monthly, quarterly, half-yearly, and yearly. These measures will allow the department manager to pick and choose good features for quick reports on the department's performance. (If the quarterly performance is poor, the half-yearly figures can be emphasized.)

After an hour or so of varying the structure, we decide that we will define the "plan" to be the original budget plus periodic reforecasts to year end. Plan is the best current guess at anticipated performance. In the present case, with only one reforecast made in June, the plan is the January-to-May Budget and the June-to-December Forecast. If a second reforecast were made in

September, the plan would have three legs: January-to-May, June-to-September, and October-to-December. Because the manager will want to see how close performance is to anticipated performance, the six areas necessary are:

Monthly plan

Monthly actual

Monthly difference

Summary plan

Summary actual

Summary difference

With these six sections, the manager can illustrate in a few pages how the business performs. The manager can wait a few days for the spreadsheet operator to adjust the Report Areas to generate the proper month's reports and graphs.

Next, we turn to the Initial Data Area to enter the data necessary to make the model real. We begin with the historical sales data because we know the model will need it to do one of the desired graphs. Then we put in the budget, the actuals to date, and the plan (which is composed of original budget numbers and later forecasts for the remainder of the year).

	A	B	C	D	E	F	G	H	I	J	K
57	Initial data and beginning assumptions										
58		May	:Current month								
59											
60	BACK DATA	Jan.	Feb.	Mar.	Apr.	May	Jun.	Jul.	Aug.	Sep.	Oct.
61	Sales 84	12	17	19	23	22	19	18	15	18	20
62	Sales 85	15	17	21	27	25	20	19	14	20	22
63	Cost of selling 84	5.5	5.5	5.5	6.0	6.0	6.0	5.5	5.5	5.5	5.5
64	Cost of selling 85	5.5	5.5	5.5	5.5	5.5	5.5	5.5	5.5	5.5	5.5
65											
66	ORIG. BUDGET	Jan.	Feb.	Mar.	Apr.	May	Jun.	Jul.	Aug.	Sep.	Oct.
67	Sales	16.0	19.0	23.0	30.0	28.0	22.0	21.0	15.0	22.0	24.0
68	Delivery costs	0.5	0.6	0.7	0.9	0.8	0.6	0.4	0.4	0.7	0.7
69	Raw material	2.4	2.8	3.4	4.5	4.2	3.3	3.0	2.2	3.3	3.6
70	Mfg costs	1.9	2.3	2.8	3.6	3.4	2.6	2.5	1.8	2.6	2.9
71	Cost of selling	5.5	5.5	5.5	6.0	6.0	5.5	5.5	5.5	5.5	5.5
72	Plant costs	1.0	1.0	1.0	1.0	1.0	1.0	1.0	1.0	1.0	1.0
73	Office costs	0.6	0.6	0.6	0.6	0.6	0.6	0.6	0.6	0.6	0.6
74	Admin. salaries	4.0	4.0	4.0	4.0	4.0	4.0	4.0	4.0	4.0	4.0
75	Profit	0.1	2.2	5	9.4	8	4.4	4	-0.5	4.3	5.7

(continued)

	A	B	C	D	E	F	G	H	I	J	K
76											
77	ACTUAL	Jan.	Feb.	Mar.	Apr.	May	Jun.	Jul.	Aug.	Sep.	Oct.
78	Sales	16.0	20.0	21.0	27.0	27.0	0.0	0.0	0.0	0.0	0.0
79	Delivery costs	0.5	0.6	0.6	0.8	0.7	0.0	0.0	0.0	0.0	0.0
80	Raw material	2.4	2.9	3.0	4.1	4.1	0.0	0.0	0.0	0.0	0.0
81	Mfg costs	1.9	2.3	2.5	3.3	3.3	0.0	0.0	0.0	0.0	0.0
82	Cost of selling	5.5	5.5	5.5	6.0	6.0	0.0	0.0	0.0	0.0	0.0
83	Plant costs	1.0	1.0	1.0	1.0	1.0	0.0	0.0	0.0	0.0	0.0
84	Office costs	0.6	0.6	0.6	0.6	0.6	0.0	0.0	0.0	0.0	0.0
85	Admin. salaries	4.0	4.0	4.0	4.0	4.0	0.0	0.0	0.0	0.0	0.0
86											
87	Plan is a combination of budget and ongoing reforecasts (6/86)										
88	PLAN	Jan.	Feb.	Mar.	Apr.	May	Jun.	Jul.	Aug.	Sep.	Oct.
89	Sales	16.0	19.0	23.0	30.0	28.0	21.0	20.0	14.0	21.0	23.0
90	Delivery costs	0.5	0.6	0.7	0.9	0.8	0.5	0.3	0.3	0.6	0.6
91	Raw material	2.4	2.8	3.4	4.5	4.2	3.1	2.8	2.0	3.1	3.4
92	Mfg costs	1.9	2.3	2.8	3.6	3.4	2.5	2.4	1.7	2.5	2.8
93	Cost of selling	5.5	5.5	5.5	6.0	6.0	5.5	5.5	5.5	5.5	5.5
94	Plant costs	1.0	1.0	1.0	1.0	1.0	1.0	1.0	1.0	1.0	1.0
95	Office costs	0.6	0.6	0.6	0.6	0.6	0.6	0.6	0.6	0.6	0.6
96	Admin. salaries	4.0	4.0	4.0	4.0	4.0	4.0	4.0	4.0	4.0	4.0
97											

After entering the data, we spend a great deal of time on the model itself. The model is really the working report—the one the department manager will use often to track the department's performance. The model spreads out the variable costs, the fixed costs, the sales, and the profits. It tracks the costs and profits as a percentage of sales so that we can see how our variable costs track our variable sales.

While we only required the December figure for 1984, we included the whole year to give ourselves some latitude for changing our mind when we return to the selling efficiency report and graph. (November and December figures are not shown in the example.) We also computed a profits line for our original budget data because we will need it in our profit report. (Actual and plan profits are computed in the Model Area.)

	A	B	C	D	E	F	G	H	I	J	K
98	Model										
99											
100	MONTHLY PLAN	May	:Current month								
101		Jan.	Feb.	Mar.	Apr.	May	Jun.	Jul.	Aug.	Sep.	Oct.
102	Sales	16.0	19.0	23.0	30.0	28.0	21.0	20.0	14.0	21.0	23.0
103	Variable costs										
104	Delivery costs	0.5	0.6	0.7	0.9	0.8	0.5	0.3	0.3	0.6	0.6
105	Raw material	2.4	2.8	3.4	4.5	4.2	3.1	2.8	2.0	3.1	3.4
106	Mfg costs	1.9	2.3	2.8	3.6	3.4	2.5	2.4	1.7	2.5	2.8
107	Total var. costs	4.8	5.7	6.9	9.0	8.4	6.1	5.5	4.0	6.2	6.8
108	(%)	30%	30%	30%	30%	30%	29%	28%	29%	30%	30%
109	Fixed costs										
110	Cost of selling	5.5	5.5	5.5	6.0	6.0	5.5	5.5	5.5	5.5	5.5
111	Plant costs	1.0	1.0	1.0	1.0	1.0	1.0	1.0	1.0	1.0	1.0
112	Office costs	0.6	0.6	0.6	0.6	0.6	0.6	0.6	0.6	0.6	0.6
113	Admin. salaries	4.0	4.0	4.0	4.0	4.0	4.0	4.0	4.0	4.0	4.0
114	Total fix costs	11.1	11.1	11.1	11.6	11.6	11.1	11.1	11.1	11.1	11.1
115	(%)	69%	58%	48%	39%	41%	53%	56%	79%	53%	48%
116											
117	Profit	0.1	2.2	5.0	9.4	8.0	3.8	3.4	-1.1	3.7	5.1
118	(%)	1%	12%	22%	31%	29%	18%	17%	-8%	17%	22%
119											
120											
121	MONTHLY ACTUAL	May	:Current month								
122		Jan.	Feb.	Mar.	Apr.	May	Jun.	Jul.	Aug.	Sep.	Oct.
123	Sales	16.0	20.0	21.0	27.0	27.0	0.0	0.0	0.0	0.0	0.0
124	Variable costs										
125	Delivery costs	0.5	0.6	0.6	0.8	0.7	0.0	0.0	0.0	0.0	0.0
126	Raw material	2.4	2.9	3.0	4.1	4.1	0.0	0.0	0.0	0.0	0.0
127	Mfg costs	1.9	2.3	2.5	3.3	3.3	0.0	0.0	0.0	0.0	0.0
128	Total var. costs	4.8	5.8	6.1	8.2	8.1	0.0	0.0	0.0	0.0	0.0
129	(%)	30%	29%	29%	30%	30%	####	####	####	####	####
130	Fixed costs										
131	Cost of selling	5.5	5.5	5.5	6.0	6.0	0.0	0.0	0.0	0.0	0.0
132	Plant costs	1.0	1.0	1.0	1.0	1.0	0.0	0.0	0.0	0.0	0.0
133	Office costs	0.6	0.6	0.6	0.6	0.6	0.0	0.0	0.0	0.0	0.0
134	Admin. salaries	4.0	4.0	4.0	4.0	4.0	0.0	0.0	0.0	0.0	0.0
135	Total fix costs	11.1	11.1	11.1	11.6	11.6	0.0	0.0	0.0	0.0	0.0
136	(%)	69%	56%	53%	43%	43%	####	####	####	####	####
137											
138	Profit	0.1	3.1	3.8	7.2	7.3	0.0	0.0	0.0	0.0	0.0
139	(%)	1%	16%	18%	27%	27%	####	####	####	####	####
140											

(continued)

	A	B	C	D	E	F	G	H	I	J	K
141											
142	MONTHLY DIFFERENCE		May	:Current month							
143	Difference = (actual - plan)/plan										
144		Jan.	Feb.	Mar.	Apr.	May	Jun.	Jul.	Aug.	Sep.	Oct.
145	Sales	0%	5%	-9%	-10%	-4%	-100%	-100%	-100%	-100%	-100%
146	Variable costs										
147	Delivery costs	0%	0%	-14%	-11%	-13%	-100%	-100%	-100%	-100%	-100%
148	Raw material	0%	4%	-12%	-9%	-2%	-100%	-100%	-100%	-100%	-100%
149	Mfg costs	0%	0%	-11%	-8%	-3%	-100%	-100%	-100%	-100%	-100%
150	Total var. costs	0%	2%	-12%	-9%	-4%	-100%	-100%	-100%	-100%	-100%
151	(%)	0%	-3%	-3%	1%	0%	####	####	####	####	####
152	Fixed costs										
153	Cost of selling	0%	0%	0%	0%	0%	-100%	-100%	-100%	-100%	-100%
154	Plant costs	0%	0%	0%	0%	0%	-100%	-100%	-100%	-100%	-100%
155	Office costs	0%	0%	0%	0%	0%	-100%	-100%	-100%	-100%	-100%
156	Admin. salaries	0%	0%	0%	0%	0%	-100%	-100%	-100%	-100%	-100%
157	Total fix costs	0%	0%	0%	0%	0%	-100%	-100%	-100%	-100%	-100%
158	(%)	0%	-5%	10%	11%	4%	####	####	####	####	####
159											
160	Profit	0%	41%	-24%	-23%	-9%	-100%	-100%	-100%	-100%	-100%
161	(%)	0%	34%	-17%	-15%	-5%	####	####	####	####	####
162											
163											

We format our differences to highlight relative differences by using percentages rather than absolute amounts. We tell the reader how we calculate our difference with a formula: difference = (actual – plan)/plan.

We repeat the basic model for our summary figures.

	A	B	C	D	E	F	G	H	I	J	K
164	SUMMARY PLAN		May	:Current month							
165		Qtr 1	Qtr 2	Qtr 3	Qtr 4		Half 1	Half 2		Year	
166	Sales	58.0	79.0	55.0	74.0		137.0	129.0		266.0	
167	Variable costs										
168	Delivery costs	1.8	2.2	1.3	2.1		4.0	3.4		7.4	
169	Raw material	8.6	11.8	8.0	11.0		20.4	19.0		39.4	
170	Mfg costs	7.0	9.5	6.5	8.8		16.5	15.3		31.8	
171	Total var. costs	17.4	23.5	15.8	21.9		40.9	37.7		78.6	
172	(%)	30%	30%	29%	30%		30%	29%		30%	
173	Fixed costs										
174	Cost of selling	16.5	17.5	16.5	17.5		34.0	34.0		68.0	
175	Plant costs	3.0	3.0	3.0	3.0		6.0	6.0		12.0	
176	Office costs	1.8	1.8	1.8	1.8		3.6	3.6		7.2	
177	Admin. salaries	12.0	12.0	12.0	12.0		24.0	24.0		48.0	
178	Total fix costs	33.3	34.3	33.3	34.3		67.6	67.6		135.2	
179	(%)	57%	43%	61%	46%		49%	52%		51%	
180											
181	Profit	7.3	21.2	5.9	17.8		28.5	23.7		52.2	
182	(%)	13%	27%	11%	24%		21%	18%		20%	

(continued)

	A	B	C	D	E	F	G	H	I	J	K
183											
184											
185	SUMMARY ACTUAL	May	:Current month								
186		Qtr 1	Qtr 2	Qtr 3	Qtr 4		Half 1	Half 2		Year	
187	Sales	57.0	54.0	0.0	0.0		111.0	0.0		111.0	
188	Variable costs										
189	Delivery costs	1.7	1.5	0.0	0.0		3.2	0.0		3.2	
190	Raw material	8.3	8.2	0.0	0.0		16.5	0.0		16.5	
191	Mfg costs	6.7	6.6	0.0	0.0		13.3	0.0		13.3	
192	Total var. costs	16.7	16.3	0.0	0.0		33.0	0.0		33.0	
193	(%)	29%	30%	####	####		30%	####		30%	
194	Fixed costs										
195	Cost of selling	16.5	12.0	0.0	0.0		28.5	0.0		28.5	
196	Plant costs	3.0	2.0	0.0	0.0		5.0	0.0		5.0	
197	Office costs	1.8	1.2	0.0	0.0		3.0	0.0		3.0	
198	Admin. salaries	12.0	8.0	0.0	0.0		20.0	0.0		20.0	
199	Total fix costs	33.3	23.2	0.0	0.0		56.5	0.0		56.5	
200	(%)	58%	43%	####	####		51%	####		51%	
201											
202	Profit	7.0	14.5	0.0	0.0		21.5	0.0		21.5	
203	(%)	12%	27%	####	####		19%	####		19%	
204											
205											
206	SUMMARY DIFFERENCE			May	:Current month						
207	Difference = (actual - plan)/plan										
208		Qtr 1	Qtr 2	Qtr 3	Qtr 4		Half 1	Half 2		Year	
209	Sales	-2%	-32%	-100%	-100%		-19%	-100%		-58%	
210	Variable costs										
211	Delivery costs	-6%	-32%	-100%	-100%		-20%	-100%		-57%	
212	Raw material	-3%	-31%	-100%	-100%		-19%	-100%		-58%	
213	Mfg costs	-4%	-31%	-100%	-100%		-19%	-100%		-58%	
214	Total var. costs	-4%	-31%	-100%	-100%		-19%	-100%		-58%	
215	(%)	-2%	1%	####	####		0%	####		1%	
216	Fixed costs										
217	Cost of selling	0%	-31%	-100%	-100%		-16%	-100%		-58%	
218	Plant costs	0%	-33%	-100%	-100%		-17%	-100%		-58%	
219	Office costs	0%	-33%	-100%	-100%		-17%	-100%		-58%	
220	Admin. salaries	0%	-33%	-100%	-100%		-17%	-100%		-58%	
221	Total fix costs	0%	-32%	-100%	-100%		-16%	-100%		-58%	
222	(%)	2%	-1%	####	####		3%	####		0%	
223											
224	Profit	-4%	-32%	-100%	-100%		-25%	-100%		-59%	
225	(%)	-2%	0%	####	####		-7%	####		-1%	
226											

The error comments are left in the model because the model is intended for the working department manager only. The error comments remind the viewer that the full year is not yet complete. The model itself is instructive in its size. While not striving to become large, our model has reached a size where a printed copy is necessary to comprehend it. Our concern for the reader is vindicated: Even the original author must be a reader. The model is far too large for the tiny screen of the computer.

The size of the model gets altered several times as we build the formulas. We change the global column width to be sure we can see as much as possible with the two- and three-digit numbers we are manipulating. Column A gets stretched to accommodate the longer titles. The model takes six hours to get right—total elapsed time is 10 hours.

With the knowledge that the model may be subject to errors, we make a note to be sure and do a good Verify Area. But, before doing that, we revisit the reports to get them finished with real data. As we work on them, we find that we must further revise our original ideas. We format the numbers in the reports to two decimal places so they will be familiar to the reader's eye.

	A	B	C	D	E	F	G	H	I	J	K
232	Department goals for the quarter										
233	-Be sure to adjust titles and formulas.										
234	12-Jun-86			OUR DEPARTMENT'S QUARTERLY PERFORMANCE							
235				FOR MONTH OF MAY (Month 2 of Quarter 2)							
236			Quarter to date			Until end of quarter					
237		Plan	Actual	Rate		Plan	To go		Rate	Comment	
238	Sales	58.0	54.0	93%		79.0	25.0		68%	Ahead of the game	
239	Costs	40.6	39.5	97%		57.8	18.3		68%	"	
240	Profits	17.4	14.5	83%		21.2	6.7		68%	"	
241											
242	We are close to being on target. Let's keep up the good work!										
243	The third month will be a big one. We can make our sales target if we										
244	continue at the level of the last two months.										
247	Department's year-to-date performance										
248	-Be sure to check titles and formulas for the current month.										
249		12-Jun-86		OUR DEPARTMENT'S YEAR-TO-DATE PERFORMANCE							
250				FOR MONTH OF MAY (Month 5 of 12)							
251		Year to date				Until end of year					
252		Plan	Actual	Rate		Plan	To go		Rate	Comment	
253	Sales	116.00	111.00	96%		266.00	155.00		42%	Try to recover 5$	
254	Costs	91.30	89.50	98%		213.84	124.34		42%	Keep control of costs	
255	Profits	24.70	21.50	87%		52.16	30.66		41%	Profit's down $3	

The first two reports are quite similar. They both report on the progress of the department—the progress during the quarter and the progress during the year. Both report areas need some directions in addition to the actual report. We include the directions at the top.

	A	B	C	D	E	F	G	H	I	J	K
251	Department cost analysis										
252	-Be sure to check titles and formulas for the current month.										
253	12-Jun-86			DEPARTMENTAL COST ANALYSIS							
254				FOR MONTH OF MAY (Month 2 of Quarter 2)							
255		Month	Plan	Dif.	YTD	Plan	Dif.	Rate	Comment		
256	Delivery costs	0.70	0.80	-0.10	3.20	3.50	-0.30	91%	Variable costs off		
257	Raw material	4.10	4.20	-0.10	16.50	17.30	-0.80	95%			
258	Mfg costs	3.30	3.40	-0.10	13.30	14.00	-0.70	95%			
259	Cost of selling	6.00	6.00	0.00	28.50	28.50	0.00	100%	Fixed costs on target		
260	Plant costs	1.00	1.00	0.00	5.00	5.00	0.00	100%			
261	Office costs	0.60	0.60	0.00	3.00	3.00	0.00	100%			
262	Admin. salaries	4.00	4.00	0.00	20.00	20.00	0.00	100%			
263											
264	Total	19.70	20.00	-0.30	89.50	91.30	-1.80	98%	Overall costs a little high		
265											

The department manager uses this report to get a fix on his or her costs. The variable costs are down because sales are down, but the fixed costs remain stubbornly at the planned level. The directions warn the user that the formulas and the title must be changed for the next month.

	A	B	C	D	E	F	G	H	I	J	K
266	Sales and selling costs										
267	-Be sure to adjust smoothing formulas for last three actuals.										
268	-If sales are zero, then costs as a % of sales is 0%.										
269	12-Jun-86		SALES AND SELLING COSTS, MONTH OF MAY								
270		Jan.	Feb.	Mar.	Apr.	May	Jun.	Jul.	Aug.	Sep.	Oct.
271	Sales	16.00	20.00	21.00	27.00	27.00	0.00	0.00	0.00	0.00	0.00
272	Costs	5.50	5.50	5.50	6.00	6.00	0.00	0.00	0.00	0.00	0.00
273	Costs as % of sales	34%	28%	26%	22%	22%	0%	0%	0%	0%	0%
274	Smoothed(5 mth)*										
275	Sales	21.4	22	22.2	25	27	0	0	0	0	0
276	Costs as % of sales	26%	25%	25%	24%	22%	0%	0%	0%	0%	0%
277											
278	*Next to last month is smoothed over 3 months, last month is unsmoothed.										
279	Note: This report is supported by the graph "Selling costs (%) down slightly in last six months"										
280											

The report reassures the manager that underneath the seasonal fluctuation in sales, the cost of selling remains under 25 percent and may be declining. The "Costs as a % of sales" formula contains an if…then function to print a 0 when sales are 0 in order to avoid some unnecessarily disturbing "error" messages in the cells of a report. Notes on important calculations are included in the report. (The report bleeds off the page here and in regular use would require printing sideways in landscape orientation or on wide paper.)

	A	B	C	D	E	F	G	H	I	J	K
281	Department performance report										
282	-Be sure to check titles and formulas for the current month.										
283	12-Jun-86				IDEAL DEPARTMENT, MONTH OF MAY						
284				YEAR-TO-DATE PERFORMANCE				REPLANNING			
285	YTD IS JAN-MAY	YTD	YTD	YTD	Actual/	Actual/		Annual	Annual		
286		Budget	Plan	Actual	Plan	Budget		Budget	Plan	Budget	
287	Sales	116.00	116.00	111.00	96%	96%		273.00	266.00	97%	
288	Variable costs	34.80	34.80	33.00	95%	95%		81.20	78.64	97%	
289	Fixed costs	56.50	56.50	56.50	100%	100%		135.20	135.20	100%	
290											
291	Profit	24.70	24.70	21.50	87%	87%		56.60	52.16	92%	
292											

The performance report to top management is a bit different than originally envisioned. More information is included in less space. This repeated improvement of the final form should convince us that making a good report is harder than we are willing to admit. We should not think of a report as merely format—a report is a way to shape the information we want to convey. Notice that the reporting date is included on every report. We spent three more hours on our reports (elapsed time is now 13 hours).

The next activity is to verify our model. We do that by introducing a yearly summary column on the monthly data and cross-footing the profit for the year against the sum of the monthly profits. We repeat this procedure at three other points in the model and at three points in our reports. Beneath the Graphing Area we construct a Verify Area to collect information from these cross-checks.

	A	B	C	D	E	F	G	H	I	J	K
353	Verify area										
354	297.16 The model verification sum										
355											
356	If an error appears here, check below and then the appropriate area of the model.										
357	(Be sure you have recalculated the whole model.)										
358	135.2 The monthly plan yearly profit										
359	21.5 The monthly actual yearly profit										
360	52.16 The summary plan yearly profit										
361	21.5 The summary actual yearly profit										
362	17.4 The qtr-to-date planned profits in										
363	Department's goals for quarter report										
364	24.7 The year-to-date planned profits in										
365	Department's year-to-date performance report										
366	24.7 The year-to-date planned profits in										
367	Department's performance report										
368											

After completing the Verify Area, we turn our attention to building the charts and graphs to accompany the reports. The graphs are changed several times as we build and review them. The originally envisioned graphs do not look as good as our hand sketches. They do, however, suggest other forms that might be improvements (see Figures 6-1 and 6-2).

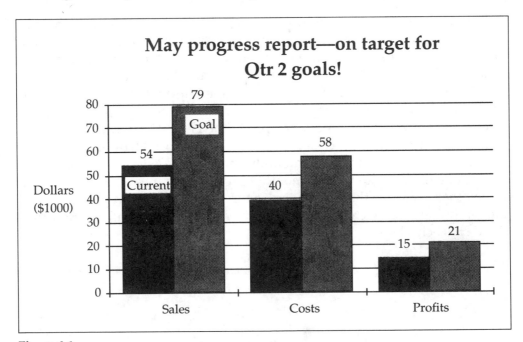

Figure 6-1.

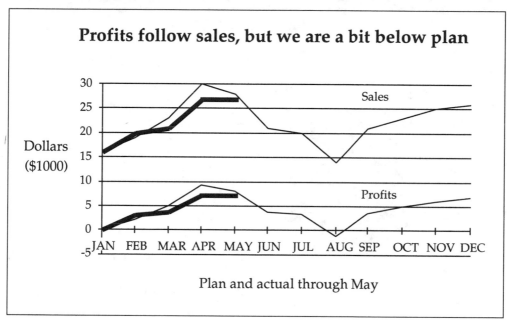

Figure 6-2.

The final charts and graphs suit the original purposes. The bar chart tells the department where they are on the way to the quarterly goals. The year-to-date sales and profit figures show how the department is performing against plan (and, incidentally, how all the costs were behaving since the difference between sales and profits is costs).

These graphs will not only be displayed for the department, they will be presented to upper management and used by the department manager. The charts in Figures 6-3 and 6-4 will be used only by the department manager.

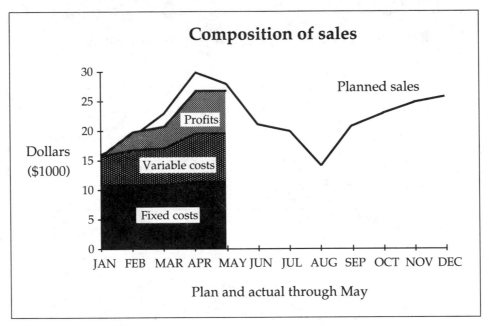

Figure 6-3.

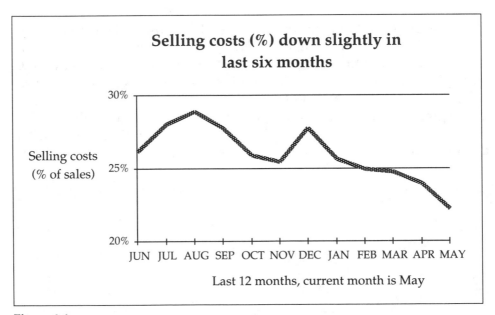

Figure 6-4.

The department manager gets a look at fixed costs versus variable costs in the composition of sales and a look at the selling efficiency in the line chart. All graphs come with extra instructions in the appropriate Graphing Area. The name of each graph is also included in the Graphing Area.

	A	B	C	D	E	F	G	H	I	J	K
293	Graph area										
294	"Qtr2 goals": Dept. Qtrly Goals, Sales, Costs, Profits—everyone										
295		Actual	Qtr plan								
296	Sales	54	79								
297	Costs	40	58								
298	Profits	15	21								
299											
300	"Sales and profits": planned vs. actual—everyone										
301	"Sales composition": fixed cst, var cst, profit—manager										
302	1. The months to come are shifted down a row to make the graph end sharply										
303	by using blank values (see Sales Composition graph).										
304					Sales			Profit			
305		Fixed	Var	Prof	Budget	Plan	Actual	Budget	Plan	Actual	
306	JAN	11.1	4.8	0.1	16.0	16.0	16.0	0.1	0.1	0.1	
307	FEB	11.1	5.8	3.1	19.0	19.0	20.0	2.2	2.2	3.1	
308	MAR	11.1	6.1	3.8	23.0	23.0	21.0	5.0	5.0	3.8	
309	APR	11.6	8.2	7.2	30.0	30.0	27.0	9.4	9.4	7.2	
310	MAY	11.6	8.1	7.3	28.0	28.0	27.0	8.0	8.0	7.3	
311	JUN				22.0	21.0	0.0	4.4	3.8	0.0	
312	JUL	0.0	0.0	0.0	21.0	20.0	0.0	4.0	3.4	0.0	
313	AUG	0.0	0.0	0.0	15.0	14.0	0.0	-0.5	-1.1	0.0	
314	SEP	0.0	0.0	0.0	22.0	21.0	0.0	4.3	3.7	0.0	
315	OCT	0.0	0.0	0.0	24.0	23.0	0.0	5.7	5.1	0.0	
316	NOV	0.0	0.0	0.0	26.0	25.0	0.0	6.6	6.0	0.0	
317	DEC	0.0	0.0	0.0	27.0	26.0	0.0	7.4	6.8	0.0	
318		0.0	0.0	0.0							
319											
320	"Selling costs (%)": last 12 months, cost of sales/smoothed sales (5-mth smoothing)—dept mgr.										
321	1. Insert a blank row at the beginning of current 12 months.										
322	2. Change the smoothing formulas near the end of the current 12 months.										
323	(Next to last is 3 month, last is raw)										
324		CST/SLS	Sales	Smoothed		Costs					
325	DEC		23.0			6.0					
326	JAN		15.0			5.5					
327	FEB	27%	17.0	20.6		5.5					
328	MAR	26%	21.0	21.0		5.5					
329	APR	25%	27.0	22.0		5.5					
330	MAY	25%	25.0	22.4		5.5					

(continued)

	A	B	C	D	E	F	G	H	I	J	K
331											
332	JUN	26%	20.0	21.0		5.5					
333	JUL	28%	19.0	19.6		5.5					
334	AUG	29%	14.0	19.0		5.5					
335	SEP	28%	20.0	19.8		5.5					
336	OCT	26%	22.0	21.2		5.5					
337	NOV	25%	24.0	21.6		5.5					
338	DEC	28%	26.0	21.6		6.0					
339	JAN	26%	16.0	21.4		5.5					
340	FEB	25%	20.0	22.0		5.5					
341	MAR	25%	21.0	22.2		5.5					
342	APR	24%	27.0	25.0	**	6.0					
343	MAY	22%	27.0	27.0	**	6.0					
344	JUN		0.0			0.0					
345	JUL		0.0			0.0					
346	AUG		0.0			0.0					
347	SEP		0.0			0.0					
348	OCT		0.0			0.0					
349	NOV		0.0			0.0					
350	DEC		0.0			0.0					
351	**formulas need work										
352											

Our Graphing Area allows us to be concerned with how the user makes graphs. We mark special formulas for revision. We give special instructions where necessary. We keep the data streams compactly arranged in vertical columns.

The Graphing Area contains odd-looking tables that help make good-looking graphs. We shift the inactive data down one month to create a blank line that causes the graphed areas to stop cleanly. By shifting the block down a line, we preserve our formulas so we only have to do simple moving, not complicated formula rebuilding, when we move on to the next month. We can also insert a blank line to clearly mark the beginning of a rolling 12-month selling efficiency graph.

We store numbers in a format that keeps us from making mistakes when we graph. A rate is displayed as .2895, a number visible between 0 and 1, and not 29 percent, a number one might mistakenly try to find between 1 and 100. The graphs take four hours to complete. Our total elapsed time is 17 hours.

We add some easy-to-follow instructions to the Introduction and feel pretty good about our completed spreadsheet. We decide to take it out for a test drive. We will add a month of June actuals and follow our instructions and see how the parts work.

	A	B	C	D	E	F	G	H	I	J	K
17	To use:										
18	1. Add new actual data.										
19	2. Be sure to restrict reforecasts to the plan from present until year end.										
20	3. Adjust report formulas and titles before printing them out.										
21	4. Adjust graphing area and graphs before printing.										
22	5. Print out selected models, reports, and graphs as needed.										

The month of June was a good month, with better than expected sales. We enter the data and alter the formulas. While we alter formulas, the verify warnings turn on twice to alert us that formulas do not cross-check. An hour later the new spreadsheet is complete. The reports make sense. The graphs neatly summarize the information. Our test drive convinces us that the model can be used repeatedly by an informed assistant. The instructions are sound and will work in practice.

We also realize that our manager might want to play "what if?" with the model, so we include some directions on how to go about doing that.

	A	B	C	D	E	F	G	H	I	J	K
23	To model various sales levels:										
24	1. Be sure to use a renamed copy of this spreadsheet; NOT THE ORIGINAL.										
25	2. Type in projected sales in Actual Initial Data.										
26	3. Use a formula of your choice to project variable costs.										
27	4. Adjust selected fixed costs (or hold constant).										
28	5. Print out selected models, reports, and graphs as needed (be sure to label as projections).										

One way of reducing a variable cost to a percentage of sales is:

Variable cost % of sales = <sum of costs so far>/<sum of sales so far>

With this percentage, the user can project sales and variable costs as a percentage of sales. We decide the instructions can withstand the test of use.

We give the model to a friend to proofread. His comments are: "I liked it. I had some questions in the Initial Data Area, but I answered them when I read the model. The spreadsheet looks like it might be useful. I may want to use a copy. The reports and graphs made sense."

As a final step, we protect against accidental alteration of a cell by explicitly unprotecting those cells that we wish to allow people to change. By explicitly unprotecting cells, we enforce the assumption that a cell will be protected unless a special effort was made to unprotect it.

We examine the time it took to build the model against the time it took to revise it and conclude that the 20-hour investment will repay our efforts with swift, error-free updates each month. The time invested in writing the model well will be repaid in time not spent awkwardly modifying an error-ridden tangle of formulas and hidden constants.

Finally, four days later, a good name for the model pops into our head: Progress. The purpose of the model is to track our department's progress against its plan. We adopt our new title, polish up our statement of purpose, note our revision, and call our job done. The entire model looks like this:

	A	B	C	D	E	F	G	H	I	J	K
1	**PROGRESS**		17 November 1986		John M. Nevison						
2	(C) Copyright 1986	by John M. Nevison									
3	10-Apr-90	Date printed									
5	**Revision history**										
6	21 Nov 86			JMN changed the title and rewrote the purpose statement							
7				and table of contents.							
9	**Description**										
10				The purpose of this model is to illustrate a well-made spreadsheet that							
11				provides a department manager with the tools he needs to track his							
12				department's budget progress against its plan. It includes:							
13				A twelve-month plan for the year,							
14				A month by month list of the actual figures as they occur.							
15				Reports and graphs for the manager							
16				Reports and graphs to be posted for the department to see							
17				Reports and graphs for upper management							
19	**To use**										
20	1. Add new actual data.										
21	2. Be sure to restrict reforecasts to the plan from present until year end.										
22	3. Adjust report formulas, and titles before printing them out.										
23	4. Adjust graphing area and graphs before printing.										
24	5. Print out selected models, reports, and graphs as needed.										
25	**To model various sales levels**										
26	1. Be sure to use a renamed copy of this spreadsheet; NOT THE ORIGINAL.										
27	2. Type in projected sales in Actual Initial Data.										
28	3. Use a formula of your choice to project variable costs.										
29	4. Adjust selected fixed costs (or hold constant).										
30	5. Print out selected models, reports, and graphs as needed (be sure to label as projections).										
32	**Contents**										
33				Introduction: title, description, contents							
34				Initial data							
35				Back data							
36				Initial budget							
37				Actual budget to date							
38				Plan (budget plus reforecasts)							
39				Twelve-month model							
40				Plan							
41				Actual							
42				Difference							

(continued)

	A	B	C	D	E	F	G	H	I	J	K
43		Summary models: quarters, halves, year									
44			Plan								
45			Actual								
46			Difference								
47		Department goals for quarter									
48		Department's year-to-date performance									
49		Department cost analysis									
50		Sales and selling costs									
51		Department performance report									
52		Graphs:									
53			Qtr2 goals								
54			Sales and profits								
55			Sales composition								
56			Selling efficiency								
57		Verify area									
60	**Initial data**										
61		May :Current month									
62											
63	BACK DATA	Jan.	Feb.	Mar.	Apr.	May	Jun.	Jul.	Aug.	Sep.	Oct.
64	Sales 84	12	17	19	23	22	19	18	15	18	20
65	Sales 85	15	17	21	27	25	20	19	14	20	22
66	Cost of selling 84	5.5	5.5	5.5	6.0	6.0	6.0	5.5	5.5	5.5	5.5
67	Cost of selling 85	5.5	5.5	5.5	5.5	5.5	5.5	5.5	5.5	5.5	5.5
68											
69	ORIGINAL BUDGET	Jan.	Feb.	Mar.	Apr.	May	Jun.	Jul.	Aug.	Sep.	Oct.
70	Sales	16.0	19.0	23.0	30.0	28.0	22.0	21.0	15.0	22.0	24.0
71	Delivery costs	0.5	0.6	0.7	0.9	0.8	0.6	0.4	0.4	0.7	0.7
72	Raw material	2.4	2.8	3.4	4.5	4.2	3.3	3.0	2.2	3.3	3.6
73	Mfg costs	1.9	2.3	2.8	3.6	3.4	2.6	2.5	1.8	2.6	2.9
74	Cost of selling	5.5	5.5	5.5	6.0	6.0	5.5	5.5	5.5	5.5	5.5
75	Plant costs	1.0	1.0	1.0	1.0	1.0	1.0	1.0	1.0	1.0	1.0
76	Office costs	0.6	0.6	0.6	0.6	0.6	0.6	0.6	0.6	0.6	0.6
77	Admin salaries	4.0	4.0	4.0	4.0	4.0	4.0	4.0	4.0	4.0	4.0
78	Profit	0.1	2.2	5	9.4	8	4.4	4	-0.5	4.3	5.7
79											
80	ACTUAL	Jan.	Feb.	Mar.	Apr.	May	Jun.	Jul.	Aug.	Sep.	Oct.
81	Sales	16.0	20.0	21.0	27.0	27.0	0.0	0.0	0.0	0.0	0.0
82	Delivery costs	0.5	0.6	0.6	0.8	0.7	0.0	0.0	0.0	0.0	0.0
83	Raw material	2.4	2.9	3.0	4.1	4.1	0.0	0.0	0.0	0.0	0.0
84	Mfg costs	1.9	2.3	2.5	3.3	3.3	0.0	0.0	0.0	0.0	0.0
85	Cost of selling	5.5	5.5	5.5	6.0	6.0	0.0	0.0	0.0	0.0	0.0
86	Plant costs	1.0	1.0	1.0	1.0	1.0	0.0	0.0	0.0	0.0	0.0
87	Office costs	0.6	0.6	0.6	0.6	0.6	0.0	0.0	0.0	0.0	0.0
88	Admin salaries	4.0	4.0	4.0	4.0	4.0	0.0	0.0	0.0	0.0	0.0
89											
90	Plan is a combination of budget and ongoing reforecasts (6/86)										
91	PLAN	Jan.	Feb.	Mar.	Apr.	May	Jun.	Jul.	Aug.	Sep.	Oct.
92	Sales	16.0	19.0	23.0	30.0	28.0	21.0	20.0	14.0	21.0	23.0
93	Delivery costs	0.5	0.6	0.7	0.9	0.8	0.5	0.3	0.3	0.6	0.6
94	Raw material	2.4	2.8	3.4	4.5	4.2	3.1	2.8	2.0	3.1	3.4
95	Mfg costs	1.9	2.3	2.8	3.6	3.4	2.5	2.4	1.7	2.5	2.8
96	Cost of selling	5.5	5.5	5.5	6.0	6.0	5.5	5.5	5.5	5.5	5.5
97	Plant costs	1.0	1.0	1.0	1.0	1.0	1.0	1.0	1.0	1.0	1.0
98	Office costs	0.6	0.6	0.6	0.6	0.6	0.6	0.6	0.6	0.6	0.6
99	Admin salaries	4.0	4.0	4.0	4.0	4.0	4.0	4.0	4.0	4.0	4.0

(continued)

	A	B	C	D	E	F	G	H	I	J	K
102	Model										
103											
104	MONTHLY PLAN	May	:Current month								
105		Jan.	Feb.	Mar.	Apr.	May	Jun.	Jul.	Aug.	Sep.	Oct.
106	Sales	16.0	19.0	23.0	30.0	28.0	21.0	20.0	14.0	21.0	23.0
107	Variable costs										
108	Delivery costs	0.5	0.6	0.7	0.9	0.8	0.5	0.3	0.3	0.6	0.6
109	Raw material	2.4	2.8	3.4	4.5	4.2	3.1	2.8	2.0	3.1	3.4
110	Mfg costs	1.9	2.3	2.8	3.6	3.4	2.5	2.4	1.7	2.5	2.8
111	Total var costs	4.8	5.7	6.9	9.0	8.4	6.1	5.5	4.0	6.2	6.8
112	(%)	30%	30%	30%	30%	30%	29%	28%	29%	30%	30%
113	Fixed costs										
114	Cost of selling	5.5	5.5	5.5	6.0	6.0	5.5	5.5	5.5	5.5	5.5
115	Plant costs	1.0	1.0	1.0	1.0	1.0	1.0	1.0	1.0	1.0	1.0
116	Office costs	0.6	0.6	0.6	0.6	0.6	0.6	0.6	0.6	0.6	0.6
117	Admin salaries	4.0	4.0	4.0	4.0	4.0	4.0	4.0	4.0	4.0	4.0
118	Total fix costs	11.1	11.1	11.1	11.6	11.6	11.1	11.1	11.1	11.1	11.1
119	(%)	69%	58%	48%	39%	41%	53%	56%	79%	53%	48%
120											
121	Profit	0.1	2.2	5.0	9.4	8.0	3.8	3.4	-1.1	3.7	5.1
122	(%)	1%	12%	22%	31%	29%	18%	17%	-8%	17%	22%
123											
124											
125	MONTHLY ACTUAL	May	:Current month								
126		Jan.	Feb.	Mar.	Apr.	May	Jun.	Jul.	Aug.	Sep.	Oct.
127	Sales	16.0	20.0	21.0	27.0	27.0	0.0	0.0	0.0	0.0	0.0
128	Variable costs										
129	Delivery costs	0.5	0.6	0.6	0.8	0.7	0.0	0.0	0.0	0.0	0.0
130	Raw material	2.4	2.9	3.0	4.1	4.1	0.0	0.0	0.0	0.0	0.0
131	Mfg costs	1.9	2.3	2.5	3.3	3.3	0.0	0.0	0.0	0.0	0.0
132	Total var costs	4.8	5.8	6.1	8.2	8.1	0.0	0.0	0.0	0.0	0.0
133	(%)	30%	29%	29%	30%	30%	#NUM!	#NUM!	#NUM!	#NUM!	#NUM!
134	Fixed costs										
135	Cost of selling	5.5	5.5	5.5	6.0	6.0	0.0	0.0	0.0	0.0	0.0
136	Plant costs	1.0	1.0	1.0	1.0	1.0	0.0	0.0	0.0	0.0	0.0
137	Office costs	0.6	0.6	0.6	0.6	0.6	0.0	0.0	0.0	0.0	0.0
138	Admin salaries	4.0	4.0	4.0	4.0	4.0	0.0	0.0	0.0	0.0	0.0
139	Total fix costs	11.1	11.1	11.1	11.6	11.6	0.0	0.0	0.0	0.0	0.0
140	(%)	69%	56%	53%	43%	43%	#NUM!	#NUM!	#NUM!	#NUM!	#NUM!
141											
142	Profit	0.1	3.1	3.8	7.2	7.3	0.0	0.0	0.0	0.0	0.0
143	(%)	1%	16%	18%	27%	27%	#NUM!	#NUM!	#NUM!	#NUM!	#NUM!
144											
145											
146	MONTHLY DIFFERENCE			May	:Current month						
147	Difference = (actual - plan)/plan										
148		Jan.	Feb.	Mar.	Apr.	May	Jun.	Jul.	Aug.	Sep.	Oct.
149	Sales	0%	5%	-9%	-10%	-4%	-100%	-100%	-100%	-100%	-100%
150	Variable costs										
151	Delivery costs	0%	0%	-14%	-11%	-13%	-100%	-100%	-100%	-100%	-100%
152	Raw material	0%	4%	-12%	-9%	-2%	-100%	-100%	-100%	-100%	-100%
153	Mfg costs	0%	0%	-11%	-8%	-3%	-100%	-100%	-100%	-100%	-100%
154	Total var costs	0%	2%	-12%	-9%	-4%	-100%	-100%	-100%	-100%	-100%
155	(%)	0%	-3%	-3%	1%	0%	#NUM!	#NUM!	#NUM!	#NUM!	#NUM!

(continued)

	A	B	C	D	E	F	G	H	I	J	K
156	Fixed costs										
157	Cost of selling	0%	0%	0%	0%	0%	-100%	-100%	-100%	-100%	-100%
158	Plant costs	0%	0%	0%	0%	0%	-100%	-100%	-100%	-100%	-100%
159	Office costs	0%	0%	0%	0%	0%	-100%	-100%	-100%	-100%	-100%
160	Admin salaries	0%	0%	0%	0%	0%	-100%	-100%	-100%	-100%	-100%
161	Total fix costs	0%	0%	0%	0%	0%	-100%	-100%	-100%	-100%	-100%
162	(%)	0%	-5%	10%	11%	4%	#NUM!	#NUM!	#NUM!	#NUM!	#NUM!
163											
164	Profit	0%	41%	-24%	-23%	-9%	-100%	-100%	-100%	-100%	-100%
165	(%)	0%	34%	-17%	-15%	-5%	#NUM!	#NUM!	#NUM!	#NUM!	#NUM!
166											
167											

	A	Qtr 1	Qtr 2	Qtr 3	Qtr 4		Half 1	Half 2		Year	
168	SUMMARY PLAN	May :Current month									
169		Qtr 1	Qtr 2	Qtr 3	Qtr 4		Half 1	Half 2		Year	
170	Sales	58.0	79.0	55.0	74.0		137.0	129.0		266.0	
171	Variable costs										
172	Delivery costs	1.8	2.2	1.3	2.1		4.0	3.4		7.4	
173	Raw material	8.6	11.8	8.0	11.0		20.4	19.0		39.4	
174	Mfg costs	7.0	9.5	6.5	8.8		16.5	15.3		31.8	
175	Total var costs	17.4	23.5	15.8	21.9		40.9	37.7		78.6	
176	(%)	30%	30%	29%	30%		30%	29%		30%	
177	Fixed costs										
178	Cost of selling	16.5	17.5	16.5	17.5		34.0	34.0		68.0	
179	Plant costs	3.0	3.0	3.0	3.0		6.0	6.0		12.0	
180	Office costs	1.8	1.8	1.8	1.8		3.6	3.6		7.2	
181	Admin salaries	12.0	12.0	12.0	12.0		24.0	24.0		48.0	
182	Total fix costs	33.3	34.3	33.3	34.3		67.6	67.6		135.2	
183	(%)	57%	43%	61%	46%		49%	52%		51%	
184											
185	Profit	7.3	21.2	5.9	17.8		28.5	23.7		52.2	
186	(%)	13%	27%	11%	24%		21%	18%		20%	
187											
188											
189	SUMMARY ACTUAL	May :Current month									
190		Qtr 1	Qtr 2	Qtr 3	Qtr 4		Half 1	Half 2		Year	
191	Sales	57.0	54.0	0.0	0.0		111.0	0.0		111.0	
192	Variable costs										
193	Delivery costs	1.7	1.5	0.0	0.0		3.2	0.0		3.2	
194	Raw material	8.3	8.2	0.0	0.0		16.5	0.0		16.5	
195	Mfg costs	6.7	6.6	0.0	0.0		13.3	0.0		13.3	
196	Total var costs	16.7	16.3	0.0	0.0		33.0	0.0		33.0	
197	(%)	29%	30%	#NUM!	#NUM!		30%	#NUM!		30%	
198	Fixed costs										
199	Cost of selling	16.5	12.0	0.0	0.0		28.5	0.0		28.5	
200	Plant costs	3.0	2.0	0.0	0.0		5.0	0.0		5.0	
201	Office costs	1.8	1.2	0.0	0.0		3.0	0.0		3.0	
202	Admin salaries	12.0	8.0	0.0	0.0		20.0	0.0		20.0	
203	Total fix costs	33.3	23.2	0.0	0.0		56.5	0.0		56.5	
204	(%)	58%	43%	#NUM!	#NUM!		51%	#NUM!		51%	
205											
206	Profit	7.0	14.5	0.0	0.0		21.5	0.0		21.5	
207	(%)	12%	27%	#NUM!	#NUM!		19%	#NUM!		19%	
208											

(continued)

	A	B	C	D	E	F	G	H	I	J	K
209											
210	SUMMARY DIFFERENCE		May :Current month								
211	Difference = (actual - plan)/plan										
212		Qtr 1	Qtr 2	Qtr 3	Qtr 4		Half 1	Half 2		Year	
213	Sales	-2%	-32%	-100%	-100%		-19%	-100%		-58%	
214	Variable costs										
215	Delivery costs	-6%	-32%	-100%	-100%		-20%	-100%		-57%	
216	Raw material	-3%	-31%	-100%	-100%		-19%	-100%		-58%	
217	Mfg costs	-4%	-31%	-100%	-100%		-19%	-100%		-58%	
218	Total var costs	-4%	-31%	-100%	-100%		-19%	-100%		-58%	
219	(%)	-2%	1%	#NUM!	#NUM!		0%	#NUM!		1%	
220	Fixed costs										
221	Cost of selling	0%	-31%	-100%	-100%		-16%	-100%		-58%	
222	Plant costs	0%	-33%	-100%	-100%		-17%	-100%		-58%	
223	Office costs	0%	-33%	-100%	-100%		-17%	-100%		-58%	
224	Admin salaries	0%	-33%	-100%	-100%		-17%	-100%		-58%	
225	Total fix costs	0%	-32%	-100%	-100%		-16%	-100%		-58%	
226	(%)	2%	-1%	#NUM!	#NUM!		3%	#NUM!		0%	
227											
228	Profit	-4%	-32%	-100%	-100%		-25%	-100%		-59%	
229	(%)	-2%	0%	#NUM!	#NUM!		-7%	#NUM!		-1%	

	A	B	C	D	E	F	G	H	I	J	K
232	**Department goals for the quarter**										
233	-Be sure to adjust titles and formulas.										
234	12-Jun-86		OUR DEPARTMENT'S QUARTERLY PERFORMANCE								
235			FOR MONTH OF MAY (Month 2 of Quarter 2)								
236			Quarter to date			Until end of quarter					
237		Plan	Actual	Rate		Plan	To go	Rate	Comment		
238	Sales	58	54.0	93%		79.0	25.0	68%	Ahead of the game		
239	Costs	40.6	39.5	97%		57.8	18.3	68%	"		
240	Profits	17.4	14.5	83%		21.2	6.7	68%	"		
241											
242	We are close to being on target. Let's keep up the good work!										
243	The third month will be a big one. We can make our sales target if we										
244	continue at the level of the last two months.										

	A	B	C	D	E	F	G	H	I	J	K
247	**Department's year-to-date performance**										
248	-Be sure to check titles and formulas for the current month.										
249		12-Jun-86	OUR DEPARTMENT'S YEAR-TO-DATE PERFORMANCE								
250			FOR MONTH OF MAY (Month 5 of 12)								
251		Year to date				Until end of year					
252		Plan	Actual	Rate		Plan	To go	Rate	Comment		
253	Sales	116.00	111.00	96%		266.00	155.00	42%	Try to recover $5		
254	Costs	91.30	89.50	98%		213.84	124.34	42%	Keep control of costs		
255	Profits	24.70	21.50	87%		52.16	30.66	41%	Profit's down $3		

(continued)

	A	B	C	D	E	F	G	H	I	J	K
258	**Department cost analysis**										
259	-Be sure to check titles and formulas for the current month.										
260	12-Jun-86			DEPARTMENTAL COST ANALYSIS							
261				FOR MONTH OF MAY (Month 2 of Quarter 2)							
262		Month		Plan	Difference	YTD		Plan	Difference	Rate	Comment
263	Delivery costs	0.70		0.80	-0.10	3.20		3.50	-0.30	91%	Variable costs off
264	Raw material	4.10		4.20	-0.10	16.50		17.30	-0.80	95%	
265	Mfg costs	3.30		3.40	-0.10	13.30		14.00	-0.70	95%	
266	Cost of selling	6.00		6.00	0.00	28.50		28.50	0.00	100%	Fixed costs on target
267	Plant costs	1.00		1.00	0.00	5.00		5.00	0.00	100%	
268	Office costs	0.60		0.60	0.00	3.00		3.00	0.00	100%	
269	Admin salaries	4.00		4.00	0.00	20.00		20.00	0.00	100%	
270											
271	Total	19.70		20.00	-0.30	89.50		91.30	-1.80	98%	Overall costs a little high
274	**Sales and selling costs**										
275	-Be sure to adjust smoothing formulas for last three actuals.										
276	-If sales are zero, then costs as a % of sales is 0%.										
277	12-Jun-86			SALES AND SELLING COSTS, MONTH OF MAY							
278		Jan.	Feb.	Mar.	Apr.	May	Jun.	Jul.	Aug.	Sep.	Oct.
279	Sales	16.00	20.00	21.00	27.00	27.00	0.00	0.00	0.00	0.00	0.00
280	Costs	5.50	5.50	5.50	6.00	6.00	0.00	0.00	0.00	0.00	0.00
281	Costs as % of sales	34%	28%	26%	22%	22%	0%	0%	0%	0%	0%
282	Smoothed(5 mth)*										
283	Sales	21.4	22	22.2	25	27	0	0	0	0	0
284	Costs as % of sales	26%	25%	25%	24%	22%	0%	0%	0%	0%	0%
285											
286	*Next to last month is smoothed over 3 months, last month is unsmoothed.										
287	Note: This report is supported by the graph "Selling costs (%) down slightly in last six months"										
290	**Department performance report**										
291	-Be sure to check titles and formulas for the current month.										
292	12-Jun-86			IDEAL DEPARTMENT, MONTH OF MAY							
293				YEAR-TO-DATE PERFORMANCE				REPLANNING			
294	YTD IS JAN-MAY	YTD	YTD	YTD	Actual/	Actual/		Annual	Annual		
295		Budget	Plan	Actual	Plan	Budget		Budget	Plan	Budget	
296	Sales	116.00	116.00	111.00	96%	96%		273.00	266.00	97%	
297	Variable costs	34.80	34.80	33.00	95%	95%		81.20	78.64	97%	
298	Fixed costs	56.50	56.50	56.50	100%	100%		135.20	135.20	100%	
299											
300	Profit	24.70	24.70	21.50	87%	87%		56.60	52.16	92%	

(continued)

	A	B	C	D	E	F	G	H	I	J	K
303	**Graph area**										
304	"Qtr2 goals": Dept. Qtrly Goals, Sales, Costs, Profits--everyone										
305		Actual	Qtr plan								
306	Sales	54	79								
307	Costs	40	58								
308	Profits	15	21								
309											
310	"Sales and profits": planned vs. actual--everyone										
311	"Sales composition": fixed cst, var cst, profit --manager										
312	1. The months to come are shifted down a row to make the graph end sharply										
313	by using blank values (see Sales Composition graph).										
314						Sales			Profit		
315		Fixed	Var	Prof	Budget	Plan	Actual	Budget	Plan	Actual	
316	JAN	11.1	4.8	0.1	16.0	16.0	16.0	0.1	0.1	0.1	
317	FEB	11.1	5.8	3.1	19.0	19.0	20.0	2.2	2.2	3.1	
318	MAR	11.1	6.1	3.8	23.0	23.0	21.0	5.0	5.0	3.8	
319	APR	11.6	8.2	7.2	30.0	30.0	27.0	9.4	9.4	7.2	
320	MAY	11.6	8.1	7.3	28.0	28.0	27.0	8.0	8.0	7.3	
321	JUN				22.0	21.0	0.0	4.4	3.8	0.0	
322	JUL	0.0	0.0	0.0	21.0	20.0	0.0	4.0	3.4	0.0	
323	AUG	0.0	0.0	0.0	15.0	14.0	0.0	-0.5	-1.1	0.0	
324	SEP	0.0	0.0	0.0	22.0	21.0	0.0	4.3	3.7	0.0	
325	OCT	0.0	0.0	0.0	24.0	23.0	0.0	5.7	5.1	0.0	
326	NOV	0.0	0.0	0.0	26.0	25.0	0.0	6.6	6.0	0.0	
327	DEC	0.0	0.0	0.0	27.0	26.0	0.0	7.4	6.8	0.0	
328		0.0	0.0	0.0							
329											
330	"Selling costs (%)": last 12 months, cost of sales/smoothed sales (5-mth smoothing)--dept manager										
331	1. Insert a blank row at the beginning of current 12 months.										
332	2. Change the smoothing formulas near the end of the current 12 months.										
333	(Next to last is 3 month, last is raw)										
334		Costs/S	Sales	Smoothed		Costs					
335	DEC		23.0			6.0					
336	JAN		15.0			5.5					
337	FEB	27%	17.0	20.6		5.5					
338	MAR	26%	21.0	21.0		5.5					
339	APR	25%	27.0	22.0		5.5					
340	MAY	25%	25.0	22.4		5.5					
341											

(continued)

	A	B	C	D	E	F	G	H	I	J	K
342	JUN	26%	20.0	21.0		5.5					
343	JUL	28%	19.0	19.6		5.5					
344	AUG	29%	14.0	19.0		5.5					
345	SEP	28%	20.0	19.8		5.5					
346	OCT	26%	22.0	21.2		5.5					
347	NOV	25%	24.0	21.6		5.5					
348	DEC	28%	26.0	21.6		6.0					
349	JAN	26%	16.0	21.4		5.5					
350	FEB	25%	20.0	22.0		5.5					
351	MAR	25%	21.0	22.2		5.5					
352	APR	24%	27.0	25.0	**	6.0					
353	MAY	22%	27.0	27.0	**	6.0					
354	JUN		0.0			0.0					
355	JUL		0.0			0.0					
356	AUG		0.0			0.0					
357	SEP		0.0			0.0					
358	OCT		0.0			0.0					
359	NOV		0.0			0.0					
360	DEC		0.0			0.0					
361	**formulas need work										

364	**Verify area**
365	297.16 The model verification sum
366	
367	If an error appears here, check below and then the appropriate area of the model.
368	(Be sure you have recalculated the whole model.)
369	135.2 The monthly plan yearly profit
370	21.5 The monthly actual yearly profit
371	52.16 The summary plan yearly profit
372	21.5 The summary actual yearly profit
373	17.4 The qtr-to-date planned profits in
374	Department's goals for quarter report
375	24.7 The year-to-date planned profits in
376	Department's year-to-date performance report
377	24.7 The year-to-date planned profits in
378	Department performance report

Modifying an Old Spreadsheet: GROWTH

The spreadsheet GROWTH was first built to appear in a book that was published in 1986. It was styled a bit at the time, but it does not follow many of the rules of style presented in Chapters 2–5. It represents a situation you may find yourself in—you want to modify an old spreadsheet to improve its structure and style.

The original spreadsheet GROWTH looks like this:

	A	B	C	D	E
1	GROWTH 15 Jan 1986 John M. Nevison				
2					
3	(C) Copyright 1983 John M. Nevison				
4					
5	Model an industry with three competing firms. Priced conveniently.				
6					
7	Reference: John M. Nevison, "Executive Computing,"				
8	Atlanta, GA: AMCEE, 1986.				
9					
10	ASSUMPTION SECTION				
11					
12					
13	Interest rate	1.10			
14	Exp curve slope	0.80			
15	Slope factor	-0.32			
16	Init mkt price	15.00			
17	Init firm costs		10.00	10.00	10.00
18					
19	Init mkt volume	9,000.00			
20	Init firm volumes		3,000.00	3,000.00	3,000.00
21					
22					
23	Market growth and share goal				
24					
25	Year	Market	Firm A	Firm B	Firm C
26	0.00	1.00	0.33	0.33	0.33
27	1.00	1.40	0.38	0.33	0.29
28	2.00	1.40	0.43	0.33	0.24
29	3.00	1.30	0.48	0.33	0.19
30	4.00	1.20	0.50	0.33	0.17
31	5.00	1.20	0.50	0.33	0.17
32	6.00	1.20	0.50	0.33	0.17
33	7.00	1.20	0.50	0.33	0.17
34	8.00	1.20	0.50	0.33	0.17
35	9.00	1.20	0.50	0.33	0.17
36	10.00	1.20	0.50	0.33	0.17
37					

(continued)

	A	B	C	D	E
38	Product price (as a function of cumulative market				
39	volume and share change)				
40		Year	Price A	Price B	Price C
41					
42		0.00	$15.00	$15.00	$15.00
43		1.00	9.83	11.32	13.27
44		2.00	8.25	9.34	11.28
45		3.00	7.21	8.05	10.17
46		4.00	6.87	7.16	8.00
47		5.00	6.47	6.47	6.47
48		6.00	5.91	5.91	5.91
49		7.00	5.44	5.44	5.44
50		8.00	5.04	5.04	5.04
51		9.00	4.68	4.68	4.68
52		10.00	4.36	4.36	4.36
53					
54					
55	MAIN MODEL				
56					
57	Year	0			
58	Annual Market	9,000.00			
59	Cum Market	9,000.00			
60	Avg Price/unit	$15.00			
61					
62	Firm		A	B	C
63		Mkt share	33%	33%	33%
64					
65		Annual units	2,970.00	2,970.00	2,970.00
66		Annual debt	$32,670.00	$32,670.00	$32,670.00
67					
68		Cum volume	2,970.00	2,970.00	2,970.00
69		Cost/unit	$10.03	$10.03	$10.03
70					
71		Price	$15.00	$15.00	$15.00
72					
73		Margin	33%	33%	33%
74					
75		Annual Sales	$44,550.00	$44,550.00	$44,550.00
76					
77		Cum cash	$11,880.00	$11,880.00	$11,880.00
78					
79					

(continued)

	A	B	C	D	E
80	Year	1			
81	Annual Market	12,600.00			
82	Cum Market	21,600.00			
83	Avg Price/unit	$11.32			
84					
85			A	A	A
86		Mkt share	38%	33%	29%
87					
88		Annual units	4,788.00	4,158.00	3,654.00
89		Annual debt	$39,770.68	$32,818.22	$27,256.26
90					
91		Cum volume	7,758.00	7,128.00	6,624.00
92		Cost/unit	$7.36	$7.57	$7.75
93					
94		Price	9.83	11.32	13.27
95					
96		Margin	25%	33%	42%
97					
98		Annual Sales	$47,051.67	$47,051.67	$48,477.48
99					
100		Cum cash	$7,280.99	$14,233.45	$21,221.22
101					
102					
103	Year	2			
104	Annual Market	17,640.00			
105	Cum Market	39,240.00			
106	Avg Price/unit	$9.34			
107					
108			A	A	A
109		Mkt share	43%	33%	24%
110					
111		Annual units	7,585.20	5,821.20	4,233.60
112		Annual debt	$53,441.07	$32,806.14	$12,744.38
113					
114		Cum volume	15,343.20	12,949.20	10,857.60
115		Cost/unit	$5.91	$6.25	$6.61
116					
117		Price	8.25	9.34	11.28
118					
119		Margin	28%	33%	41%
120					
121		Annual Sales	$62,589.97	$54,354.45	$47,766.03
122					
123		Cum cash	$9,148.90	$21,548.31	$35,021.65
124					
125					

(continued)

	A	B	C	D	E
126	Year	3			
127	Annual Market	22,932.00			
128	Cum Market	62,172.00			
129	Avg Price/unit	$8.05			
130					
131			A	A	A
132		Mkt share	48%	33%	19%
133					
134		Annual units	11,007.36	7,567.56	4,357.08
135		Annual debt	$61,533.22	$28,282.69	($6,846.01)
136					
137		Cum volume	26,350.56	20,516.76	15,214.68
138		Cost/unit	$4.97	$5.39	$5.93
139					
140		Price	7.21	8.05	10.17
141					
142		Margin	31%	33%	42%
143					
144		Annual Sales	$79,394.52	$60,930.68	$44,313.22
145					
146		Cum cash	$17,861.30	$32,647.99	$51,159.23
147					
148					
149	Year	4			
150	Annual Market	27,518.40			
151	Cum Market	89,690.40			
152	Avg Price/unit	$7.16			
153					
154			A	A	A
155		Mkt share	50%	33%	17%
156					
157		Annual units	13,759.20	9,081.07	4,678.13
158		Annual debt	$55,548.17	$17,879.98	($25,763.91)
159					
160		Cum volume	40,109.76	29,597.83	19,892.81
161		Cost/unit	$4.34	$4.79	$5.44
162					
163		Price	6.87	7.16	8.00
164					
165		Margin	37%	33%	32%
166					
167		Annual Sales	$94,516.88	$64,980.35	$37,412.93
168					
169		Cum cash	$38,968.71	$47,100.37	$63,176.84
170					
171					

(continued)

	A	B	C	D	E
172	Year	5			
173	Annual Market	33,022.08			
174	Cum Market	122,712.48			
175	Avg Price/unit	$6.47			
176					
177			A	A	A
178		Mkt share	50%	33%	17%
179					
180		Annual units	16,511.04	10,897.29	5,613.75
181		Annual debt	$35,954.09	$5,557.61	($35,908.54)
182					
183		Cum volume	56,620.80	40,495.12	25,506.56
184		Cost/unit	$3.88	$4.33	$5.02
185					
186		Price	6.47	6.47	6.47
187					
188		Margin	40%	33%	22%
189					
190		Annual Sales	$106,804.90	$70,491.24	$36,313.67
191					
192		Cum cash	$70,850.81	$64,933.62	$72,222.21
193					
194					
195	Year	6			
196	Annual Market	39,626.50			
197	Cum Market	162,338.98			
198	Avg Price/unit	$5.91			
199					
200			A	A	A
201		Mkt share	50%	33%	17%
202					
203		Annual units	19,813.25	13,076.74	6,736.50
204		Annual debt	$6,711.75	($9,193.67)	($42,240.81)
205					
206		Cum volume	76,434.05	53,571.86	32,243.07
207		Cost/unit	$3.53	$3.95	$4.66
208					
209		Price	5.91	5.91	5.91
210					
211		Margin	40%	33%	21%
212					
213		Annual Sales	$117,124.35	$77,302.07	$39,822.28
214					
215		Cum cash	$110,412.60	$86,495.74	$82,063.09
216					
217					

(continued)

	A	B	C	D	E
218	Year	7			
219	Annual Market	47,551.80			
220	Cum Market	209,890.77			
221	Avg Price/unit	$5.44			
222					
223			A	A	A
224		Mkt share	50%	33%	17%
225					
226		Annual units	23,775.90	15,692.09	8,083.81
227		Annual debt	($29,229.56)	($26,899.04)	($48,869.50)
228					
229		Cum volume	100,209.95	69,263.95	40,326.87
230		Cost/unit	$3.23	$3.64	$4.33
231					
232		Price	5.44	5.44	5.44
233					
234		Margin	41%	33%	20%
235					
236		Annual Sales	$129,392.99	$85,399.38	$43,993.62
237					
238		Cum cash	$158,622.55	$112,298.42	$92,863.12
239					
240					
241	Year	8			
242	Annual Market	57,062.15			
243	Cum Market	266,952.93			
244	Avg Price/unit	$5.04			
245					
246			A	A	A
247		Mkt share	50%	33%	17%
248					
249		Annual units	28,531.08	18,830.51	9,700.57
250		Annual debt	($73,056.26)	($48,133.26)	($55,921.71)
251					
252		Cum volume	128,741.02	88,094.47	50,027.44
253		Cost/unit	$2.98	$3.37	$4.04
254					
255		Price	5.04	5.04	5.04
256					
257		Margin	41%	33%	20%
258					
259		Annual Sales	$143,704.18	$94,844.76	$48,859.42
260					
261		Cum cash	$216,760.45	$142,978.02	$104,781.13
262					
263					

(continued)

	A	B	C	D	E
264	Year	9			
265	Annual Market	68,474.59			
266	Cum Market	335,427.51			
267	Avg Price/unit	$4.68			
268					
269			A	A	A
270		Mkt share	50%	33%	17%
271					
272		Annual units	34,237.29	22,596.61	11,640.68
273		Annual debt	($126,153.58)	($73,541.95)	($63,504.89)
274					
275		Cum volume	162,978.32	110,691.08	61,668.12
276		Cost/unit	$2.76	$3.13	$3.78
277					
278		Price	4.68	4.68	4.68
279					
280		Margin	41%	33%	19%
281					
282		Annual Sales	$160,223.78	$105,747.70	$54,476.09
283					
284		Cum cash	$286,377.36	$179,289.65	$117,980.98
285					
286					
287	Year	10			
288	Annual Market	82,169.50			
289	Cum Market	417,597.01			
290	Avg Price/unit	$4.36			
291					
292			A	A	A
293		Mkt share	50%	33%	17%
294					
295		Annual units	41,084.75	27,115.94	13,968.82
296		Annual debt	($190,125.76)	($103,859.07)	($71,718.65)
297					
298		Cum volume	204,063.07	137,807.01	75,636.93
299		Cost/unit	$2.57	$2.92	$3.54
300					
301		Price	4.36	4.36	4.36
302					
303		Margin	41%	33%	19%
304					
305		Annual Sales	$179,173.58	$118,254.56	$60,919.02
306					
307		Cum cash	$369,299.34	$222,113.63	$132,637.67
308					
309					

(continued)

	A	B	C	D	E
310	GRAPHING SECTION				
311					
312	Year	Cum Cash A	Cum Cash B	Cum Cash C	
313	0	11,880.00	11,880.00	11,880.00	
314	1	7,280.99	14,233.45	21,221.22	
315	2	9,148.90	21,548.31	35,021.65	
316	3	17,861.30	32,647.99	51,159.23	
317	4	38,968.71	47,100.37	63,176.84	
318	5	70,850.81	64,933.62	72,222.21	
319	6	110,412.60	86,495.74	82,063.09	
320	7	158,622.55	112,298.42	92,863.12	
321	8	216,760.45	142,978.02	104,781.13	
322	9	286,377.36	179,289.65	117,980.98	
323	10	369,299.34	222,113.63	132,637.67	
324					
325	Year	% Cum Cash A	% Cum Cash B	% Cum Cash C	
326	0	0.33	0.33	0.33	
327	1	0.17	0.33	0.50	
328	2	0.14	0.33	0.53	
329	3	0.18	0.32	0.50	
330	4	0.26	0.32	0.42	
331	5	0.34	0.31	0.35	
332	6	0.40	0.31	0.29	
333	7	0.44	0.31	0.26	
334	8	0.47	0.31	0.23	
335	9	0.49	0.31	0.20	
336	10	0.51	0.31	0.18	
337					
338	Year	Margin A	Margin B	Margin C	
339	0	0.33	0.33	0.33	
340	1	0.25	0.33	0.42	
341	2	0.28	0.33	0.41	
342	3	0.31	0.33	0.42	
343	4	0.37	0.33	0.32	
344	5	0.40	0.33	0.22	
345	6	0.40	0.33	0.21	
346	7	0.41	0.33	0.20	
347	8	0.41	0.33	0.20	
348	9	0.41	0.33	0.19	
349	10	0.41	0.33	0.19	
350					

(continued)

	A	B	C	D	E
351	Year	Mkt Share A	Mkt Share B	Mkt Share C	
352	0	0.33	0.33	0.33	
353	1	0.38	0.33	0.29	
354	2	0.43	0.33	0.24	
355	3	0.48	0.33	0.19	
356	4	0.50	0.33	0.17	
357	5	0.50	0.33	0.17	
358	6	0.50	0.33	0.17	
359	7	0.50	0.33	0.17	
360	8	0.50	0.33	0.17	
361	9	0.50	0.33	0.17	
362	10	0.50	0.33	0.17	

As you can see, the model has followed some of the rules. It has an Introduction, an Initial Data Area, a Model Area, and a Graph Area. The model's major weakness is that the Model Area is really a Report Area. The form of the 11 years' calculations is very inconvenient. It was difficult to set up the original Graph Areas, and we know now that it will be difficult to modify them in the future if we wish to elaborate the model in any major way.

We decide that we want to streamline the Model Area and create a Report Area with Year 1 and Year 10. At the same time, we want to improve the overall model in any way that we can by checking it against the template of FULLRULE.

The original model's outline looks like this:

Introduction
Assumptions
    Factors
    Market growth and share assumptions
    Market price assumptions
Main model
    Yearly 0 report for firm A, B, C
    Year 1 report for firm A, B, C
      .
      .
      .
    Year 10 report for firm A, B, C
Graphing area
    Cumulative cash
    Cumulative cash (%)
    Profit margin (%)
    Market share (%)

What we wish to do (First Design On Paper) is:

Introduction
Initial data
    Factors
    Market growth and share assumptions
    Market price assumptions
Model area
    Firm A, years 0 to 10
    Firm B, years 0 to 10
    Firm C, years 0 to 10
Report area
    Year 1 report for firm A, B, C
    Year 10 report for firm A, B, C
Graphing area
    Cumulative cash
    Cumulative cash (%)
    Profit margin (%)
    Market share (%)

We see from our outline that our improvements will be focused in the Model Area with a little work in the Report Area. As a by-product of that work, we expect our Introduction and Initial Data Area to change a little. We decide to do our first round of work on the old model. Then, later, we will compare our result to the template of FULLRULE.

First Work Session

We call up the model and go to work. We begin by moving the four lines of market information up into a line. This effort is speeded by splitting the screen and jumping between the source and the destination of the move. Next, we move up the figures for each firm for each year. After completing the rearrangement, we delete the blank rows that we wish to remove from our model and make sure the numbers are formatted the way we want to work with them.

Our new model area is much more compact than our old arrangement of 10 years' worth or reports. It looks like this:

	A	B	C	D	E	F	G	H
102	Year	0	1	2	3	4	5	6
103	Annual Market	9,000	12,600	17,640	22,932	27,518	33,022	39,626
104	Cum Market	9,000	21,600	39,240	62,172	89,690	122,712	162,339
105	Avg Price/unit	$15.00	$11.32	$9.34	$8.05	$7.16	$6.47	$5.91
106	Firm A							
107	Mkt share	33%	38%	43%	48%	50%	50%	50%
108	Annual units	2,970	4,788	7,585	11,007	13,759	16,511	19,813
109	Annual debt	32,670	39,771	53,441	61,533	55,548	35,954	6,712
110	Cum volume	2,970	7,758	15,343	26,351	40,110	56,621	76,434
111	Cost/unit	$10.03	$7.36	$5.91	$4.97	$4.34	$3.88	$3.53
112	Price	$15.00	$9.83	$8.25	$7.21	$6.87	$6.47	$5.91
113	Margin	33%	25%	28%	31%	37%	40%	40%
114	Annual Sales	44,550	47,052	62,590	79,395	94,517	106,805	117,124
115	Cum cash	11,880	7,281	9,149	17,861	38,969	70,851	110,413
116	Firm B							
117	Mkt share	33%	33%	33%	33%	33%	33%	33%
118	Annual units	2,970	4,158	5,821	7,568	9,081	10,897	13,077
119	Annual debt	32,670	32,818	32,806	28,283	17,880	5,558	(9,194)
120	Cum volume	2,970	7,128	12,949	20,517	29,598	40,495	53,572
121	Cost/unit	$10.03	$7.57	$6.25	$5.39	$4.79	$4.33	$3.95
122	Price	$15.00	$11.32	$9.34	$8.05	$7.16	$6.47	$5.91
123	Margin	33%	33%	33%	33%	33%	33%	33%
124	Annual Sales	44,550	47,052	54,354	60,931	64,980	70,491	77,302
125	Cum cash	11,880	14,233	21,548	32,648	47,100	64,934	86,496
126	Firm C							
127	Mkt share	33%	29%	24%	19%	17%	17%	17%
128	Annual units	2,970	3,654	4,234	4,357	4,678	5,614	6,737
129	Annual debt	32,670	27,256	12,744	(6,846)	(25,764)	(35,909)	(42,241)
130	Cum volume	2,970	6,624	10,858	15,215	19,893	25,507	32,243
131	Cost/unit	$10.03	$7.75	$6.61	$5.93	$5.44	$5.02	$4.66
132	Price	$15.00	$13.27	$11.28	$10.17	$8.00	$6.47	$5.91
133	Margin	33%	42%	41%	42%	32%	22%	21%
134	Annual Sales	44,550	48,477	47,766	44,313	37,413	36,314	39,822
135	Cum cash	11,880	21,221	35,022	51,159	63,177	72,222	82,063

	I	J	K	L
102	7	8	9	10
103	47,552	57,062	68,475	82,170
104	209,891	266,953	335,428	417,597
105	$5.44	$5.04	$4.68	$4.36
106				
107	50%	50%	50%	50%
108	23,776	28,531	34,237	41,085
109	(29,230)	(73,056)	(126,154)	(190,126)
110	100,210	128,741	162,978	204,063
111	$3.23	$2.98	$2.76	$2.57
112	$5.44	$5.04	$4.68	$4.36
113	41%	41%	41%	41%
114	129,393	143,704	160,224	179,174
115	158,623	216,760	286,377	369,299
116				
117	33%	33%	33%	33%
118	15,692	18,831	22,597	27,116
119	(26,899)	(48,133)	(73,542)	(103,859)
120	69,264	88,094	110,691	137,807
121	$3.64	$3.37	$3.13	$2.92
122	$5.44	$5.04	$4.68	$4.36
123	33%	33%	33%	33%
124	85,399	94,845	105,748	118,255
125	112,298	142,978	179,290	222,114
126				
127	17%	17%	17%	17%
128	8,084	9,701	11,641	13,969
129	(48,870)	(55,922)	(63,505)	(71,719)
130	40,327	50,027	61,668	75,637
131	$4.33	$4.04	$3.78	$3.54
132	$5.44	$5.04	$4.68	$4.36
133	20%	20%	19%	19%
134	43,994	48,859	54,476	60,919
135	92,863	104,781	117,981	132,638

We leave one set of labels below the model to use for our Report Area. We add the appropriate border to separate the two areas, save our work, and take a break. Elapsed time is 1 hour.

Second Work Session

We begin by recreating the report area for Year 1 and Year 10. After experimenting with several forms, we decide to arrange it like this:

	A	B	C	D	E	F	G	H
138	**Report area**							
139	Year	1				10		
140	Annual Market	12,600				82,170		
141	Cum Market	21,600				417,597		
142	Avg Price/unit	$11.32				$4.36		
143								
144	Firms	A	B	C		A	B	C
145	Mkt share	38%	33%	29%		50%	33%	17%
146								
147	Annual units	4,788	4,158	3,654		41,085	27,116	13,969
148	Annual debt	39,771	32,818	27,256		(190,126)	(103,859)	(71,719)
149	(surplus)							
150	Cum volume	7,758	7,128	6,624		204,063	137,807	75,637
151	Cost/unit	$7.36	$7.57	$7.75		$2.57	$2.92	$3.54
152								
153	Price	$9.83	$11.32	$13.27		$4.36	$4.36	$4.36
154								
155	Margin	25%	33%	42%		41%	33%	19%
156								
157	Annual Sales	47,052	47,052	48,477		179,174	118,255	60,919
158								
159	Cum cash	7,281	14,233	21,221		369,299	222,114	132,638

We recheck our graphs to verify that the basic numbers remain correct and note that this work took 30 minutes.

We are now ready to begin part two of our effort—combining the model GROWTH with the model FULLRULE. Here, we almost make a mistake. We paste GROWTH into FULLRULE and lose the chart references! Before we save our work, we realize our error and begin again. We paste FULLRULE into GROWTH (Import with Care). Our spreadsheet looks like Figure 6-5 as we begin work.

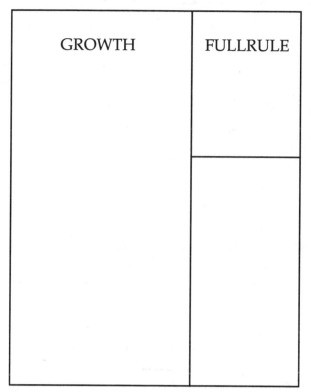

Figure 6-5. Position of combined spreadsheets.

We methodically work down the list of FULL RULE. It reminds us of several things: Include the date printed; revise the references; improve the statement of purpose; give better directions (later); and map the contents with a table of contents. We make the titles of the sections refer to those in the table of contents. We improve our typography as we go.

By doing quite a bit of moving, we have established those areas that we really need, added several new features to our Introduction, and reminded ourselves that our initial plan overlooked two important features, a Verify Area and a set of instructions. The revised end is in sight:

Introduction
Initial data
    Factors
    Market growth and share assumptions
    Market price assumptions

Model area
    Firm A, years 0 to 10
    Firm B, years 0 to 10
    Firm C, years 0 to 10
Report area
    Year 1 report for firm A, B, C   Year 10 report for firm A, B, C
Graphing area
    Cumulative cash
    Cumulative cash (%)
    Profit margin (%)
    Market share (%)
Verify area

We decide to pause again and look at our watch. Our second session took 1.5 hours, so our total elapsed time to this point is 2.5 hours.

Third Work Session

As we begin our third session, we decide to add a list of formulas to our Model Area to explain how the model works (Model to Explain). We spend three quarters of an hour typing in the list and revising the terms to be sure they are clear. The result looks like this:

	A	B	C	D	E	F	G	H
83	**Model**							
84	Market formulas:							
85	Annual Market = last year's market * market growth factor							
86	Cumulative Market = last year's cumulative market + current annual market							
87	Avg Price/unit = initial price * (cum market/initial market) ^ experience factor							
88								
89	Firm formulas:							
90	Market share = assumption							
91	Annual units = annual market * market share							
92	Annual debt = (cost to make - last year's cash) * interest rate							
93	where cost to make = annual units * last year's cost per unit							
94	Cumulative units = last year's cumulative units + annual units							
95	Cost/unit = initial cost * (cum volume/initial volume) ^ experience factor							
96	Price/unit = (last year's share/current share) * average price per unit							
97	Margin = (Price-cost)/Price							
98	Annual Sales = Annual units * Price							
99	Cumulative cash = Annual sales - debt							
100								
101								

While this list is about as clear as it can be, it still requires that the reader be familiar with the idea of an experience curve and exactly how debt is used in the current example. We decide to refer the reader to the references for additional details.

Next, we look at the set of price assumptions in the model and realize that, when the user explores the model, he will be surprised to find so many formulas in the Initial Data Area. We provide a brief explanation of how he can make use of these assumptions if he wishes to march off on an independent course. We also revise our initial directions on how to use the model. Our time to complete this work was half an hour.

We begin to work on our Verify Area and discover that our work really is not to be performed in the Verify Area, but in the other areas of the model. We spend quite a while trying to figure out why our total cumulative market is 90 units more than the sum of our three firms' markets. Finally, we realize that in the very first year we let each firm be 33 percent (not 33.33 percent) and we lost 1 percent of 9,000 units, 90 units. We choose to preserve the model in the present form and we write our IF statement to reflect this initial minor difference.

IF(ABS((tenth year cumulative market) - (sum of firms' cumulative markets)) < 90.1, (tenth year cumulative market), "ERR")

We put this statement in the appropriate location in the model and wire up a Verify Area entry to this cell.

Next, we decide to put an IF statement in our Report Area to be sure that the results we have pointed to in the Model Area remain consistent. The statement reads:

IF(ABS((tenth year Firm C cumulative cash) - ((tenth year Firm C annual sales) - (tenth year Firm C annual debt)) < .000001, (tenth year Firm C cumulative cash), "ERR")

We wire up a verify entry for this cell and then turn to our initial data. We examine this data and ask the question "What likely errors can we guard against?" We hit upon the entry of market share goals for the three firms. The goals of the three firms should always add up to 1.00. (We have made an exception in our start-up year to make everything balance at the beginning.) We decide to add a column called "Check sums" to our initial data. Each check sum reads:

IF(ABS((sum of three firms' market shares) - 1.00) < .000001, (sum of three firms' market shares), "ERR")

The entry in our Verify Area is a SUM function that covers the whole column of check sums, so that if any one of them signals an ERR, our Verify Area element will also. The statement reads:

SUM(the column of check sums in the Initial Data Area)

The Verify Area took an hour and a quarter to complete.

	A	B	C	D	E	F	G	H
195	Verify area							
196	550244.68 Verification sum							
197	If an error appears here, check below and the appropriate area of the							
198	spreadsheet. (Be sure that you have recalculated the whole model.)							
199	10.00 Initial data's market share years 2-10 sum of check sums							
200	417597.01 Model's year 10 cumulative market							
201	132637.67 Report Year 10 Firm C's cumulative cash							

Our spreadsheet modification is all done. Our third session took 2.5 hours and our whole modification effort took 5 hours. The explanation of the model's ideas that follows shows why it was worthwhile to have a robust version of this model around.

We summarize our experience in a set of guidelines for future work.

How to Fix an Old Spreadsheet

1. Study it and decide what you want it to look like (**First design on paper**). Sometimes it helps to decide what area or areas it most resembles. If it is primarily raw data with almost no formulas, it resembles an Initial Data Area. If it is a thicket of formulas, it resembles a Model Area.

2. Find what you can check to be sure that the spreadsheet is still correct after you have changed it (**Verify critical work**). Sometimes this can be a printed copy of a report, and other times it can be a set of graphs that depend on everything being correct. If nothing exists, **build the Verify Area before you change anything**.

3. Import your whole old spreadsheet into the appropriate area of a fresh template like FULLRULE, or import a template with the rules into your old spreadsheet (**Import with care**).

4. Rename it and save it under its new name.

5. Systematically work through the old spreadsheet and move items to the appropriate area. Raw data goes in the Initial Data Area (**Surface and label every assumption**), formal introductions go in the Introduction, title line goes at the top of the Introduction, and so on.

6. Using the template as a guide, add new introductory features that your old spreadsheet lacked. You may begin with the title line, you probably will need a table of contents, you may wish to improve your references and your directions.

7. Continuing to use the template as your guide, build areas that need to be added (**Give a new function a new area**). A Verify Area can be a big help. You may need a Report Area or a Graphing Area.

8. Erase extraneous template material from your results.

9. Unprotect appropriate areas and protect everything else.

10. Test your results to be sure they are correct (**Test and edit**).

11. Save the result and consider it as a possible template for some of your future work.

An Explanation of the Ideas in the Revised GROWTH

In order to understand many spreadsheet models, special knowledge is required. The discussion that follows is both an explanation of some of the ideas in GROWTH and an example of how to present a discussion around the parts of a long and complex model. (For additional examples, see the next chapter.)

GROWTH illustrates what the economics of the experience curve can mean to business competition. A powerful way to learn about the experience curve is to examine the competitive interplay of three firms in an integrated spreadsheet model.

The Value of Experience

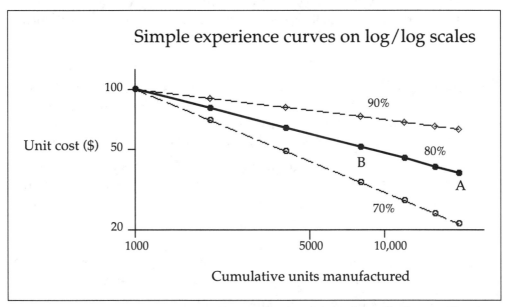

Figure 6-6.   As an activity is repeated, it gets performed quicker and cheaper. The curve appears on log/log paper so that the bend in the line is straightened out. Constant percentage changes make straight lines. Notice that a firm that has produced more goods, Point A, has a lower unit cost than a less experienced firm, Point B. The dotted lines show 70% and 90% curves that indicate the range of frequently encountered curves.

The idea of the experience curve dates back to the early 1950s when some industries noted an experience curve in their costs: Their cost per unit (in constant dollars) dropped as their lifetime total number of units—their experience—grew (see Figure 6-1). Because of this long-term economy of scale, a firm that understands its industry experience curve tries to produce more units than its competitors and gain the profit advantage of lower unit costs.

To sell more units than its competitor and capture a bigger share of the market, a firm must begin by cutting its price. To understand exactly how to cut your price, you must have a clear idea of how you, your competitors, and your market all interact.

The Integrated Model

The integrated model begins with the growth of the market and each firm's market share goals and shows how each firm will grow. Let us suppose that three firms—one gaining share, one preserving share, and one losing share—are competing for a single new market.

The first interaction between the firm and the market is based on how big the market is expected to become and, as a consequence, how much the firm must manufacture and sell to meet its share goal. After the firm decides how many units to make, it must figure out how to price its units to sell them all.

If the firm wishes simply to preserve its share of the market, it sets its price at the projected industry "ideal" price (estimated from the experience curve). The firm sets its price lower than the projected standard in order to gain market share and higher if it is willing to lose. (Why a firm might be willing to lose share will be discussed later.) The actual market price is the weighted average of all the firm's prices. This pricing mechanism successfully integrates the activities of the individual firms with each other and with the market.

The Spreadsheet Model GROWTH

You can understand these ideas better by looking at an actual spreadsheet and tracing the detailed cause and effect cycle for one of the three firms and for the market itself. Look at the introduction and initial assumptions of the actual spreadsheet model.

	A	B	C	D	E	F	G	H
1	**GROWTHA**	3 Jan 1989	John M. Nevison					
2	(Revised from a 1986 model GROWTH)							
3	® Copyright 1989 John M. Nevison							
4	12-Sep-89 Date printed							
6	**Description**							
7		Model an industry with three competing firms whose						
8		costs follow an experience curve. Prices follow a						
9		market experience curve, but can be revised to be						
10		another independent assumption.						
12	**Reference**							
13		John M. Nevison, "Excel Spreadsheet Design," New York,						
14		NY: Brady Books, 1990.						
15		John M. Nevison, "Executive Computing Using Spreadsheets and Graphs,"						
16		Atlanta, GA: AMCEE, 1986.						
18	**To use**							
19		Vary initial conditions and check the graphs and reports to						
20		see how the model reacts. You may alter growth strategies,						
21		market share strategies, and even price strategies. See						
22		references for further details.						
24	**Contents**							
25		Introduction: title, description, contents						
26		Initial data						
27		Model						
28		Report area						
29		Graph area						
30		Verify area						
33	**Initial data**							
34	Interest rate	1.10						
35	Exp curve slope	80%						
36	Slope factor	-0.32						
37	Init mkt price	15.00						
38	Init firm costs		10.00	10.00	10.00			
40	Init mkt volume	9000.00						
41	Init firm volumes		3000.00	3000.00	3000.00			
42								

(continued)

	A	B	C	D	E	F	G	H
43		Market growth and share goal						
45		Year	Market	Firm A	Firm B	Firm C		Check sum
46		0	1.00	0.33	0.33	0.33		
47		1	1.40	0.38	0.33	0.29		1.00
48		2	1.40	0.43	0.33	0.24		1.00
49		3	1.30	0.48	0.33	0.19		1.00
50		4	1.20	0.50	0.33	0.17		1.00
51		5	1.20	0.50	0.33	0.17		1.00
52		6	1.20	0.50	0.33	0.17		1.00
53		7	1.20	0.50	0.33	0.17		1.00
54		8	1.20	0.50	0.33	0.17		1.00
55		9	1.20	0.50	0.33	0.17		1.00
56		10	1.20	0.50	0.33	0.17		1.00
57								
58	Product price (as a function of cumulative market							
59	volume and share change)							
60		The prices in the data area are calculated functions						
61		rather than independent terms. If you wish to make them						
62		independent terms:						
63		1. Give your new version a NEW NAME and save it.						
64		2. Enter prices you think are consistent with your share						
65		goals and your competition.						
66		3. Examine the results of your assumptions.						
67								
68		Year	Price A	Price B	Price C			
70		0.00	$15.00	$15.00	$15.00			
71		1.00	9.83	11.32	13.27			
72		2.00	8.25	9.34	11.28			
73		3.00	7.21	8.05	10.17			
74		4.00	6.87	7.16	8.00			
75		5.00	6.47	6.47	6.47			
76		6.00	5.91	5.91	5.91			
77		7.00	5.44	5.44	5.44			
78		8.00	5.04	5.04	5.04			
79		9.00	4.68	4.68	4.68			
80		10.00	4.36	4.36	4.36			

Notice that, in the Introduction, two references are given for further details (one of which you are reading now). The Initial Data Area contains the fundamental assumptions about the model. The first list identifies the environmental constants of the model: the starting year, the interest rate, the interest factor, the experience curve slope, and the slope factor. The example begins in 1991 to make the years easy to track. The interest rate is 10 percent, which makes the interest factor 1.10 (one plus the per-unit interest rate).

The experience curve for this example is set at 80 percent. This means that when the cumulative volume doubles, the dollars per unit drops to 80 percent of its original value. The slope factor is computed from the 80 percent figure by the following formula.

$$<slope\ factor> = log<experience\ curve\ slope>\ /\ log<2>$$

$$= log<.80>\ /\ log<2>$$

$$= -0.32$$

Experience curves vary from 70 to 90 percent. An 80 percent curve is a medium-size experience curve. A 70 percent curve has a lot of drop; a 90 percent curve hardly drops at all (see Figure 6-6).

The next initial data in the spreadsheet describes the start-up period background of the three firms and the market. Assume that 1) during the start-up period the market in this example is 9,000 units; 2) each of the three firms has 33 percent of the market and manufactures 3,000 units; 3) the initial market price per unit is $15 and the initial cost per unit is $10; and 4) each firm's actual total profit (after $300 of interest costs) is $12,000. (While these numbers are related to one another, they may all be entered in the Initial Data Area as raw numbers.)

The third set of initial data is the year-to-year sequence for the market growth and the firms' market share goals. The market takes a big 40 percent leap in growth in the first two years (1.40 growth rate factor), eases off to 30 percent in the third year, and stabilizes at a solid 20 percent for the next seven years. Real markets can expand even faster than this model. Between 1955 and 1960, the motorcycle market in Japan grew at a rate of 42 percent a year.

The market share goals of the Initial Data are graphed in Figure 6-5. Over the first four years after the start-up, Firm A increased its share to 50 percent of the market, Firm B preserved its share, and Firm C lost some of its share. Each firm's market share remained stable for the rest of the 10-year period.

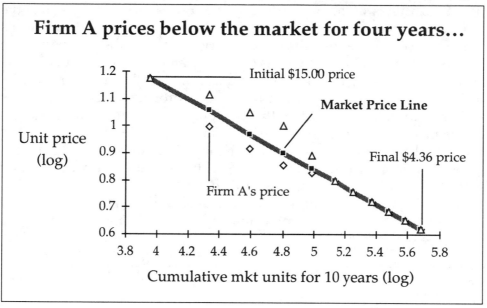

Figure 6-7.

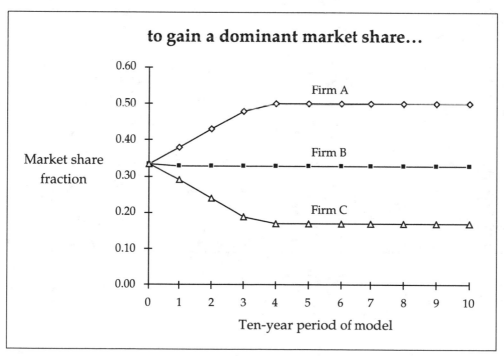

Figure 6-8.

The final values in the initial data are the prices that make possible the changes in market share. Notice that because Firm B always preserves its share, its price matches the ideal market price in all but the first year. (The $0.17 discrepancy in the first year is caused by an initial drop from a 33.333 percent to a 33.0 percent share.) Firm A gains share in the first four years by pricing below the market, while Firm C fails to drop its prices as fast as the market and loses share in each of the first four years. From the fifth year on, all three firms preserve share by maintaining the ideal market price. Figure 6-3 shows the prices graphed against the logarithm of cumulative market volume. The actual weighted average of the firms' prices is mathematically identical to the ideal market price in each year.

To understand the logic of the formulas, look at the first year (Year 1) of the spreadsheet model and examine how the expressions for the yearly cycle are derived for Firm A.

	A	B	C	D	E	F	G	H
138	**Report area**							
139	Year	1				10		
140	Annual Market	12,600				82,170		
141	Cum Market	21,600				417,597		
142	Avg Price/unit	$11.32				$4.36		
143								
144	Firms	A	B	C		A	B	C
145	Mkt share	38%	33%	29%		50%	33%	17%
146								
147	Annual units	4,788	4,158	3,654		41,085	27,116	13,969
148	Annual debt	39,771	32,818	27,256		(190,126)	(103,859)	(71,719)
149	(surplus)							
150	Cum volume	7,758	7,128	6,624		204,063	137,807	75,637
151	Cost/unit	$7.36	$7.57	$7.75		$2.57	$2.92	$3.54
152								
153	Price	$9.83	$11.32	$13.27		$4.36	$4.36	$4.36
154								
155	Margin	25%	33%	42%		41%	33%	19%
156								
157	Annual Sales	47,052	47,052	48,477		179,174	118,255	60,919
158								
159	Cum cash	7,281	14,233	21,221		369,299	222,114	132,638

The yearly cycle begins with the market. The number of units brought to market in any given year will be the annual market growth times the number produced in the previous year. (In the discussion of the initial year, the "previous" year is the start-up period, Year 0.)

<market units> = <market growth> * <market units prior year>

12,600 = 1.4 * 9,000

After the total number of units in the market are predicted, each firm must manufacture its share of these units. This number depends on the firm's desired market share goal. (Remember that .38, or 38 percent, is Firm A's goal.)

<firm units> = <firm market share goal> * <market units>

4,788 = .38 * 12,600

Assume for the moment that each firm will sell all its units through appropriate pricing. First, the firm must pay to make all its units. This is a conservative calculation because you produce the current year's units at a cost based on the unit cost at the end of the prior year. (This cost includes all the firm's expenses except interest payments.) If your costs drop over the course of the year, as you expect them to, the actual costs will be lower.

You borrow the money to cover the cost of the units you need and you pay interest on the money for the whole year. To find how much you need to borrow, you begin with the number of units you want to make this year multiplied by the cost per unit at the end of the prior year. If you have some cash from the profit of last year, you invest it in this year's production. You borrow the rest and pay interest on it. (Honda borrowed heavily in Japan between 1955 and 1960 to capture share in the Japanese motorcycle market.)

<firm annual debt> = (<cost per unit, prior year> * <units to be made> − <cumulative profit, prior year>) * <interest rate>

39,468 = (10.00 * 4,788 − 12,000) * 1.10

After a while, the profits may grow large enough to cover the new year's costs and the debt will turn negative. Negative debt simply means you have excess cash that you are investing at the same interest rate you paid on your debt. Earning only the interest rate on your cash is a conservative assumption that will understate profits.

After you finance your annual production, you accumulate unit volumes for the industry (for price) and for the firm (for cost).

<cumulative market volume> = <cumulative market volume prior year> + <annual market volume>

21,600 = 9,000 + 12,600

<cumulative firm volume> = <cumulative firm volume prior year> + <annual firm volume>

7,788 = 3,000 + 4,788

The individual unit costs are computed from the firm's cumulative volume on the cost-experience curve.

<firm unit cost> = <initial cost> * (<cumulative firm volume>/<initial firm volume>) ^ <slope factor>

7.36 = 10 * (7,788 / 3,000) ^ (–.32)

The cost per unit is computed from Firm A's cumulative volume on the cost skill experience curve, that is, start-up cost times cumulative units divided by start-up units raised to the power of the experience factor. The slope factor is the experience factor for the 80 percent curve. (See "An Afterword on Experience Curve Mathematics," later in this chapter, for additional details.)

The ideal industry price is computed using the price-experience curve. The price is the low, end-of-the-year, most conservative price. It understates profits.

<ideal market unit price> = <initial price> * (<cumulative market volume>/<initial market volume>) ^ <slope factor>

11.32 = 15 * (21,600 / 9,000) ^ (–.32)

The ideal industry price is from the price–experience curve—the start-up price times the cumulative market divided by the start-up market raised to the power of the experience curve factor.

Each firm's actual price is computed as a function of the ideal price and the year-to-year change in market share. The calculation has several desirable properties. First, if you want to build share, you must price below your competitors. Second, if you wish to preserve share, you must drop your price every year to stay with the market. Third, the results of the individual firm pricing decisions compose a weighted average market price that is mathematically identical to the ideal market price.

<firm price> = (<firm share prior year> / <firm share>) * <ideal market unit price>

9.93 = (.33/.38) * 11.32

In the spreadsheet model, the price cell with the formula is found in the price section of the Initial Data Area. The price cell in the model points to the price in the Initial Data Area. By collecting prices in the Initial Data Area, you allow a future user to plug in his or her own independent price assumptions. (In practice, Firm A would price as much below its competitors as was needed to sell all its goods.)

The unit margin is price minus cost divided by price.

<unit margin> = (<unit price> – <unit cost>)/<unit price>

.26 = (9.93–7.36)/9.83

The firm's sales for the year are the number of units sold times the price per unit. This is also a conservative figure because you use the end-of-year (lowest) price per unit to compute your dollar sales. If prices were higher during the year, some of the sales would have been made at the higher prices and the final total would be higher.

<firm annual sales> = <firm annual units> * <firm price>

47,527 = 4,788 * 9.93

Last, the firm's cumulative profit is what the firm sold minus its annual debt (or plus the beginning surplus cash put out at interest for the year). In either case, the annual debt folds the interest payments in with all the other costs.

<firm cumulative profit> = <firm annual sales> – <annual debt>

8,259 = 47,527 – 39,468

Firm B and C have similar formulas.

The Results of the Model

After looking at only one year of growth, one might think that Firm A is in trouble. While Firm C nets $20,553 and B nets $14,989, Firm A nets only about $8,259.

Figures for the tenth year, however, show that Firm A's cumulative profit of $369,299 is 50 percent more than the $222,113 of Firm B, which decided to preserve share, and almost three times the $132,637 of Firm C, which lost share. The model shows that gaining market share can pay off handsomely after only a few years. (By 1960, Honda dominated the motorcycle market in Japan.)

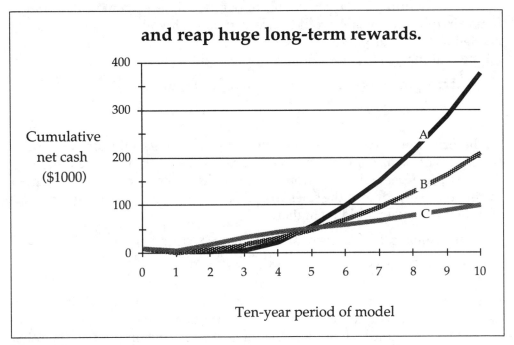

Figure 6-9.

Some products have very short life cycles. The present model can illustrate a short life cycle by simply assuming each time period is, say, four months, instead of a year. The interest rate must be adjusted to the rate of the period. Everything else can remain the same.

All 10 years of cumulative profit appear in the above chart. Firm A, which aggressively pursued market share in the early years, paid for the share with a big dip in its initial cumulative profits. Firm C initially benefitted from its high prices with large profits. As time passed, however, the market share shift depresses Firm C and boosts Firm A. Firm A rises because it sells more units and because it makes a higher profit on each unit. The course from initial loss to subsequent gain takes foresight, courage, and forbearance.

By the end of the fourth year, Firm A controls the market and in each succeeding year it increases its command by increasing its relative per unit profit margin. In 1964, Honda's old rival, the market leader of 1950, declared bankruptcy.

The integrated model shows us several other things that are worth noting. The ideal price in the market steeply declines at the outset where each year yields a large increase in the cumulative number of units. Firm C might very well in real life have priced the way it did in the model out of ignorance: It did not understand how fast it must reduce its price to remain competitive. The 80 percent curve used in the model was not as steep as many real experience curves. The price decline in real life can be even more precipitous. The prices of digital watches and hand-held calculators in the United States in the early 1970s fell faster than some firms ever imagined possible.

Another reason Firm C might hold its price steady is the need for short-term performance. Indeed, if all three firms needed to hold up prices, you might see the actual market price appear above the ideal price curve. This is a common phenomenon in real life. The price does not sustain itself up there for long, however. When competition heats up, most markets experience a steep price drop as prices descend to the ideal curve. This steep descent is called a market shakeout. When the shakeout occurs, the weaker firms frequently discover that they cannot afford to stay in business.

Our integrated model helps us to understand one of the major economic shifts of the 20th century: the Japanese capture of several major U.S. markets. Experience curve competition works best in rapidly growing markets. The Japanese firms cut their teeth in the domestic Japanese markets that had been expanding rapidly over many years as they recovered from the Second World War.

The Japanese firm prizes share growth while the U.S. firm prizes return on stockholder's equity. In Japan, where 80 percent of a company's equity is debt and 20 percent is common stock (exactly the opposite proportions from in the U.S.), a firm has to listen to many fewer voices clamoring for quarter-to-quarter profits and annual dividends. The Japanese firm is encouraged to plan for the longer term.

While in the model no firm went heavily into debt, in real life a firm gaining market share often incurs heavy debt. Japanese banks strongly encourage aggressive experience curve competition by tolerating debt/equity ratios of 2:1 (versus 0.7:1 for a typical U.S. firm).

The Implications of the Model

You might wish to explore some of the following possibilities with the model.

- The effect of loan limitations;

- The effect of different sloped experience curves (70 percent versus 90 percent);

- The effect of a head start (what if the mix starts at 6000, 2000, 1000?);

- The effect of coming from behind (how much debt does the 1000 player above need to get in the game?);

- The effects of working in an old market (what happens when the market grows at less than 10 percent a year?);

- The effects of leapfrogging the curve (stealing technology; substitute several thousand synthetic units for a company);

- The effect of market collapse (what happens when the market declines?); or

- The effect of oversupply (firms produce shares that add up to more than 100 percent).

The full model looks like this:

	A	B	C	D	E	F	G	H
1	**GROWTHA** 3 Jan 1989 John M. Nevison							
2	(Revised from a 1986 model GROWTH)							
3	® Copyright 1989 John M. Nevison							
4	12-Sep-89 Date printed							
6	**Description**							
7	Model an industry with three competing firms whose							
8	costs follow an experience curve. Prices follow a							
9	market experience curve, but can be revised to be							
10	another independent assumption.							
12	**Reference**							
13	John M. Nevison, "Excel Spreadsheet Design," New York,							
14	NY: Brady Books, 1990.							
15	John M. Nevison, "Executive Computing Using Spreadsheets and Graphs,"							
16	Atlanta, GA: AMCEE, 1986.							
18	**To use**							
19	Vary initial conditions and check the graphs and reports to							
20	see how the model reacts. You may alter growth strategies,							
21	market share strategies, and even price strategies. See							
22	references for further details.							
24	**Contents**							
25	Introduction: title, description, contents							
26	Initial data							
27	Model							
28	Report area							
29	Graph area							
30	Verify area							
33	**Initial data**							
34	Interest rate	1.10						
35	Exp curve slope	80%						
36	Slope factor	-0.32						
37	Init mkt price	15.00						
38	Init firm costs		10.00	10.00	10.00			
40	Init mkt volume	9000.00						
41	Init firm volumes		3000.00	3000.00	3000.00			
42								

(continued)

	A	B	C	D	E	F	G	H
43		Market growth and share goal						
45		Year	Market	Firm A	Firm B	Firm C		Check sum
46		0	1.00	0.33	0.33	0.33		
47		1	1.40	0.38	0.33	0.29		1.00
48		2	1.40	0.43	0.33	0.24		1.00
49		3	1.30	0.48	0.33	0.19		1.00
50		4	1.20	0.50	0.33	0.17		1.00
51		5	1.20	0.50	0.33	0.17		1.00
52		6	1.20	0.50	0.33	0.17		1.00
53		7	1.20	0.50	0.33	0.17		1.00
54		8	1.20	0.50	0.33	0.17		1.00
55		9	1.20	0.50	0.33	0.17		1.00
56		10	1.20	0.50	0.33	0.17		1.00
57								
58	Product price (as a function of cumulative market							
59	volume and share change)							
60			The prices in the data area are calculated functions					
61			rather than independent terms. If you wish to make them					
62			independent terms:					
63			1. Give your new version a NEW NAME and save it.					
64			2. Enter prices you think are consistent with your share					
65			goals and your competition.					
66			3. Examine the results of your assumptions.					
67								
68			Year	Price A	Price B	Price C		
70			0.00	$15.00	$15.00	$15.00		
71			1.00	9.83	11.32	13.27		
72			2.00	8.25	9.34	11.28		
73			3.00	7.21	8.05	10.17		
74			4.00	6.87	7.16	8.00		
75			5.00	6.47	6.47	6.47		
76			6.00	5.91	5.91	5.91		
77			7.00	5.44	5.44	5.44		
78			8.00	5.04	5.04	5.04		
79			9.00	4.68	4.68	4.68		
80			10.00	4.36	4.36	4.36		

(continued)

	A	B	C	D	E	F	G	H
83	**Model**							
84	Market formulas:							
85	Annual Market = last year's market * market growth factor							
86	Cumulative Market = last year's cumulative market + current annual market							
87	Avg Price/unit = initial price * (cum market/initial market) ^ experience factor							
88								
89	Firm formulas:							
90	Market share = assumption							
91	Annual units = annual market * market share							
92	Annual debt = (cost to make - last year's cash) * interest rate							
93	where cost to make = annual units * last year's cost per unit							
94	Cumulative units = last year's cumulative units + annual units							
95	Cost/unit = initial cost * (cum volume/initial volume) ^ experience factor							
96	Price/unit = (last year's share/current share) * average price per unit							
97	Margin = (Price-cost)/Price							
98	Annual Sales = Annual units * Price							
99	Cumulative cash = Annual sales - debt							
100								
101								
102	Year	0	1	2	3	4	5	6
103	Annual Market	9,000	12,600	17,640	22,932	27,518	33,022	39,626
104	Cum Market	9,000	21,600	39,240	62,172	89,690	122,712	162,339
105	Avg Price/unit	$15.00	$11.32	$9.34	$8.05	$7.16	$6.47	$5.91
106	Firm A							
107	Mkt share	33%	38%	43%	48%	50%	50%	50%
108	Annual units	2,970	4,788	7,585	11,007	13,759	16,511	19,813
109	Annual debt	32,670	39,771	53,441	61,533	55,548	35,954	6,712
110	Cum volume	2,970	7,758	15,343	26,351	40,110	56,621	76,434
111	Cost/unit	$10.03	$7.36	$5.91	$4.97	$4.34	$3.88	$3.53
112	Price	$15.00	$9.83	$8.25	$7.21	$6.87	$6.47	$5.91
113	Margin	33%	25%	28%	31%	37%	40%	40%
114	Annual Sales	44,550	47,052	62,590	79,395	94,517	106,805	117,124
115	Cum cash	11,880	7,281	9,149	17,861	38,969	70,851	110,413
116	Firm B							
117	Mkt share	33%	33%	33%	33%	33%	33%	33%
118	Annual units	2,970	4,158	5,821	7,568	9,081	10,897	13,077
119	Annual debt	32,670	32,818	32,806	28,283	17,880	5,558	(9,194)
120	Cum volume	2,970	7,128	12,949	20,517	29,598	40,495	53,572
121	Cost/unit	$10.03	$7.57	$6.25	$5.39	$4.79	$4.33	$3.95
122	Price	$15.00	$11.32	$9.34	$8.05	$7.16	$6.47	$5.91
123	Margin	33%	33%	33%	33%	33%	33%	33%
124	Annual Sales	44,550	47,052	54,354	60,931	64,980	70,491	77,302
125	Cum cash	11,880	14,233	21,548	32,648	47,100	64,934	86,496

(continued)

	A	B	C	D	E	F	G	H
126	Firm C							
127	Mkt share	33%	29%	24%	19%	17%	17%	17%
128	Annual units	2,970	3,654	4,234	4,357	4,678	5,614	6,737
129	Annual debt	32,670	27,256	12,744	(6,846)	(25,764)	(35,909)	(42,241)
130	Cum volume	2,970	6,624	10,858	15,215	19,893	25,507	32,243
131	Cost/unit	$10.03	$7.75	$6.61	$5.93	$5.44	$5.02	$4.66
132	Price	$15.00	$13.27	$11.28	$10.17	$8.00	$6.47	$5.91
133	Margin	33%	42%	41%	42%	32%	22%	21%
134	Annual Sales	44,550	48,477	47,766	44,313	37,413	36,314	39,822
135	Cum cash	11,880	21,221	35,022	51,159	63,177	72,222	82,063
138	**Report area**							
139	Year	1				10		
140	Annual Market	12,600				82,170		
141	Cum Market	21,600				417,597		
142	Avg Price/unit	$11.32				$4.36		
143								
144	Firms	A	B	C		A	B	C
145	Mkt share	38%	33%	29%		50%	33%	17%
146								
147	Annual units	4,788	4,158	3,654		41,085	27,116	13,969
148	Annual debt	39,771	32,818	27,256		(190,126)	(103,859)	(71,719)
149	(surplus)							
150	Cum volume	7,758	7,128	6,624		204,063	137,807	75,637
151	Cost/unit	$7.36	$7.57	$7.75		$2.57	$2.92	$3.54
152								
153	Price	$9.83	$11.32	$13.27		$4.36	$4.36	$4.36
154								
155	Margin	25%	33%	42%		41%	33%	19%
156								
157	Annual Sales	47,052	47,052	48,477		179,174	118,255	60,919
158								
159	Cum cash	7,281	14,233	21,221		369,299	222,114	132,638

(continued)

	A	B	C	D	E	F	G	H
162	**Graph area**							
163	1. "Firm pricing" -- three firms in the market							
164	2. "Market share" -- three firms' market share over 10 years							
165	3. "Cumulative cash" -- three firms' 10-year net cash							
166			Price				Log(price)	
167		Year	Price A	Price B	Price C	Firm A	Firm B	Firm C
168		0	15.00	15.00	15.00	1.18	1.18	1.18
169		1	9.83	11.32	13.27	0.99	1.05	1.12
170		2	8.25	9.34	11.28	0.92	0.97	1.05
171		3	7.21	8.05	10.17	0.86	0.91	1.01
172		4	6.87	7.16	8.00	0.84	0.85	0.90
173		5	6.47	6.47	6.47	0.81	0.81	0.81
174		6	5.91	5.91	5.91	0.77	0.77	0.77
175		7	5.44	5.44	5.44	0.74	0.74	0.74
176		8	5.04	5.04	5.04	0.70	0.70	0.70
177		9	4.68	4.68	4.68	0.67	0.67	0.67
178		10	4.36	4.36	4.36	0.64	0.64	0.64
179								
180			Market share			Cumulative cash ($1000)		
181		Year	A	B	C	A	B	C
182		0	0.33	0.33	0.33	12	12	12
183		1	0.38	0.33	0.29	7	14	21
184		2	0.43	0.33	0.24	9	22	35
185		3	0.48	0.33	0.19	18	33	51
186		4	0.50	0.33	0.17	39	47	63
187		5	0.50	0.33	0.17	71	65	72
188		6	0.50	0.33	0.17	110	86	82
189		7	0.50	0.33	0.17	159	112	93
190		8	0.50	0.33	0.17	217	143	105
191		9	0.50	0.33	0.17	286	179	118
192		10	0.50	0.33	0.17	369	222	133
195	**Verify area**							
196	550244.68 Verification sum							
197	If an error appears here, check below and the appropriate area of the							
198	spreadsheet. (Be sure that you have recalculated the whole model.)							
199	10.00 Initial data's market share years 2-10 sum of check sums							
200	417597.01 Model's year 10 cumulative market							
201	132637.67 Report Year 10 Firm C's cumulative cash							

An Afterword on Experience Curve Mathematics

An experience curve such as the one in Figure 6-6 is a function of the cumulative volume that yields the current unit cost. The unit cost is calculated from the start-up unit cost, the cumulative volume, the start-up volume, and the experience curve "slope." When the cumulative volume doubles, the unit cost drops to a fixed percentage, say 80 percent, of its prior value. For example, if your initial start-up unit cost was $100 and your start-up volume was 1,000 units, when you reach 2,000 units the unit cost will be $80, and when you reach 4,000 units the cost will be $64. The 80 percent is called the "slope" of the experience curve.

The full experience curve formula appears below. (In the formula, asterisk (*) means multiply, caret (^) means to-the-power-of, and lg means logarithm.)

<unit cost> = <start-up unit cost> * (<cumulative volume>/<start-up volume>) ^ (lg(<experience curve slope>)/lg(2))

The unit cost is a function, f(x), where x is the cumulative volume.

f(x) = <start-up unit cost> * (x /<start-up volume>) ^ (lg(<experience curve slope>)/lg(2))

Using the example above at cumulative volumes of 1,000, 2,000, 4,000 the formulas work out like this:

f(1000) = 100 * (1000/1000) ^ (lg(.8)/lg(2))

= 100 * 1 = 100

because one raised to any power is one.

f(2000) = 100 * (2000/1000) ^ (lg(.8)/lg(2))

= 100 * 2 ^ (lg(.8)/lg(2)

take the log of both sides,

$$lg(f(2000)) = lg(100 * 2 \wedge (lg(.8)/lg(2))$$
$$= lg(100) + lg(2 \wedge (lg(.8)/lg(2))$$
$$= lg(100) + (lg(.8)/lg(2)) * lg(2)$$
$$= lg(100) + lg(.8)$$
$$= lg(100*.8)$$
$$lg(f(2000)) = lg (80)$$

take the inverse of the log—exponentiate both sides,

$$f(2000) = 80.$$
$$f(4000) = 100 * (4000/1000) \wedge (lg(.8)/lg(2))$$
$$= 100 * 4 \wedge (lg(.8)/lg(2))$$

take the log of both sides,

$$lg(f(4000)) = lg(100 * 4 \wedge (lg(.8)/lg(2))$$
$$= lg(100) + lg(4 \wedge (lg(.8)/lg(2))$$
$$= lg(100) + (lg(.8)/lg(2)) * lg(4)$$
$$= lg(100) + (lg(.8)/lg(2)) * lg(2*2)$$
$$= lg(100) + (lg(.8)/lg(2)) * (lg(2) + lg(2))$$
$$= lg(100) + lg(.8) + lg(.8)$$
$$= lg(100*.8*.8)$$
$$lg(f(4000)) = lg (64)$$

take the inverse of the log—exponentiate both sides,

$$f(4000) = 64.$$

Because the ratio of two logarithms is the active term, the logarithms may be either log, base 10, or ln, base e.

As the experience (cumulative volume) grows from 1,000 to 2,000 to 4,000, the unit cost diminishes from 100 to 80 to 64.

Conclusion

In this chapter we have seen how the rules of style helped to write a large new spreadsheet and to modify a large existing spreadsheet. We have also seen an example of a business explanation of a somewhat sophisticated spreadsheet model. The rules helped significantly. The spreadsheets possess sound forms, perform correctly, are capable of being modified, and explain themselves clearly to the attentive reader.

7

Examples

IF WISHES WERE HORSES
If wishes were horses, beggars would ride.
If turnips were watches, I would wear one by my side.
    And if "ifs" and " ands"
    Were pots and pans,
There'd be no work for tinkers!

The Model QUEST

The model QUEST helps make a decision between alternatives evaluated with several conflicting criteria for choice. Read in its entirety, QUEST provides a good example of what a model built for use and reuse might look like.

	A	B	C	D	E	F	G	H
1	**QUEST**	15 October 1495		King Henry				
2	® Copyright 1989 by John M. Nevison							
3	13-Sep-89 Date Printed							
5	**Description**							
6	Pick the best land to gain glory with a quest.							
8	Decide which choice best satisfies several required and desired objectives.							
9	List the choices, then list and weight the objectives to be met. Rank the choices							
10	against each other and pick the choice with the highest weighted score.							
12	**Reference**							
13	Kepner, Charles H., and Tregoe, Benjamin B., "The New Rational Manager,"							
14	Princeton, NJ: Princeton Research Press, 1981, pp. 83-102.							

(continued)

	A	B	C	D	E	F	G	H
16	**Contents**							
17			Introduction: title, description, contents, and directions					
18			Initial data					
19			Decision model					
20			Choice's bar graph.					
22	**Directions**							
23	In the initial data area:							
24	1. State the decision and the desired result.							
25	2. Put in choices and make comments.							
26	3. Enter "must" objectives--things that must be satisfied.							
27	4. Enter "want" objectives--things that you would like to have.							
28	5. Weight the importance of the "want" objectives and comment.							
29	6. Rate or rank the choices against each objective.							
30	For example, rate the best choice (of four) as 4 and let the others have 3,							
31	2, or 1. You may have ties if you wish. You may rate a choice 0 if you wish.							
32	In the decision model							
33	7. Examine the model's results and graph.							
34	8. Revise and reexamine the importance of objectives, the rank of choices,							
35	and other features to be sure of your choice.							
36	9. List the adverse consequences of the best choice to see if it will work.							

The Introduction covers a lot of important ground including a brief reference to a source that explains the full method behind the spreadsheet. The directions give step-by-step guidance to the user.

	A	B	C	D	E	F	G	H
39	**Initial data**							
41	DECISION AND RESULT:							
42			Pick the best land to gain glory with a quest.					
44	CHOICES		COMMENTS					
46	Northumberland		Nice country, lots of dwarves.					
47	Easton		Tough country, magic rings in abundance.					
48	Southington		No known questing beast.					
49	Westerly		Good roads, friendly elves.					
50								
51	"MUST" OBJECTIVES		COMMENTS					
53	Questing Beast		A questing beast to be slain					
54	Maiden in distress		A maiden to be rescued					
55	Holy relic		A relic to bring back to the Church					
56								

(continued)

	A	B	C	D	E	F	G	H
57	"WANT" OBJECTIVES		IMPORTANCE AND COMMENTS					
59	Elves		10	Have magic, can be big help on quest				
60	Magic rings		10	Help in the quest				
61	Good camps		9	Water and firewood for camps				
62	Smooth roads		7	Easy to travel				
63	Golden treasures		5	Nice to find				
64	Dwarves		4	Can help on the quest				
65	Friendly castles		2	Places to stay				
66	Trolls		1	Some help with bridges				
67								

The Initial Data Area tells quite a story. The King needs to choose which of four kingdoms to explore on a quest. He needs to bring back a holy relic, needs to slay a questing beast, and he needs to rescue a maiden in distress. He would like to have the help of elves and magic rings. He would like good travel conditions. Of less importance to him are the presence of golden treasures, dwarves, friendly castles, and trolls.

The first part of the Initial Data Area is mostly text. Notice, however, that the names of the four lands can be data for some spreadsheets that allow pointing to a label. The most important feature about this first part of the Initial Data Area is that it provides room for the necessary information to be spread out and, not only identified, but commented upon where appropriate. The most important data entered here is the relative importance given to the various criteria by which the user shall evaluate the choices.

	A	B	C	D	E	F	G	H
68		North	East	South	West			
70	Questing Beast	1	1	0	1			
71	Maiden in distress	1	1	1	1			
72	Holy relic	1	1	1	0			
73								
74			Relative scores					
75	Elves	2	2	3	4			
76	Magic rings	1	4	1	4			
77	Good camps	4	1	3	2			
78	Smooth roads	1	3	2	4			
79	Golden treasures	4	3	2	1			
80	Dwarves	4	4	2	1			
81	Friendly castles	4	4	2	4			
82	Trolls	3	4	1	3			

The second part of the Initial Data Area contains the real meat of the model. The cross rating of each alternative by each criteria. When the user has completed the entry of this data, the model can grind out a conclusion.

	A	B	C	D	E	F	G	H
85	Decision model							
86				CHOICES				
87	"MUST" OBJECTIVES		North	East	South	West		
89	Questing Beast		1	1	0	1		
90	Maiden in distress		1	1	1	1		
91	Holy relic		1	1	1	0		
92								Check
93	"WANT" OBJECTIVES	Importance		Weighted scores				sums
95	Elves	10	20	20	30	40		110
96	Magic rings	10	10	40	10	40		100
97	Good camps	9	36	9	27	18		90
98	Smooth roads	7	7	21	14	28		70
99	Golden treasure	5	20	15	10	5		50
100	Dwarves	4	16	16	8	4		44
101	Friendly castles	2	8	8	4	8		28
102	Trolls	1	3	4	1	3		11
104	Totals		120	133	104	146		503
105								
106	First choice: Easton							
107	Adverse effects of first choice (see also relative scores in initial data area):							
108	--Be prepared for tough camping							
109	--Try to stay at castles as much as possible							
110	--Double-check on Westerly's lack of a holy relic.							

The model evaluates the data collected in the Initial Data Area and illustrates, in this case, which alternative should be chosen: Easton. (Two of our alternatives failed one or more of the "must" objectives.) The model includes a Check Sums column to allow a cross-check of the results. Beneath the arithmetic of the model is a written summary of the adverse consequences of the first choice. Note that one of the items in the list is a reminder to double-check on the existence of a relic in Westerly. If Westerly could pass that "must" objective, it would be the most preferred choice.

	A	B	C	D	E	F	G	H
113	Choice's bar graph.							
115	Northumberland	120						
116	Easton	133						
117	Southington	104						
118	Westerly	146						

The Graph Area compactly collects the data for display. The bottom two choices are valid, and the top two are invalid because they failed a "must" criteria. The graph itself visually reinforces how important it is to be sure that Westerly is disqualified. It is the clear winner of the "want" criteria rating.

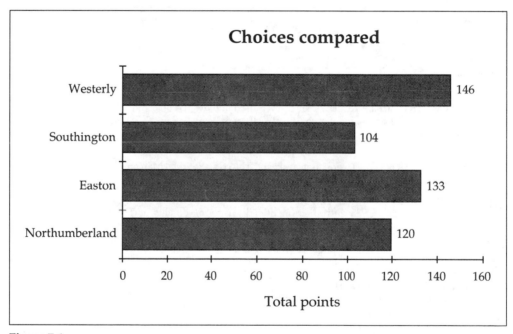

Figure 7-1.

QUEST shows how the parts of the basic form can reinforce one another. The Introduction tells you quickly what is going on and that directions exist where you need them. The Initial Data Area supports and elaborates on the Introduction with concrete data and explanatory comments. The Initial Data Area makes it easy for a new user to ask "what if" questions with this model. Finally, the directions make it possible for a new user not only to modify the present model, but to completely revise it to make a new decision. The next model, LADY, illustrates a version the Queen developed to choose a new lady in waiting.

The Model LADY

Queen Elizabeth wanted a new lady in waiting with diplomatic talents. She had had some success in modifying other tools of her husband to suit her own needs, so she renamed a version of QUEST and set to work. The first thing she did was set down her goal and reexamine the Introduction to alter any other details. Because most of the Introduction was a generic description, she quickly completed the initial work.

	A	B	C	D	E	F	G	H
1	**LADY**		16 November 1495		Queen Elizabeth of York			
2	® Copright 1989 by John M. Nevison							
3		13-Sep-89	Date printed					
5	**Description**							
6	Choose a lady in waiting who will have diplomatic talents.							
8	Decide which choice best satisfies several required and desired objectives.							
9	List the choices, then list and weight the objectives to be met. Rank the choices							
10	against each other and pick the choice with the highest weighted score.							
12	**Reference**							
13	Kepner, Charles H., and Tregoe, Benjamin B., "The New Rational Manager,"							
14	Princeton, NJ: Princeton Research Press, 1981, pp. 83-102.							
16	**Contents**							
17	Introduction: title, description, contents, and directions							
18	Initial data							
19	Decision model							
20	Choice's bar graph							
22	**Directions**							
23	In the initial comments area:							
24	1. State the decision and the desired result.							
25	In the initial assumptions area:							
26	2. Put in choices and make comments.							
27	3. Enter "must" objectives--things that must be satisfied.							
28	4. Enter "want" objectives--things that you would like to have.							
29	5. Weight the importance of the "want" objectives and comment.							
30	6. Rate or rank the choices against each objectives.							
31	For example, rate the best choice (of four) as 4 and let the others have 3,							
32	2, or 1. You may have ties if you wish. You may rate a choice 0 if you wish.							
33	In the decision model							
34	7. Examine the model's results and graph.							
35	8. Revise and reexamine the importance of objectives, the rank of choices,							
36	and other features to be sure of your choice.							
37	9. List the adverse consequences of the best choice to see if it will work.							

Because the model was new to her, the Queen spent a good deal of time going over the fundamental rules to be sure she understood how to use it herself. She read the "must" objectives and the "want" objectives and spent a good deal of time making and revising her own list for her lady in waiting. She also spent considerable time deciding who the likely candidates were. When she had completed her homework, she entered her results in the first part of the Initial Data Area.

	A	B	C	D	E	F	G	H
40	Initial data							
42	DECISION AND RESULT:							
43		Choose a lady in waiting who will have diplomatic talents.						
45	CHOICES		COMMENTS					
47	Jane	Beautiful, English, skilled at music, wealthy family.						
48	Kate	English, of good family, skilled at poetry.						
49	Anne	Stunning, skilled in languages, French, poor family.						
50	Mary	German, wealthy family, exquisite manners.						
51								
52	"MUST" OBJECTIVES		COMMENTS					
54	Noble blood		To be a lady at court, she must be from a noble family.					
55	Speaks English		She must speak English fluently (if she is from					
56			the continent).					
57								
58	"WANT" OBJECTIVES		IMPORTANCE AND COMMENTS					
60	Good looks	10	To be effective, she must be stunning.					
61	Money	9	She should bring money when she comes to court.					
62	Spanish	7	Able to understand important visitors.					
63	French	7	Able to understand important visitors.					
64	Table manners	6	Because so many gatherings are around meals.					
65	Music	4	Able to play an instrument, sing, and dance.					
66	Poetry	4	Accomplishment becoming a lady.					
67	Needlework	1	A skill I must say I considered, but do not value highly.					
68								

Her four choices were two English ladies, Jane and Kate; one French lady, Anne; and one German lady, Mary. Each had her own accomplishments.

Her "must objectives" had to include noble blood and fluent English. Nobility was required for her to gain access to the influential lords. They did not care whether a lady was of high or low nobility, but she could not, by custom, be admitted to their social affairs if not of pedigreed birth. Fluency in English was an absolute requirement for a person who would be used to influence diplomatic gatherings. The subtle shades of the language must be understood. Of course it was also desirable to be fluent in other languages for similar reasons.

Among her "want" criteria, good looks was the only traditional feminine virtue to be of much value. Money and ability with languages accounted for more than the traditional accomplishments of a lady. Traditional accomplishments, however, could not be wholly ignored, and together they might outweigh some of the more sober virtues.

The next part was hard for the Queen. She rated and rerated her four choices on her 10 criteria. Two were easy, but the eight "want" objectives were time consuming. After several tries, she was finally satisfied she had done as much as she could to get it right.

	A	B	C	D	E	F	G	H
69		Jane	Kate	Anne	Mary			
71	Noble blood	1	1	1	1			
72	Speaks English	1	1	1	1			
73								
74			Relative scores					
75	Good looks	3	3	4	2			
76	Money	3	2	1	4			
77	Spanish	2	0	4	2			
78	French	4	4	4	0			
79	Table manners	1	3	4	4			
80	Music	4	2	2	2			
81	Poetry	1	4	3	2			
82	Needlework	3	3	4	1			

All four passed the muster of the "must" criteria. Among the other criteria, Anne was the poorest, but the most beautiful; Mary, was the richest, but plain; and Jane and Kate were in between. French Anne, however, was a master of several languages—at least among the four choices she was the strongest in Spanish and French. The four's skills in traditional accomplishments were varied.

The Queen examined the results of her evaluation with great interest.

	A	B	C	D	E	F	G	H
85	**Decision model**							
86				CHOICES				
87	"MUST" OBJECTIVES		Jane	Kate	Anne	Mary		
89	Noble blood		1	1	1	1		
90	Speaks English		1	1	1	1		
91								
92	"WANT" OBJECTIVES	Importance		Weighted scores				Check sums
94	Good looks	10	30	30	40	20		120
95	Money	9	27	18	9	36		90
96	Spanish	7	14	0	28	14		56
97	French	7	28	28	28	0		84
98	Table manners	6	6	18	24	24		72
99	Music	4	16	8	8	8		40
100	Poetry	4	4	16	12	8		40
101	Needlework	1	3	3	4	1		11
103	Totals		128	121	153	111		513
104								

French Anne won hands down. The check sum column was clear, so no errors had crept into her reworking of her husband's model. Anne won on her looks, language skills, and better-than-average mastery of the traditional accomplishments of a lady. The Queen studied the results for a while to be sure she had been fair to each candidate. Then she made a list of the adverse consequences of her first choice.

	A	B	C	D	E	F	G	H
105	Adverse effects of first choice (see also relative scores in initial data area):							
106	--Lady Anne will not bring a strong dowry to court.							
107	--This means that the treasury will be poorer than anticipated this year.							
108	--Must find another means of raising some money.							

The Queen knew how to deal with raising money. In order to secure the approval of her husband, she followed his example and graphed the results of LADY.

	A	B	C	D	E	F	G	H
111	**Choice's bar graph**							
113	Jane	128						
114	Kate	121						
115	Anne	153						
116	Mary	111						

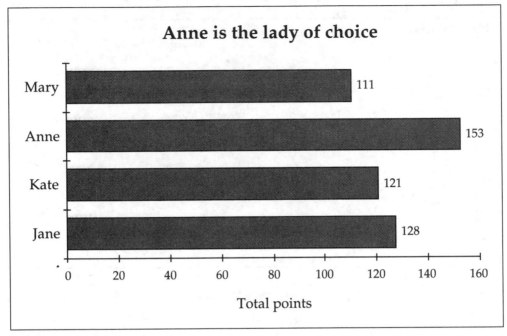

Figure 7-2.

The King gave his approval. As the original author, he was pleased that the Queen had used his model to such good effect. He understood her decision and could explain it to the English fathers of Jane and Kate. The Queen offered Anne the job as her new lady in waiting. Anne was a huge success.

The Model RAINCOAT

Sometimes while using a spreadsheet such as QUEST to arrive at a decision, the decision maker needs additional help to assess the adverse future consequences of an alternative. Sometimes the future remains uncertain. The next two spreadsheets, RAINCOAT and PIETEST, can help you assess the consequences of an uncertain future and make decisions under this uncertainty.

The classic problem of uncertain future is the weather. The classic decision made under this uncertainty is whether to wear a raincoat on a cloudy day. The cloudy day is important. Notice it is not a rainy day. You don't know whether or not it will rain. As a matter of fact, the weather forecast is a 50 percent chance of rain.

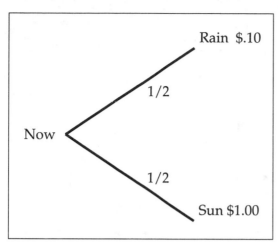

Figure 7-3.   Nature's game on a cloudy day.

The cloudy day represents nature's uncertain future. Figure 7-3 is one way of diagramming the predicament. If you were to get a dime when it rained and a dollar when the sun came out, then the expected value of the situation is the total of the reward times the chance of getting the reward; that is:

Expected value = (1/2) * 10 + (1/2) * 100

= 55

If the weather forecast is only a one-third chance of rain, the odds in this game would change and the expected value would change as well:

Expected value = (1/3) * 10 + (2/3) * 100

= 70

Notice that as the odds shift toward a favorable outcome, the expected value of the forecast goes up. This is only common sense.

The reason this chance game of nature is important is that it will influence your decision. Suppose for a moment that having a raincoat when it rains pleased you 10 points; having to carry your raincoat when the sun shines displeased you −20 points; not having a raincoat when it rains displeased you −50 points; and not having your raincoat on a sunny day pleased you 80 points.

With values for the possible outcomes, you are ready to make your decision in the face of the weather's uncertainty. You could diagram your situation as in Figure 7-4.

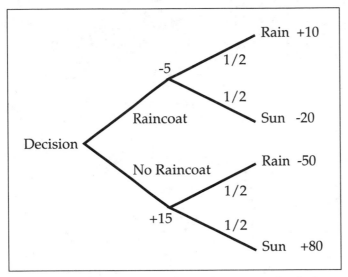

Figure 7-4.   The decision to take a raincoat on a cloudy day.

Your must decide between two different plays of nature's game. The reason for the two plays is that the outcomes have different values:

Raincoat Game   = (1/2) * 10 + (1/2) * -20

    = –5

No raincoat game   = (1/2) * –50 + (1/2) * 80

    = 15

Fifteen points is better than -5, so you choose not to take a raincoat when the forecast is only a 50 percent chance of rain.

Notice that you could repeat the evaluation of chancy situations for different alternatives with different payoff criteria and use the results of these various games of nature to fill in values in the decision table of QUEST or LADY. The table might be:

Table 7-1. Example of a decision table

	Raincoat	No Raincoat
First person's criteria	-5	15
Second person's values	.	.
	.	.	.
	.	.	.
	.	.	.

You could fill in the table with the results of different payoffs others might have for the same uncertain futures. The model RAINCOAT allows you to see this decision played out in front of your eyes.

	A	B	C	D	E	F	G	H	I
1	**RAINCOAT**		30 Dec 1988	J. M. Nevison					
2	® Copyright 1988 by John M. Nevison								
3	13-Sep-89	Date printed							
5	Description								
6	Show how the raincoat decision can be represented as a tree.								
8	Reference								
9	John M. Nevison, "Excel Spreadsheet Design," New York, NY: Brady								
10	Books, 1990.								
12	Contents								
13	Introduction: title, description, contents								
14	Initial data								
15	Decision tree								
18	Initial data								
20	50.0%	Chance of rain							
21	50.0%	Chance of sun							
22	Outcome payoffs								
23	10	Wear raincoat and it rains							
24	-20	Wear raincoat and the sun shines							
25	-50	No raincoat and it rains							
26	80	No raincoat and the sun shines							

(continued)

	A	B	C	D	E	F	G	H	I
29	**Decision tree**								
30	Tricky formulas:								
31	value of decision = maximum of (alternatives)								
32	value of chance game = sum of (chance of outcome x value of outcome)								
33									
34		Decision		Chance games			Primary outcomes		
35							(* indicates end of branch)		
36	15	Decision	-5	Raincoat	50%	10	*Rain		
37					50%	-20	*Sun		
38									
39			15	No raincoat	50%	-50	*Rain		
40					50%	80	*Sun		

The Initial Data Area clearly distinguishes what you must know at the beginning: the chance of rain and how you value the various outcomes. Should the chance of rain or your feeling about the payoffs change, you may quickly revise your model.

The model itself calculates from right to left to allow the reader to progress from left to right, from final answer back to initial conditions. The reader is free to browse through as many or as few details as necessary to understand the result. The ends of the branches of the decision tree are indicated with an asterisk (*).

One interesting experiment you can conduct with this model is to alter the chance of rain to find out at what percentage your outcome payoffs are evenly balanced (in this case, it's a 62.5 percent chance of rain).

	A	B	C	D	E	F	G	H	I
18	Initial data								
20	62.5%	Chance of rain							
21	37.5%	Chance of sun							
22	Outcome payoffs								
23	10	Wear raincoat and it rains							
24	-20	Wear raincoat and the sun shines							
25	-50	No raincoat and it rains							
26	80	No raincoat and the sun shines							
29	**Decision tree**								
30	Tricky formulas:								
31	value of decision = maximum of (alternatives)								
32	value of chance game = sum of (chance of outcome x value of outcome)								
33									
34			Decision		Chance games		Primary outcomes		
35							(* indicates end of branch)		
36		-1.25	Decision	-1	Raincoat	63%	10	*Rain	
37						38%	-20	*Sun	
38									
39				-1	No raincoat	63%	-50	*Rain	
40						38%	80	*Sun	

The Model PIETEST

A more elaborate problem with different kinds of uncertainty was faced by the Pieman whom Simple Simon met. The Pieman wanted to bring to market a new kind of pie. He figured there was a 75 percent chance folks would like it and a 25 percent chance they would not. If it failed, he would lose 50 ducats of materials and time from his current business of 200 ducats. If it succeeded, he would add 80 ducats of new profit to his current business.

The simple decision looks easy.

	B	C	D	E	F	G	H	I
40		247.5	No test	247.5	Release	75%	280	*Like
41				200	*Continue	25%	150	*Don't like

The game has a value of 247.5 versus a stand pat decision of 200. The Pieman should decide to release the new pie into production. But what if the Pieman has the chance to do a little market research?

A market test will consist of a friend walking about the market place and asking customers if they would like the new pie. The friend will charge only 2 ducats and the Pieman is convinced he will know with 90 percent certainty whether or not the market likes his new idea. Should he conduct the market test?

The decision trees for what he would find out look like this.

	F	G	H	I	J	K	L
34	267	Like	267	Release	90%	280	*Like
35		Decision	200	*Continue	10%	150	*Don't like
36							
37	200	Don`t like	163	Release	10%	280	*Like
38		Decision	200	*Continue	90%	150	*Don't like

These trees, assembled with his previous knowledge, gather into a test decision that looks like this.

	A	B	C	D	E	F	G	H	I	J	K	L
34	250.25	Decision	250.25	Test	75%	267	Like	267	Release	90%	280	*Like
35							Decision	200	*Continue	10%	150	*Don't like
36												
37					25%	200	Don`t like	163	Release	10%	280	*Like
38							Decision	200	*Continue	90%	150	*Don't like
39												
40			247.5	No test	247.5	Release	75%	280	*Like			
41					200	*Continue	25%	150	*Don't like			

The Pieman sees that the value of the test is 2.75 ducats and decides to pay his friend 2 ducats to conduct a market test. If the friend had charged 3 ducats, the Pieman would have declined doing the test.

The full spreadsheet looks like this.

	A	B	C	D	E	F	G	H	I	J	K	L
1	**PIETEST**		30 December 1620		P. Pieman							
2	® Copyright 1988 by John M. Nevison											
3	13-Sep-90 Date printed											
5	**Description**											
6			Evaluate a decision to pay for some market research.									
8	**Reference**											
9			John M. Nevison, "Excel Spreadsheet Design," New York, NY: Brady									
10			Books, 1990.									
12	**Contents**											
13			Introduction: title, description, contents									
14			Initial data									
15			Decision tree									
18	**Initial data**											
19		75%	Chance market will like new product									
20		25%	Chance market will hate new product									
21		90%	Test certainty									
22	Payoff structure											
23			280	Value if market likes new product								
24			150	Value if market hates new product								
25			200	Value if present product is continued								
28	**Decision tree**											
29	Tricky formulas:											
30		value of decision = maximum of (alternatives)										
31		value of chance game = sum of (chance of outcome x value of outcome)										
32	(* indicates end of branch)											
33												
34	250.25	Decision	250.25	Test	75%		267	Like	267	Release	90%	280 *Like
35								Decision	200	*Continue	10%	150 *Don't like
36												
37					25%		200	Don`t like	163	Release	10%	280 *Like
38								Decision	200	*Continue	90%	150 *Don't like
39												
40			247.5	No test	247.5	Release	75%		280	*Like		
41					200	*Continue	25%		150	*Don't like		

The Model SEASON

When figures vary on a regular basis over the course of a year, a common way to look for the trend in the data is to seasonally adjust the figures. When you try to look beyond the last known figure, often you fit a line through the seasonally adjusted points and figure the next month off the line. Sometimes the figure is unadjusted to find out what next month's actual result is predicted to be. The model SEASON does just that. Its result is a graph, shown in Figure 7-5.

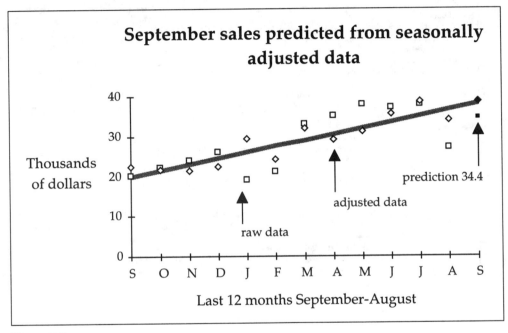

Figure 7-5.

The result of SEASON contains the raw data of the last 12 months, the seasonally adjusted data, the best-fit line, and the projections for next month's figure. If you look closely at the raw data you will see that it fluctuates over the year.

This fluctuation is confirmed by the seasonal factors that are computed from the four back years of data.

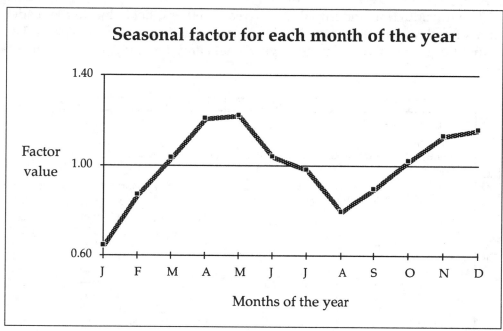

Figure 7-6.

The year begins low and works to a high in April, declines through the summer, and then rises toward a second high in December. The seasonal effect is pronounced.

The spreadsheet SEASON starts off with no surprises.

	A	B	C	D	E	F	G	H	I	J	K	L
1	**SEASON**		28 August 1640		J. Sprat							
2	® Copyright 1989 John M. Nevison											
3	13-Sep-89	Date printed										
5	Description											
6		Predict next month's figure by using a best-fit line through										
7		adjusted data. The seasonal adjustment is made using factors										
8		that are computed from four prior years of monthly data.										
10	Contents											
11		Introduction: title, description, contents										
12		Initial data										
13		Model										
14		Seasonal factors										
15		Project next month's figure										
16		Graph area										

The Introduction and Initial Data Area together quickly locate the reader and show him or her that the Model Area will do its work in two parts. The Initial Data Area shows four back year's data and the first part of the current year.

	A	B	C	D	E	F	G	H	I	J	K	L
36	**Model**		Seasonal factors									
38	Tricky formulas:											
39	Monthly factor = <raw monthly factor>/<average raw yearly factor>											
40	Seasonal factor = average(four monthly factors)											
42		Raw Monthly Data					Monthly Factors					Seasonal
43		1Yr	2Yr	3Yr	4Yr		1Yr	2Yr	3Yr	4Yr		Factors
45	January	10	10	12	15		0.69	0.55	0.63	0.72		0.65
46	February	14	15	17	17		0.96	0.82	0.89	0.82		0.87
47	March	16	19	19	21		1.10	1.04	1.00	1.01		1.04
48	April	18	20	23	27		1.23	1.10	1.21	1.30		1.21
49	May	20	21	22	25		1.37	1.15	1.15	1.20		1.22
50	June	16	20	19	20		1.10	1.10	1.00	0.96		1.04
51	July	15	19	18	19		1.03	1.04	0.94	0.91		0.98
52	August	13	15	15	14		0.89	0.82	0.79	0.67		0.79
53	September	11	17	18	20		0.75	0.93	0.94	0.96		0.90
54	October	13	20	20	22		0.89	1.10	1.05	1.06		1.02
55	November	14	22	23	24		0.96	1.21	1.21	1.15		1.13
56	December	15	21	23	26		1.03	1.15	1.21	1.25		1.16
57												
58	Average	14.6	18.3	19.1	20.8		1.00	1.00	1.00	1.00		1.00
59	--											

The first part of the Model Area computes the seasonal factors. The two tricky formulas are presented first, followed by the calculations laid out from leftmost initial data to rightmost final result. The reader can methodically step across the page and follow the calculations at each step. Every factor column reiterates its formula in the bottom "Average" row where the correct answer 1.00 reassures the reader that the calculation is, in fact, correct.

After calculating the seasonal factors, the model turns its attention to projecting next month's figure.

	A	B	C	D	E	F	G	H	I	J	K	L
60	Project next month's figure											
61					The twelve months begin in September.							
62												
63	Fit a line to a set of points (x(i),s(i)), where each s(i) is the seasonally adjusted											
64	version of y(i). Use the line to predict the succeeding point, s(13), and seasonally											
65	adjust it to find y(13).											
66												
67	(For details on the line-fitting calculation see the model LINEFIT in											
68	"Executive Computing: How to get it done with Spreadsheets and Graphs," by											
69	John M. Nevison, Atlanta, GA: AMCEE, 1986.)											
70												
71	Tricky formulas:											
72	s(i) = y(i)/<seasonal factor for month>											
73	Each x' = x(i) - average x(i)											
74	Each s' = s(i) - average s(i)											
75	Slope of line, M = sum(x'*s')/sum(x'*x')											
76	Intercept of line, B = <average s(i)> - M * <average x(i)>											
77	Best fit line = M * x(i) + B											
78	Seasonally adjusted predicted month = M * 13 + B											
79	Raw predicted month = <seasonally adjusted predicted month> *											
80								<seasonal factor for month>				
81												Best
82					Seasonal				Calculations			Fit
83			x(i)	y(i)	Fctrs	s(i)		x'	s'	x'*s'	x'*x'		Line
85	September	1	20	0.90	22.3		-5.5	-6.2	33.91	30.25		20.1
86	October	2	22	1.02	21.5		-4.5	-6.9	31.26	20.25		21.6
87	November	3	24	1.13	21.2		-3.5	-7.2	25.30	12.25		23.1
88	December	4	26	1.16	22.5		-2.5	-6.0	15.01	6.25		24.6
89	January	5	19	0.65	29.4		-1.5	1.0	-1.46	2.25		26.2
90	February	6	21	0.87	24.1		-0.5	-4.4	2.19	0.25		27.7
91	March	7	33	1.04	31.9		0.5	3.4	1.71	0.25		29.2
92	April	8	35	1.21	29.0		1.5	0.5	0.78	2.25		30.7
93	May	9	38	1.22	31.2		2.5	2.7	6.81	6.25		32.3
94	June	10	37	1.04	35.7		3.5	7.2	25.27	12.25		33.8
95	July	11	38	0.98	38.7		4.5	10.3	46.22	20.25		35.3
96	August	12	27	0.79	34.1		5.5	5.6	30.80	30.25		36.8
98	Average	6.5			28.5		Sums		217.8	143.0		
99										1.52	= M	
100										18.56	= B	
101	Equation :		y =	1.52	* x +	18.56						
102	Seasonally adjusted predicted month:											
103		x =	13		y =	38.4						
104	Predicted month:											
105				34.4		0.90	Seasonal factor					

This part begins with some words of introduction followed by another set of tricky formulas. The deeper explanation of the computations is deferred to a formal reference, but the details of what the formulas are is revealed in the model. The numbers are arranged, again, in a left-to-right progression across the page, arriving at the coordinates of the best-fit line on the right edge.

Below the first pass of calculations, the details of the predicted month, Month 13, unfold. The predicted point on the line is 38.4, and the seasonally unadjusted figure is 34.4.

Using Excel's TREND function you can simplify the Model Area. The tricky formulas use array notation and are explained in the excerpt below.

	A	B	C	D	E	F	G	H	I	J	K	L
71	Tricky formulas:											
72	s(i) = y(i)/<seasonal factor for month>											
73	Best fit line {= TREND(<list of s(i)'s>,<list of x(i)'s>)}											
74	Seasonally adjusted predicted month = TREND(<list of s(i)'s>,<list of x(i)'s>,13)											
75	Raw predicted month = <seasonally adjusted predicted month> * <seasonal factor for month>											
76												
77								Best				
78					Seasonal			Fit				
79			x(i)	y(i)	Fctrs	s(i)		Line				
80												
81	September	1	20	0.90	22.3		20.1					
82	October	2	22	1.02	21.5		21.6					
83	November	3	24	1.13	21.2		23.1					
84	December	4	26	1.16	22.5		24.6					
85	January	5	19	0.65	29.4		26.2					
86	February	6	21	0.87	24.1		27.7					
87	March	7	33	1.04	31.9		29.2					
88	April	8	35	1.21	29.0		30.7					
89	May	9	38	1.22	31.2		32.3					
90	June	10	37	1.04	35.7		33.8					
91	July	11	38	0.98	38.7		35.3					
92	August	12	27	0.79	34.1		36.8					
94	Average	6.5			28.5							
95												
96	Seasonally adjusted predicted month:											
97	x =	13			y =	38.4						
98	Predicted month:											
99			34.4		0.90	Seasonal factor						

After the model has finished its computational work, it must arrange its results in a way convenient to graph.

	A	B	C	D	E	F	G	H	I	J	K	L
108	**Graph area**											
109	1. "Next month's sales"											
110	2. "Seasonal factors"											
111	Next month's sales							Seasonal factors				
112	x-label	x(i)	y(i)	s(i)	Line	s(13)	y(13)	x-label				
114	S	1	20	22.3	20.1			J	0.65	1		
115	O	2	22	21.5	21.6			F	0.87	1		
116	N	3	24	21.2	23.1			M	1.04	1		
117	D	4	26	22.5	24.6			A	1.21	1		
118	J	5	19	29.4	26.2			M	1.22	1		
119	F	6	21	24.1	27.7			J	1.04	1		
120	M	7	33	31.9	29.2			J	0.98	1		
121	A	8	35	29.0	30.7			A	0.79	1		
122	M	9	38	31.2	32.3			S	0.90	1		
123	J	10	37	35.7	33.8			O	1.02	1		
124	J	11	38	38.7	35.3			N	1.13	1		
125	A	12	27	34.1	36.8			D	1.16	1		
126	S	13			38.4	38.4	34.4					

The Graph Area takes advantage of its space to list the graphs by name, to set up a column of labels for the graph of the most recent 12 months, to reserve special columns for s(13) and y(13), and to reserve a column of all ones to draw a line through the center of a set of factors. Exactly how each of these columns works is unimportant. What is important is that the Graph Area allows the author enough room so that he or she can create exactly the right graph. The graph remains the most important point of this spreadsheet.

The Model TASKTIME

When a planner gets several chores lined up and looks at the uncertainty associated with any one of these, it may seem as if the whole project is in real danger of never getting done. Actually, just the opposite is true: If you can estimate the parts of a job well, the composite whole is easier to estimate. In the spreadsheet TASKTIME, King Henry puts together a model to help him estimate the length of time it might take to gain control of a neighboring kingdom.

The beginning of the spreadsheet introduces the reader to the method employed.

	A	B	C	D	E	F	G	H
1	**TASKTIME**		14 Sept 1521		King Henry			
2	® Copyright 1986, 1989 by John M. Nevison							
3			13-Sep-89 Date printed					
5	**Description**							
6	Estimate the project completion time from the estimates of the component activities.							
8	The component activities are serial -- one must be completed before the next is begun.							
9	In a large project these activities all lie on the critical path.							
11	**To use**							
12	1. Count your tasks -- each should depend on the one before.							
13	2. If you need more tasks, insert copies of an old task row in the middle of the list;							
14	if fewer, delete a few rows from the middle of the list.							
15	3. Enter the name, low, likely, and high estimates for your tasks.							
16	4. Adjust the model to the size of your initial data.							
18	**Contents**							
19			Introduction: title, description, contents					
20			Initial data					
21			Model					
22			Report area					
23			Graph area					

The instructions emphasize the requirement that the tasks follow one another and that each depends on the one before. Two sets of tasks that have these properties are the tasks on a critical path of a large project and the tasks you, as an individual, set out to do on any given day. (Many times some of the personal tasks may be independent, but if they all must be finished by one person, the set's time requirements behave as if the individual tasks were serially dependent.)

	A	B	C	D	E	F	G	H
26	**Initial data**							
27	-Low has a 1/1000 chance of happening -- very optimistic estimate,							
28	everything goes right.							
29	-High has a 1/1000 chance of happening -- extremely pessimistic estimate,							
30	everything goes completely wrong.							
31	-Likely is the most likely single estimate (the mode),							
32	everything is completely normal.							
33								
34	Task name		Low	Likely	High			
36	Make nails		8	10	20			
37	Make shoes		5	15	30			
38	Shoe horses		4	8	15			
39	Train riders		5	10	25			
40	Win battles		21	35	180			
41	Gain kingdom		20	30	60			

The Initial Data Area has some reminders that help the user enter the right kind of estimates for each task. King Henry estimated his tasks. The first two make use of his blacksmith shop. He must make nails before he can make shoes. After the manufacturing is complete, the same smithy must shoe all the horses. If his cousin can learn the job and work a second shift each day, and if his cousin is good, the job will proceed quickly; if either gets sick, the job will be slowed. Because of the new shoes, the riders must train themselves and their mounts for battle. Winning a battle involves finding the foe and engaging him (victory is assumed). Whether the foe stands and fights or runs and must be cornered leads to great uncertainty in the time it will take to conclude a major victory in battle. The formalities of assuming the crown could be done in three weeks, but if the ceremonies must stand on the attendance of certain visiting royalty, then it might be delayed several weeks.

When he had finished entering the initial data, the King turned his attention to the model itself.

	A	B	C	D	E	F	G	H
44	**Model**							
45	Tricky formulas:							
46	Expected = (low + 4*likely + high)/6							
47	Standard deviation = (high - low)/6							
48	Variance = (standard deviation)^2							
49	Project standard deviation = square root(project variance)							
50								
51	Task name	Low	Likely	High	Expected	Variance		
53	Make nails	8	10	20	11.3	4.0		
54	Make shoes	5	15	30	15.8	17.4		
55	Shoe horses	4	8	15	8.5	3.4		
56	Train riders	5	10	25	11.7	11.1		
57	Win battles	21	35	180	56.8	702.3		
58	Gain kingdom	20	30	60	33.3	44.4		
59							Standard deviation	
60	Project totals				137.5	782.5	28.0	
62	Check sums	63	108	330	137.5			

The model itself begins with a list of the tricky formulas employed in the calculations. With that help the King can see how his individual task estimates were combined into an estimate for the whole project. He examines the results closely because he doesn't believe it should take so long. After reviewing the individual tasks, confirming to himself that the individual tasks could not be doubled up, and reviewing how this project compared to the last one like it, he decides the estimate is accurate.

He checks his old Report Area and Graph Area to see if they still work.

	A	B	C	D	E	F	G	H
65	**Report area**							
66	26-Nov-40	**ESTIMATED PROJECT COMPLETION TIME**						
67		(Working Days)						
68	6	Number of activities on the project critical path						
69	137.5	Project mean completion time (50-50 chance)						
70	28.0	Project completion time standard deviation						
71								
72				PROJECT COMPLETION TIMETABLE				
73	Time:	54	102	114	123	131	138	
74	Probability:	~0%	10%	20%	30%	40%	50%	
75								
76	Time:	138	144	152	161	173	221	
77	Probability:	50%	60%	70%	80%	90%	~100%	
78								
81	**Graph area**							
82	"Timely's completion time": the project probable completion time							
83		Std. devs	Curve	Prob.	Times			
84		-3.00	0.02	0.1%	54	54		
85		-2.50	0.07	0.6%				
86		-2.00	0.21	2.3%				
87		-1.50	0.51	6.7%	96	96		
88		-1.00	0.95	15.9%				
89		-0.50	1.39	30.9%				
90		0.00	1.57	50.0%	138	138		
91		0.50	1.39	69.1%				
92		1.00	0.95	84.1%				
93		1.50	0.51	93.3%	179	179		
94		2.00	0.21	97.7%				
95		2.50	0.07	99.4%				
96		3.00	0.02	99.9%	221	221		

After he looks at them for a few minutes, he remembers that they both depend on only three numbers from the Model Area: the number of tasks, the project mean, and project standard deviation. The answers appear to be correct.

Finally he calls up the graph called "Project's probable completion time."

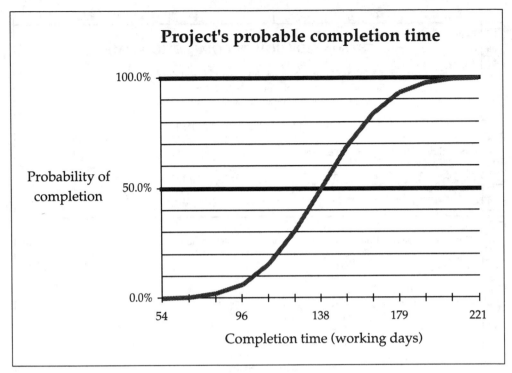

Figure 7-7.

The curve tells him the campaign will be over in four to six months. The model tells him the campaign's completion depends heavily on how fast he can engage the enemy. After he prints out copies for his files, he saves a copy of the model for later adjustment as the project unfolds.

To save a general tool that he can use later on another project, the King enters an appropriate set of initial test data and checks the model to be sure it correctly manipulates the test data.

	A	B	C	D	E	F	G	H
51	**Model**							
53	Tricky formulas:							
54	Expected = (low + 4*likely + high)/6							
55	Standard deviation = (high - low)/6							
56	Variance = (standard deviation)^2							
57	Project standard deviation = square root(project variance)							
59	Task name	Low	Likely	High	Expected	Variance		
61	Activity 1	2	5	14	6.0	4.0		
62	Activity 2	2	5	14	6.0	4.0		
63	Activity 3	2	5	14	6.0	4.0		
64	Activity 4	2	5	14	6.0	4.0		
65	Activity 5	2	5	14	6.0	4.0		
66	Activity 6	2	5	14	6.0	4.0		
67	Activity 7	2	5	14	6.0	4.0		
68	Activity 8	2	5	14	6.0	4.0		
69	Activity 9	2	5	14	6.0	4.0		
70							Standard deviation	
71	Project total				54.0	36.0	54.0	
72	Check sums	18	45	126	54.0			

The answers are correct. He saves this version of the model for his next project and goes to bed.

The Model ACTIVITY

This model tracks a project's many activities as they are opened and closed through the different phases of the project. A discussion of most of the model appears in Chapter 2, and a discussion of the graphing portion appears in Chapter 4. The whole model is included here to make it easy to find for future reference.

	A	B	C	D	E	F	G	H	I	J	K	L	M	N	O	P	Q
1	**ACTIVITY (Activity Tracking)**								3 January 1520 T. Tittlemouse								
2	(C) Copyright 1985 by John M. Nevison																
3	13-Sep-89 Date printed																
5	**Description**																
6			Track the number of assigned activities during a project.														
7			The project is to build a new catapult.														
9	**To use**																
10			1. Enter the new weekly data in the Initial Data														
11			2. Examine the model														
12			3. Print the graphs														
14	**Contents**																
15			Introduction: title, description, contents														
16			Initial data														
17			Quarterly model														
18			Graphing area														
19			Verify area														
22	**Initial data**																
23		Activities as they occurred															
24	Week number	1	2	3	4	5	6	7	8	9	10	11	12	13	14	15	16
25	Design activities																
26	Assigned	5	6	7	7	7	8	7	6	6	5	4	4	3	3	3	2
27	Completed	0	3	4	5	6	7	7	6	5	4	5	6	5	4	4	4
28	Build activities																
29	Assigned	0	0	0	0	0	0	3	4	5	4	4	5	6	7	5	6
30	Completed	0	0	0	0	0	0	0	2	4	5	4	5	5	6	6	4
31	Test activities																
32	Assigned	0	0	0	0	0	0	0	0	0	0	0	0	0	0	0	0
33	Completed	0	0	0	0	0	0	0	0	0	0	0	0	0	0	0	0

	R	S	T	U	V	W	X	Y	Z	AA	AB	AC	AD	AE	AF	AG	AH	AI	AJ	AK
22																				
23																				
24	17	18	19	20	21	22	23	24	25	26	27	28	29	30	31	32	33	34	35	36
25																				
26	2	1	0	0	0	0	0	0	0	0	0	0	0	0	0	0	0	0	0	0
27	3	3	3	2	0	0	0	0	0	0	0	0	0	0	0	0	0	0	0	0
28																				
29	7	7	7	8	7	6	6	5	4	4	3	3	3	2	2	1	0	0	0	0
30	4	5	6	7	7	6	5	4	5	6	5	4	4	4	0	4	4	3	0	0
31																				
32	2	3	3	3	4	3	2	3	3	3	3	4	4	3	3	2	2	4	2	2
33	0	0	1	3	3	2	2	2	2	2	3	4	2	2	2	2	2	3	2	2

	AL	AM	AN	AO	AP	AQ	AR	AS	AT	AU	AV	AW	AX	AY	AZ	BA
22																
23																
24	37	38	39	40	41	42	43	44	45	46	47	48	49	50	51	52
25																
26	0	0	0	0	0	0	0	0	0	0	0	0	0	0	0	0
27	0	0	0	0	0	0	0	0	0	0	0	0	0	0	0	0
28																
29	0	0	0	0	0	0	0	0	0	0	0	0	0	0	0	0
30	0	0	0	0	0	0	0	0	0	0	0	0	0	0	0	0
31																
32	0	2	2	1	0	0	0	0	0	0	0	0	0	0	0	0
33	2	4	5	5	4	1	1	0	0	0	0	0	0	0	0	0

	A	B	C	D	E	F	G	H	I	J	K	L	M	N	O	P	Q
36	**Quarterly model**																
37			THE CATAPULT PROJECT: activities completed in early autumn.														
38			1520														
39		Qtr 1		Otr 2		Otr 3		Qtr 4		Total			Date: 3 January 1521				
40	Design activities																
41	Assigned	75		11		0		0		86							
42	Completed	63		23		0		0		86							
43	Build activities																
44	Assigned	31		79		14		0		124							
45	Completed	25		71		28		0		124							
46	Test activities																
47	Assigned	0		29		33		1		63							
48	Completed	0		17		35		11		63							
49																	
50	Total activities																
51	Assigned	106		119		47		1		273							
52	Completed	88		111		63		11		273							

	A	B	C	D	E	F	G	H	I	J	K	L	M	N	O	P	Q
55	**Graphing area**																
57	Graphs supported include:																
58	1. "Catapult project activities (actual)"																
59	2. "Total activity"																
60	Cumulative counts																
61	Week number	1	2	3	4	5	6	7	8	9	10	11	12	13	14	15	16
62	Design activities																
63	Assigned	5	11	18	25	32	40	47	53	59	64	68	72	75	78	81	83
64	Completed	0	3	7	12	18	25	32	38	43	47	52	58	63	67	71	75
65	Build activities																
66	Assigned	0	0	0	0	0	0	3	7	12	16	20	25	31	38	43	49
67	Completed	0	0	0	0	0	0	0	2	6	11	15	20	25	31	37	41
68	Test activities																
69	Assigned	0	0	0	0	0	0	0	0	0	0	0	0	0	0	0	0
70	Completed	0	0	0	0	0	0	0	0	0	0	0	0	0	0	0	0
71	Total activities																
72	Assigned	5	11	18	25	32	40	50	60	71	80	88	97	106	116	124	132
73	Completed	0	3	7	12	18	25	32	40	49	58	67	78	88	98	108	116
74																	
75	Open activities																
76	Design	5	8	11	13	14	15	15	15	16	17	16	14	12	11	10	8
77	Build	0	0	0	0	0	0	3	5	6	5	5	5	6	7	6	8
78	Test	0	0	0	0	0	0	0	0	0	0	0	0	0	0	0	0
79																	
80	Total (check)	5	8	11	13	14	15	18	20	22	22	21	19	18	18	16	16
81	Week axis label	1												13			

	R	S	T	U	V	W	X	Y	Z	AA	AB	AC	AD	AE	AF	AG	AH	AI	AJ	AK
61	17	18	19	20	21	22	23	24	25	26	27	28	29	30	31	32	33	34	35	36
62																				
63	85	86	86	86	86	86	86	86	86	86	86	86	86	86	86	86	86	86	86	86
64	78	81	84	86	86	86	86	86	86	86	86	86	86	86	86	86	86	86	86	86
65																				
66	56	63	70	78	85	91	97	102	106	110	113	116	119	121	123	124	124	124	124	124
67	45	50	56	63	70	76	81	85	90	96	101	105	109	113	113	117	121	124	124	124
68																				
69	2	5	8	11	15	18	20	23	26	29	32	36	40	43	46	48	50	54	56	58
70	0	0	1	4	7	9	11	13	15	17	20	24	26	28	30	32	34	37	39	41
71																				
72	143	154	164	175	186	195	203	211	218	225	231	238	245	250	255	258	260	264	266	268
73	123	131	141	153	163	171	178	184	191	199	207	215	221	227	229	235	241	247	249	251
74																				
75																				
76	7	5	2	0	0	0	0	0	0	0	0	0	0	0	0	0	0	0	0	0
77	11	13	14	15	15	15	16	17	16	14	12	11	10	8	10	7	3	0	0	0
78	2	5	7	7	8	9	9	10	11	12	12	12	14	15	16	16	16	17	17	17
79																				
80	20	23	23	22	23	24	25	27	27	26	24	23	24	23	26	23	19	17	17	17
81									26											

	AL	AM	AN	AO	AP	AQ	AR	AS	AT	AU	AV	AW	AX	AY	AZ	BA
61	37	38	39	40	41	42	43	44	45	46	47	48	49	50	51	52
62																
63	86	86	86	86	86	86	86	86	86	86	86	86	86	86	86	86
64	86	86	86	86	86	86	86	86	86	86	86	86	86	86	86	86
65																
66	124	124	124	124	124	124	124	124	124	124	124	124	124	124	124	124
67	124	124	124	124	124	124	124	124	124	124	124	124	124	124	124	124
68																
69	58	60	62	63	63	63	63	63	63	63	63	63	63	63	63	63
70	43	47	52	57	61	62	63	63	63	63	63	63	63	63	63	63
71																
72	268	270	272	273	273	273	273	273	273	273	273	273	273	273	273	273
73	253	257	262	267	271	272	273	273	273	273	273	273	273	273	273	273
74																
75																
76	0	0	0	0	0	0	0	0	0	0	0	0	0	0	0	0
77	0	0	0	0	0	0	0	0	0	0	0	0	0	0	0	0
78	15	13	10	6	2	1	0	0	0	0	0	0	0	0	0	0
79																
80	15	13	10	6	2	1	0	0	0	0	0	0	0	0	0	0
81			39													52

	A	B	C	D	E	F	G	H	I	J	K	L	M	N	O	P	Q	R	S
84	**Verify area**																		
85	1302 The model verification sum																		
86																			
87	If an error appears here, check below and then the appropriate area of the model.																		
88	(Be sure you have recalculated the whole model.)																		
89																			
90	273 The total completed activities in the Model Area																		
91	86 The design completed cumulative check in week 52 in the Graphing Area																		
92	124 The build completed cumulative check in week 52 in the Graphing Area																		
93	63 The test completed cumulative check in week 52 in the Graphing Area																		
94	756 A sum of the check totals in the Graphing Area.																		

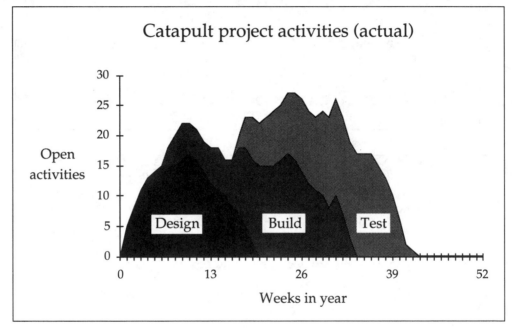

Figure 7-8.

The Model PRESENT

Sometimes a spreadsheet can be an excellent tool for explaining an idea to a colleague or a business associate. PRESENT exists to explain how discounted cash flow works. Discounted cash flow allows you to evaluate and compare different business deals that involve future sums of money. To understand the spreadsheet you need a little bit of background.

Present Value

The fundamental idea behind this spreadsheet is the present value of money. Money today is worth more than money tomorrow. To convince yourself of this, ask whether you would like to receive a million dollars now, or one year from now. After a second's thought you would say now because you know you can earn interest on your money. The million now would be worth a million and some interest in a year.

People who work with money every day calculate this interest with a shortcut that gets the answer in a single step. When they calculate interest, say 7 percent on $100, they multiply the $100 by a factor of 1.07 to get $107. An interest factor for a 15 percent interest rate is 1.15, while an interest factor for 3% is 1.03. In your problem with the million dollars, let I be the interest factor. The future value, F, is equal to the present value, P, times the interest factor, I.

<future value> = <present value> * <interest factor>

$$F = P * I$$

$$1{,}070{,}000 = 1{,}000{,}000 * 1.07 \text{ (if the interest rate is 7\%)}$$

Not only do you have a way of computing one year's interest, you can quickly extend your use of factors to cover several years. Here is what your million dollars would look like in three years.

<future value> = <present value> * <int. factor> * <int. factor> * <int. factor>

$$F = P * I * I * I$$

$$1{,}225{,}043 = 1{,}000{,}000 * 1.07 * 1.07 * 1.07$$

or

$$F = P * I^3$$

$$1{,}225{,}043 = 1{,}000{,}000 * (1.07)^3 \text{ (for those who remember exponents).}$$

To find out what the future value is, we continue to multiply by interest factors until we get to the right year.

You turn future value on its head to get present value. Ask yourself another question. How much would you accept right now in lieu of getting a million dollars in one year? The answer is whatever amount would yield a million after a year's interest. The answer—the present value P, times the interest factor, I—would be $1,000,000, if the interest rate is 7 percent.

<amount you accept now> * <interest factor> = <million at the end of the year>

<present value> * <interest factor> = <future value>

$$P * I = \$1,000,000$$

$$P * 1.07 = \$1,000,000$$

$$P = \$1,000,000 * (1/1.07)$$

$$P = \$1,000,000 * .93457943$$

$$P = \$934,579.43$$

So we would accept $934,579.43 now because we know that at the end of the year we would have a million dollars. This answer depended on the number (1/1.07), or about .935, the discount factor, D, associated with a 7 percent interest rate.

<discount factor> = (1/<interest factor>)

$$D = (1/I)$$

$$.935 = (1/1.07)$$

The discount factor works in a similar fashion to the interest factor for several years. What is the present value of a million dollars three years from now? It's a million dollars times the discount factor three times.

<pres. value> = <million in 3 years> * <dis. factor> * <dis. factor> * < dis. factor>

<pres. value> = <future value> * <dis. factor> * <dis. factor> * < dis. factor>

$$P = F * D * D * D$$

$$817,400 = 1,000,000 * .935 * .935 * .935$$

or

$$P = F * D3$$

$$817,400 = 1,000,000 * .935^3$$

The present value of a future amount is that future amount times the discount factor for however many years it takes to get back to the present.

Now we are in a position to understand all the entries in the Initial Data Area of the spreadsheet. The interest rate yields the interest factor and the discount factor. The stream of future cash flows is entered just as it occurs.

Most business deals have differing amounts of money arriving at different times. This stream of cash payments, the cash flow, is irregular, so no simple formula will work on it. For example, two different apartment houses have different purchase prices, different kinds of major repairs needed in the near future (one a furnace, and the other a new roof), and different rent schedules for the future (and different laws in different towns governing when the rents may be increased). Which is the best buy? To decide this question you first need to estimate what the future stream of cash payments is for each apartment house. After you compute the two streams of cash flows, you will notice that they are irregular in time and different in amounts.

Table 7-2.   Two apartment investments with two different cash flows

Year	Apartment A	Apartment B	
0	-10,000	-10,000	(Purchase)
1	2,000	1,000	(Rents - expenses)
2	3,000	2,000	
3	5,000	3,000	
4	5,000	4,000	
5	8,000	15,000	(Sale)

To decide which is the best deal, you must now discount each year's cash flow back to its present value and add up all the present values. This answer is the **net present value** of the **discounted cash flow**.

	A	B	C	D	E	F	G
1	**PRESENT**	5 Feb 1989	J. M. Nevison				
2	® Copyright 1988 by John M. Nevison						
3	13-Sep-89	Date printed					
5	Description						
6		Illustrate how to calculate the net present value of a					
7		series of future payments. If the result is positive,					
8		then the investment is a good one.					
10	Reference						
11		John M. Nevison, "Excel Spreadsheet Design," New York, NY:					
12		Brady Books, 1990.					
14	Contents						
15		Introduction: title, description, contents					
16		Initial data					
17		Model					
20	Initial data						
21		10%	The company cost of capital (or the inflation rate)				
22		1.10	Cost of capital factor (= 1 + cost of capital)				
23		0.91	Discount factor (= 1/(cost of capital factor))				
24							
25		YEAR	PAYMENT				
26		0	($10,000)				
27		1	2,000				
28		2	3,000				
29		3	5,000				
30		4	5,000				
31		5	8,000				
34	Model						
35	Tricky formulas:						
36	This year's factor = last year's factor * discount factor						
37							
38		10%	The company cost of capital (or the inflation rate)				
39		0.91	Discount factor (= 1/(cost of capital factor))				
40							
41			Cash	Discount	Present		
42		Year	Payment	Factor	Value		
44		0	(10,000)	1.00	($10,000)		
45		1	2,000	0.91	1,818		
46		2	3,000	0.83	2,479		
47		3	5,000	0.75	3,757		
48		4	5,000	0.68	3,415		
49		5	8,000	0.62	4,967		
50							
51		Totals	13,000		6,437		

The first stream of numbers in our spreadsheet shows a net present value of $6,437. This means your $10,000 invested in Apartment House A will yield future amounts totaling $16,437. When you plug in the numbers for Apartment House B you get a different present value.

	A	B	C	D	E	F	G
34	**Model**						
35	Tricky formulas:						
36	This year's factor = last year's factor * discount factor						
37							
38	10%	The company cost of capital (or the inflation rate)					
39	0.91	Discount factor (= 1/(cost of capital factor))					
40							
41		Cash	Discount	Present			
42	Year	Payment	Factor	Value			
44	0	(10,000)	1.00	($10,000)			
45	1	1,000	0.91	909			
46	2	2,000	0.83	1,653			
47	3	3,000	0.75	2,254			
48	4	4,000	0.68	2,732			
49	5	15,000	0.62	9,314			
50							
51	Totals	15,000		6,862			

The net present value for this apartment house is $6,862. So you can use the net present value to compare two very different business deals and decide that Apartment House B is a better deal.

Notice in the spreadsheet that the interest rate is called the "corporate cost of capital." If you are using this spreadsheet for a private calculation, you would want to use the inflation rate. However, if you are a corporation with stock that is traded and bonds that you have borrowed, then you have a corporate cost of capital that you would want to use to determine your discount rate. Details on how to calculate this rate can be found in Copeland and Weston in the References.

If you decide to play with the inflation rate, you can find one that balances the cost against the rewards so the net present value is 0. You will have found the internal rate of return for the deal.

	A	B	C	D	E	F	G
34	**Model**						
35	Tricky formulas:						
36	This year's factor = last year's factor * discount factor						
37							
38	28%	The company cost of capital (or the inflation rate)					
39	0.78	Discount factor (= 1/(cost of capital factor))					
40							
41		Cash	Discount	Present			
42	Year	Payment	Factor	Value			
44	0	(10,000)	1.00	($10,000)			
45	1	2,000	0.78	1,564			
46	2	3,000	0.61	1,835			
47	3	5,000	0.48	2,391			
48	4	5,000	0.37	1,870			
49	5	8,000	0.29	2,340			
50							
51	Totals	13,000		0			

For the first investment, a rate of about 28 percent (really 27.871 percent) balances the cost against the reward and is the internal rate of return.

In fact, PRESENT illustrates the calculations behind several Excel functions. The calculations of net present value illustrate how the function NPV(rate,values) works. "Values" includes the series of future cash flows and "rate" is the discounted periodic interest rate.

The internal rate of return can be calculated automatically by the Excel function IRR(values,guess) where "values" is the series of cash flows, and "guess" is an initial guess at the answer. The function figures out the exact answer. The short spreadsheet PRESENTS illustrates the IRR function and the NPV function in action.

	A	B	C	D	E	F	G
1	**PRESENTS**		5 Feb 1989	J. M. Nevison			
2	® Copyright 1988 by John M. Nevison						
3	13-Sep-89 Date printed						
5	Description						
6	Illustrate how to calculate the net present value (NPV) and the internal						
7	rate of return (IRR) of a series of future payments. If the NPV is						
8	positive, then the investment is a good one. This spreadsheet makes use of						
9	the Excel NPV and IRR functions.						
11	Reference						
12		John M. Nevison, "Excel Spreadsheet Design,"					
13		New York, NY: Brady Books, 1989.					
15	Contents						
16		Introduction: title, description, contents					
17		Initial data					
18		Model					
21	**Initial data**						
22	10%	The company cost of capital (or the inflation rate)					
24	YEAR	PAYMENT					
25	0	($10,000)					
26	1	2,000					
27	2	3,000					
28	3	5,000					
29	4	5,000					
30	5	8,000					
33	**Model**						
34	Tricky formulas:						
35	<net present value> = NPV<rate,years 1-5> - <year 0>						
36	<internal rate of return> = IRR<years 0-5,guess>						
38	10%	The company cost of capital (or the inflation rate)					
39							
40	$6,437	The net present value.					
41	27.9%	The internal rate of return.					

Notice that the NPV function works on years 1 to 5 so the formula had to subtract (or add the negative amount of) the initial year 0 payment to get the full net present value of the entire cash flow.

If you have a series of even payments, two other Excel functions, PV(rate,-nper,pmt,fv,type) and FV(rate,nper,pmt,pv,type), will compute the present value or future value given the payment, pmt, periodic interest rate, rate, and the number of payment periods, nper.

The Models SIMPLPAY and PAYMENTS

The next two spreadsheets also illustrate some basic financial ideas; in this case, the schedule of even loan payments that a bank loan or a mortgage loan requires for repayment. The first spreadsheet SIMPLPAY illustrates a straightforward example.

	A	B	C	D	E	F
1	**SIMPLPAY**		29 Nov 88	J. M. Nevison		
2	® Copyright 1988 by John M. Nevison					
3	13-Sep-89	Date printed				
5	**Description**					
6		Show how a payment schedule's principle				
7		percentage varies as the interest rate increases.				
9	**Reference**					
10		John M. Nevison, "Excel Spreadsheet Design,"				
11		New York, NY: Brady Books, 1989.				
13	**Contents**					
14		Introduction: title, description, contents				
15		Initial data				
16		Yearly model				
17		Verify area				
20	**Initial data**					
21	1000.00	Amount borrowed				
22	10	Number of years				
23	10.0%	Annual interest rate				
24	162.75	Yearly payment = PMT(interest rate, number of years, -amount)				

(continued)

	A	B	C	D	E	F
27	**Yearly model**					
28	Tricky formulas:					
29	Interest = Beginning balance * interest rate					
30	Principal = Yearly payment - interest					
31	New beginning balance = Old beginning balance - principal					
32						
33			10.0%	Interest rate		
34			162.75	Yearly payment		
35		Beginning			Principal	
36	Year	Balance	Interest	Principal	(% of payment)	
38	1	1000.00	100.00	62.75	39%	
39	2	937.25	93.73	69.02	42%	
40	3	868.23	86.82	75.92	47%	
41	4	792.31	79.23	83.51	51%	
42	5	708.80	70.88	91.87	56%	
43	6	616.93	61.69	101.05	62%	
44	7	515.88	51.59	111.16	68%	
45	8	404.72	40.47	122.27	75%	
46	9	282.45	28.25	134.50	83%	
47	10	147.95	14.80	147.95	91%	
49	Totals		627.45	1000.00		
52	**Verify area**					
53		1000.00	Verification sum			
54	If an error appears here, check below and then the appropriate area of					
55	the spreadsheet. (Be sure you have recalculated the whole model.)					
56						
57		1000.00	Yearly principal total cross-check			

The spreadsheet finds the amount of the periodic payment by using the Excel function PMT(rate,nper,pv) where "rate" is the periodic interest rate, "nper" is the number of payment periods, and "pv" is the principal borrowed.

If you look at the Model Area, you can see that beginning with the interest rate and the even monthly payment, the spreadsheet works out how much interest is due each year, subtracts that from the payment, and applies the remaining payment against the principal of the loan to reduce the outstanding balance. This procedure is repeated each year until the loan is paid off.

The point of the spreadsheet is to illustrate what percentage of the payment is principal as the loan is being paid off. This is illustrated in the last column entitled "Principal (% of Payment)." As you can see, the first year's payments are more interest than principal; in year four, the principal becomes more than half the payment, and, by year 10, almost all the payment is principal. This is precisely the pattern a schedule of mortgage payments follows.

The spreadsheet uses a sum of $1,000 and a rate of 10 percent because it is easy to check that the calculations are correct. The spreadsheet also compares the sum of the principal payments and the initial sum borrowed to verify that the calculations are being done correctly.

The only shortcoming of this model is that it produces a schedule that is paid on an annual basis, not on a monthly basis. The second spreadsheet, PAYMENTS, attempts to remedy this shortcoming by producing a monthly schedule with an annual summary.

	A	B	C	D	E	F
1	**PAYMENTS**		21 Nov 88	J. M. Nevison		
2	® Copyright 1988 by John M. Nevison					
3	13-Sep-89	Date printed				
5	Description					
6			Show how a payment schedule's principle			
7			percentage varies as the interest rate increases.			
9	Reference					
10			John M. Nevison, "Excel Spreadsheet Design,"			
11			New York, NY: Brady Books, 1990.			
13	Contents					
14			Introduction: title, description, contents			
15			Initial data			
16			Yearly model			
17			Monthly model			
18			Verify area			
21	Initial data					
22		1000.00	Amount borrowed			
23		10	Number of years			
24		15.0%	Annual interest rate			
25		120	Number of months = 12 * number of years			
26		1.3%	Monthly interest rate = Annual rate/12			
27		16.13	Monthly payment = PMT(mthly int. rate,num of mo.,amt.)			
28		193.60	Yearly payment = 12 * monthly payment			

(continued)

	A	B	C	D	E	F
31	**Yearly model**			Interest	15.0%	
32				Payment	193.60	
33		Beginning				
34	Year	Balance	Interest	Principal	Principal (%)	
36	1	1000.00	146.87	46.73	24%	
37	2	953.27	139.36	54.24	28%	
38	3	899.03	130.64	62.96	33%	
39	4	836.07	120.52	73.08	38%	
40	5	762.99	108.77	84.83	44%	
41	6	678.16	95.14	98.46	51%	
42	7	579.70	79.31	114.29	59%	
43	8	465.41	60.94	132.67	69%	
44	9	332.74	39.61	153.99	80%	
45	10	178.75	14.85	178.75	92%	
47	Totals		936.02	1000.00		
50	**Monthly model**			Interest	1.3%	
51				Payment	16.13	
52		Beginning				
53	Month	Balance	Interest	Principal	Principal (%)	
55	1	1000.00	12.50	3.63	23%	
56	2	996.37	12.45	3.68	23%	
57	3	992.69	12.41	3.72	23%	
58	4	988.96	12.36	3.77	23%	
59	5	985.19	12.31	3.82	24%	
60	6	981.37	12.27	3.87	24%	
61	7	977.51	12.22	3.91	24%	
62	8	973.59	12.17	3.96	25%	
63	9	969.63	12.12	4.01	25%	
64	10	965.61	12.07	4.06	25%	
65	11	961.55	12.02	4.11	26%	
66	12	957.44	11.97	4.17	26%	
67	13	953.27	11.92	4.22	26%	
68	14	949.05	11.86	4.27	26%	
69	15	944.78	11.81	4.32	27%	
70	16	940.46	11.76	4.38	27%	

(continued)

	A	B	C	D	E	F
71	17	936.08	11.70	4.43	27%	
72	18	931.65	11.65	4.49	28%	
73	19	927.16	11.59	4.54	28%	
74	20	922.62	11.53	4.60	29%	
75	21	918.02	11.48	4.66	29%	
76	22	913.36	11.42	4.72	29%	
77	23	908.64	11.36	4.78	30%	
78	24	903.87	11.30	4.84	30%	
79	25	899.03	11.24	4.90	30%	
80	26	894.14	11.18	4.96	31%	
81	27	889.18	11.11	5.02	31%	
82	28	884.16	11.05	5.08	31%	
83	29	879.08	10.99	5.15	32%	
84	30	873.93	10.92	5.21	32%	
85	31	868.73	10.86	5.27	33%	
86	32	863.45	10.79	5.34	33%	
87	33	858.11	10.73	5.41	34%	
88	34	852.70	10.66	5.47	34%	
89	35	847.23	10.59	5.54	34%	
90	36	841.69	10.52	5.61	35%	
91	37	836.07	10.45	5.68	35%	
92	38	830.39	10.38	5.75	36%	
93	39	824.64	10.31	5.83	36%	
94	40	818.81	10.24	5.90	37%	
95	41	812.91	10.16	5.97	37%	
96	42	806.94	10.09	6.05	37%	
97	43	800.89	10.01	6.12	38%	
98	44	794.77	9.93	6.20	38%	
99	45	788.57	9.86	6.28	39%	
100	46	782.30	9.78	6.35	39%	
101	47	775.94	9.70	6.43	40%	
102	48	769.51	9.62	6.51	40%	
103	49	762.99	9.54	6.60	41%	
104	50	756.40	9.45	6.68	41%	
105	51	749.72	9.37	6.76	42%	
106	52	742.96	9.29	6.85	42%	
107	53	736.11	9.20	6.93	43%	
108	54	729.18	9.11	7.02	44%	
109	55	722.16	9.03	7.11	44%	
110	56	715.05	8.94	7.20	45%	

(continued)

	A	B	C	D	E	F
111	57	707.86	8.85	7.29	45%	
112	58	700.57	8.76	7.38	46%	
113	59	693.20	8.66	7.47	46%	
114	60	685.73	8.57	7.56	47%	
115	61	678.16	8.48	7.66	47%	
116	62	670.51	8.38	7.75	48%	
117	63	662.76	8.28	7.85	49%	
118	64	654.91	8.19	7.95	49%	
119	65	646.96	8.09	8.05	50%	
120	66	638.91	7.99	8.15	50%	
121	67	630.77	7.88	8.25	51%	
122	68	622.52	7.78	8.35	52%	
123	69	614.17	7.68	8.46	52%	
124	70	605.71	7.57	8.56	53%	
125	71	597.15	7.46	8.67	54%	
126	72	588.48	7.36	8.78	54%	
127	73	579.70	7.25	8.89	55%	
128	74	570.81	7.14	9.00	56%	
129	75	561.81	7.02	9.11	56%	
130	76	552.70	6.91	9.22	57%	
131	77	543.48	6.79	9.34	58%	
132	78	534.14	6.68	9.46	59%	
133	79	524.68	6.56	9.57	59%	
134	80	515.11	6.44	9.69	60%	
135	81	505.41	6.32	9.82	61%	
136	82	495.60	6.19	9.94	62%	
137	83	485.66	6.07	10.06	62%	
138	84	475.60	5.94	10.19	63%	
139	85	465.41	5.82	10.32	64%	
140	86	455.09	5.69	10.44	65%	
141	87	444.65	5.56	10.58	66%	
142	88	434.07	5.43	10.71	66%	
143	89	423.36	5.29	10.84	67%	
144	90	412.52	5.16	10.98	68%	
145	91	401.55	5.02	11.11	69%	
146	92	390.43	4.88	11.25	70%	
147	93	379.18	4.74	11.39	71%	
148	94	367.78	4.60	11.54	72%	
149	95	356.25	4.45	11.68	72%	
150	96	344.57	4.31	11.83	73%	

(continued)

	A	B	C	D	E	F
151	97	332.74	4.16	11.97	74%	
152	98	320.77	4.01	12.12	75%	
153	99	308.64	3.86	12.28	76%	
154	100	296.37	3.70	12.43	77%	
155	101	283.94	3.55	12.58	78%	
156	102	271.35	3.39	12.74	79%	
157	103	258.61	3.23	12.90	80%	
158	104	245.71	3.07	13.06	81%	
159	105	232.65	2.91	13.23	82%	
160	106	219.42	2.74	13.39	83%	
161	107	206.03	2.58	13.56	84%	
162	108	192.48	2.41	13.73	85%	
163	109	178.75	2.23	13.90	86%	
164	110	164.85	2.06	14.07	87%	
165	111	150.78	1.88	14.25	88%	
166	112	136.53	1.71	14.43	89%	
167	113	122.10	1.53	14.61	91%	
168	114	107.49	1.34	14.79	92%	
169	115	92.70	1.16	14.97	93%	
170	116	77.73	0.97	15.16	94%	
171	117	62.57	0.78	15.35	95%	
172	118	47.22	0.59	15.54	96%	
173	119	31.67	0.40	15.74	98%	
174	120	15.93	0.20	15.93	99%	
176	Totals		936.02	1000.00		
179	**Verify area**					
180		2000.00	Verification sum			
181	If an error appears here, check below and then the appropriate area of					
182	the spreadsheet. (Be sure you have recalculated the whole model.)					
184		1000.00	Yearly principal total cross-check			
185		1000.00	Monthly principal total cross-check			

One of the most interesting aspects of this spreadsheet is that it placed the Model Area at the bottom. While the model may be of some interest while the spreadsheet is being developed, it is not very interesting to the spreadsheet's user. After the user is sure that the spreadsheet is correct (simple initial data and a Verify Area help a lot), he or she is much more interested in varying the initial interest rates to see the size of the payments, the total interest (report), and pattern of percentage principal repayments (graph). Here are the results for interest rates of 7.5, 10, and 15 percent.

	A	B	C	D	E	F
31	**Yearly model**			Interest	7.5%	
32				Payment	142.44	
33		Beginning				
34	Year	Balance	Interest	Principal	Principal (%)	
36	1	1000.00	72.63	69.81	49%	
37	2	930.19	67.21	75.23	53%	
38	3	854.96	61.37	81.07	57%	
39	4	773.89	55.08	87.36	61%	
40	5	686.53	48.30	94.14	66%	
41	6	592.38	40.99	101.45	71%	
42	7	490.93	33.11	109.33	77%	
43	8	381.60	24.62	117.82	83%	
44	9	263.78	15.48	126.96	89%	
45	10	136.82	5.62	136.82	96%	
47	Totals		424.42	1000.00		

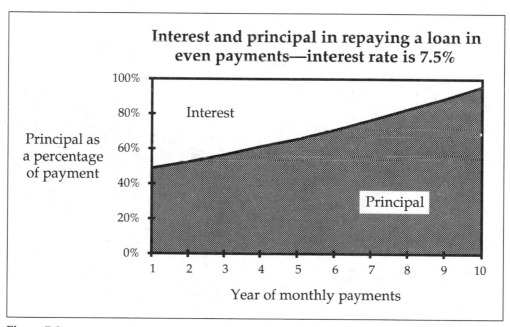

Figure 7-9.

	A	B	C	D	E	F
31	Yearly model			Interest	10.0%	
32				Payment	158.58	
33		Beginning				
34	Year	Balance	Interest	Principal	Principal (%)	
36	1	1000.00	97.24	61.34	39%	
37	2	938.66	90.82	67.77	43%	
38	3	870.89	83.72	74.86	47%	
39	4	796.03	75.88	82.70	52%	
40	5	713.33	67.22	91.36	58%	
41	6	621.97	57.65	100.93	64%	
42	7	521.05	47.09	111.49	70%	
43	8	409.55	35.41	123.17	78%	
44	9	286.38	22.51	136.07	86%	
45	10	150.31	8.27	150.31	95%	
47	Totals		585.81	1000.00		

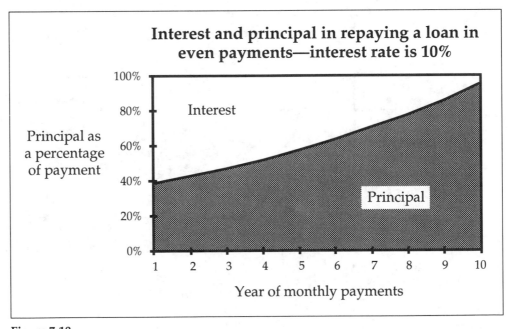

Figure 7-10.

	A	B	C	D	E	F
31	Yearly model			Interest	15.0%	
32				Payment	193.60	
33		Beginning				
34	Year	Balance	Interest	Principal	Principal (%)	
36	1	1000.00	146.87	46.73	24%	
37	2	953.27	139.36	54.24	28%	
38	3	899.03	130.64	62.96	33%	
39	4	836.07	120.52	73.08	38%	
40	5	762.99	108.77	84.83	44%	
41	6	678.16	95.14	98.46	51%	
42	7	579.70	79.31	114.29	59%	
43	8	465.41	60.94	132.67	69%	
44	9	332.74	39.61	153.99	80%	
45	10	178.75	14.85	178.75	92%	
47	Totals		936.02	1000.00		

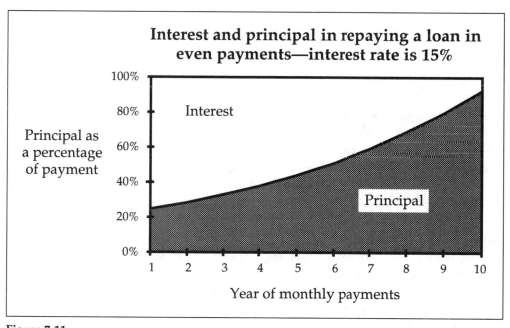

Figure 7-11.

Notice how, when the rate is 15 percent, the principal payment crosses the 50 percent mark in year 6 and the total interest almost equals the amount borrowed! When the rate is 7.5 percent, the principal payment crosses the 50 percent mark in year 2 and the total interest is much lower. You can see that lower interest rates help three ways: lower monthly and annual payments, faster payoff of the principal, and lower total interest paid.

The Model BUYBORO

The financial ideas of PRESENT and PAYMENTS suggest that if the interest rates and the inflation rates are not exactly the same, there may be some advantage to borrowing money. Clearly, it is advantageous to borrow when the interest rate is lower than the inflation rate. As a general rule it is not a good idea to borrow when the interest rate is higher than the inflation rate unless some tax break affects the interest rate. A third consideration remains, however, for those purchases that are considered to be "capital investments."

A capital investment is one where the benefits will be felt for many years—for example, a farmer's new tractor, a manufacturer's new factory, or an office's new copying machine. In order to spread out the payment of the purchase to match the benefits of the machine, the tax laws require that the capital be "depreciated over the investment's useful life." For example, if a tractor costs $100,000 and its useful life is five years, the farmer would be allowed to enter $20,000 of tractor costs in year one, $20,000 in year two, and so on. If the farmer paid cash for the tractor, he would be in trouble because he would only be allowed to write down $20,000 of costs; the other $80,000 of costs would only be written down in later years.

The discrepancy between when something was really paid for and when the tax laws allow a cost to be entered into personal or business tax calculations sometimes makes it advisable to borrow money to purchase a capital investment even when you have the cash to buy it. BUYBORO combines the effects of depreciation, present value, and schedules of loan payments to determine when it is appropriate to pay cash and when it is appropriate to borrow money to make a capital purchase.

To begin to look at this issue, examine the Initial Data Area.

	A	B	C	D	E	F	G
20	Initial data						
21					Depreciation Schedule		
23	1000	Amount borrowed			1	20%	
24	5	Number of periods			2	20%	
25	10%	Interest rate			3	20%	
26	263.80	Period payment			4	20%	
27	10%	Inflation rate			5	20%	
28	0.91	Discount factor = 1/(1 + inflation rate)					

Here, you see all the familiar factors: the amount borrowed, the number of periods, the interest rate, the loan period payment, the inflation rate, and the discount factor. Here, you also see a new actor, the depreciation schedule.

Notice that initially the interest rate and the inflation rate are the same (so the cash costs of buying versus borrowing should be exactly the same). Notice also that the depreciation schedule is for straight-line depreciation over five years, that is, 20 percent a year for five years.

To get a preview of buying versus borrowing, look at the summary report from the model.

	A	B	C	D	E	F	G
31	Buy versus borrow summary						
32	13-Sep-89	Buy versus Borrow					
33							
34		Buy	Borrow				
36	Cash costs	1000.00	1000.00				
37	Delay costs	241.84	-13.62				
39	Total costs	1241.84	986.38				
40	Advantage of borrowing			255.47			

Here, you see that the costs have two components: the cash costs and the delay costs. The cash costs are associated with the actual cash involved. The delay costs are associated with the comparison between the schedule of payments and the schedule of depreciation credits.

Look at the cash costs for a moment. If the interest rate of borrowing equals the inflation rate, then the discount factor on money makes the cash costs the same. If, for some reason, our inflation rate (or corporate cost of capital) gets higher than the interest rate, the cash costs would favor borrowing over buying. Here's what happens if the corporate cost of capital (the inflation rate) is 12 percent and the interest rate remains 10 percent:

	A	B	C	D	E	F	G
20	Initial data						
21					Depreciation Schedule		
23	1000	Amount borrowed			1	20%	
24	5	Number of periods			2	20%	
25	10%	Interest rate			3	20%	
26	263.80	Period payment			4	20%	
27	12%	Inflation rate			5	20%	
28	0.89	Discount factor = 1/(1 + inflation rate)					
31	Buy versus borrow summary						
32	13-Sep-89	Buy versus Borrow					
33							
34		Buy	Borrow				
36	Cash costs	1000.00	950.93				
37	Delay costs	279.04	-15.37				
39	Total costs	1279.04	935.56				
40	Advantage of borrowing			343.48			

As you can see, the cash costs of borrowing ($950.93) are lower than buying ($1,000.00) because the discount factor makes it cheaper to pay with future dollars rather than with present dollars.

The delay costs in both of these examples show that borrowing puts off the paying for the item until after the depreciation has let us take credit for it. The negative cost, −13.62 in the first example, is actually a credit! The delay costs of buying, 241.84 in the first example, show how much the depreciation schedule penalizes the buyer who pays cash today for this capital good.

The final line of the report says that in both of the first two examples borrowing represents a real saving over buying. In the first example, borrowing represents a $255.47, or 25 percent, advantage.

To find out more about the details behind the report, take a look at the Model Area's supporting calculations.

	A	B	C	D	E	F	G
43	Model of supporting calculations						
44							
45	Basic calculations						
46		Beginning				Discount	
47	Period	Balance	Interest	Principal	Depreciation	factor	
49	0	0	0	0	0	1.00	
50	1	1000.00	100.00	163.80	200.00	0.91	
51	2	836.20	83.62	180.18	200.00	0.83	
52	3	656.03	65.60	198.19	200.00	0.75	
53	4	457.83	45.78	218.01	200.00	0.68	
54	5	239.82	23.98	239.82	200.00	0.62	
56	Totals		318.99	1000.00	1000.00		
57							
58	--						
59			Costs of cash (Buy versus Borrow)				
60							
61		Present value of				Present value of	
62	Period	Buy payment			Borrow payments	Borrow payments	
64	0	1000.00			0.00	0.00	
65	1	0.00			263.80	239.82	
66	2	0.00			263.80	218.01	
67	3	0.00			263.80	198.19	
68	4	0.00			263.80	180.18	
69	5	0.00			263.80	163.80	
71	Totals	1000.00				1000.00	
72	--						

The first table you see here is "Basic calculations," which includes the interest payment schedule, the depreciation schedule, and a set of discount factors. These payments will be used later to compute the cash costs and the delay costs.

The second table compares the cash costs of buying and borrowing. The present value of buying is simple—it's the money you spend today, at time 0 ($1,000.00). The present value of borrowing is a little more complicated—it's the present value of those future cash payments (each is $263.80), also $1,000.00, when the inflation rate exactly matches the interest rate. Remember you saw earlier that if the inflation rate went up to 12 percent, the present value of the future borrowed payments went down to $950.93.

The delay costs each take a table.

	A	B	C	D	E	F	G
73							
74		Delay costs of borrowing					
75							
76		Principal			Present value of		
77	Period	Payments	Depreciation		Payments	Depreciation	
79	0	0	0		0.00	0.00	
80	1	163.80	200		148.91	181.82	
81	2	180.18	200		148.91	165.29	
82	3	198.19	200		148.91	150.26	
83	4	218.01	200		148.91	136.60	
84	5	239.82	200		148.91	124.18	
86	Totals	1000.00	1000.00		744.53	758.16	
87	Delay costs	-13.62					
88	---						
89							
90		Delay costs of buying					
91							
92					Present value of		
93	Period	Payments	Depreciation		Payments	Depreciation	
95	0	1000.00	0.00		1000.00	0.00	
96	1	0.00	200.00		0.00	181.82	
97	2	0.00	200.00		0.00	165.29	
98	3	0.00	200.00		0.00	150.26	
99	4	0.00	200.00		0.00	136.60	
100	5	0.00	200.00		0.00	124.18	
102	Totals	1000.00	1000.00		1000.00	758.16	
103	Delay costs	241.84					

The delay costs of borrowing are the difference between the present value of the future principal payments ($744.53) and the present value of the future depreciation credits ($758.16). You find that when you borrow the effects of time give you a $13.62 credit.

The delay costs of buying are the difference between the present value of the cash payments ($1,000.00) and the present value of the future depreciation credits ($758.16). You find that when you buy the effects of time cost you $241.84.

The summary table you looked at earlier tallied up the even cash costs and the delay costs that favored borrowing and showed a $255.47 advantage to borrowing.

The final part of the spreadsheet is the Verify Area.

	A	B	C	D	E	F	G
106	Verify area						
108		3000 Verification sum					
109	If an error appears here, check below and then the appropriate area of						
110	the spreadsheet. (Be sure you have recalculated the whole model.)						
112		1000 Total principal in model intermediate calculations					
113		1000 Total principal in delay costs of borrowing					
114		1000 Total depreciation in delay costs of buying					

The three points of verification should reassure a future user that this model can reliably be experimented with. In order to look one more time at the model, here are two additional scenarios.

	A	B	C	D	E	F	G
20	Initial data				Sum of year's digits		
21					Depreciation Schedule		
23		1000 Amount borrowed			1	33%	
24		5 Number of periods			2	27%	
25		10% Interest rate			3	20%	
26		263.80 Period payment			4	13%	
27		10% Inflation rate			5	7%	
28		0.91 Discount factor = 1/(1 + inflation rate)					
31	Buy versus borrow summary						
32		13-Sep-89 Buy versus Borrow					
33							
34			Buy	Borrow			
36	Cash costs		1000.00	1000.00			
37	Delay costs		193.86	-61.61			
39	Total costs		1193.86	938.39			
40	Advantage of borrowing				255.47		

Notice that while depreciation's effects are blunted by taking the credit for the expense sooner and both of the delay costs are lower, they are lower by the same amount, and the borrowing strategy maintains exactly the same advantage of $255.47! Notice, however, that the total cost of borrowing, the chosen alternative, has been reduced to $938.39 thanks to our ability to delay the payment of our principal until well after we have taken depreciation credit. The accelerated depreciation of the sum-of-years'-digits method has saved you about $48, or 4.8 percent, on the cost of the purchase.

The formula for the sum-of-year's-digits method is

<Years depreciation> = <principal> * <years remaining>/<sum of years digits>

or, for year 3 in a 5 year schedule,

<Year 3 depreciation> = 10000 * (5- 3 +1) / 15

<Year 3 depreciation> = 2000.

The same effect can be obtained using the Excel function SYD(cost,salvage, life,period) where, in our example, it would look like SYD(10000,0,5,3) = 2000. The other common accelerated depreciation method has an Excel function called double declining balance, DDB(cost,salvage,life,period). See your Excel Manual for details.

NOTE: When to use which depreciation scheme is a matter of law, not logic. Before you use any depreciation schedule in a real business decision, consult a qualified accountant.

Finally, here is the full original example with the original schedule of straight-line depreciation with a 12 percent corporate cost of capital (inflation rate) and a 10 percent interest rate on a loan. You can see in detail how both the cash costs and the delay costs are affected by the difference between the two rates.

	A	B	C	D	E	F	G
1	**BUYBORO (Buy versus Borrow)**				21 Nov 88	J.M. Nevison	
2	® Copyright 1988 by John M. Nevison						
3	13-Sep-89 Date printed						
5	Description						
6		Show when its better to borrow than to buy					
8	Reference						
9		John M. Nevison, "Excel Spreadsheet Design,"					
10		New York, NY: Brady Books, 1990.					
12	Contents						
13		Introduction: title, description, contents					
14		Initial data					
15		Buy versus borrow summary					
16		Model of supporting calculations					
17		Verify area					

(continued)

	A	B	C	D	E	F	G
20	Initial data						
21					Depreciation Schedule		
23		1000	Amount borrowed		1	20%	
24		5	Number of periods		2	20%	
25		10%	Interest rate		3	20%	
26		263.80	Period payment		4	20%	
27		12%	Inflation rate		5	20%	
28		0.89	Discount factor = 1/(1 + inflation rate)				
31	**Buy versus borrow summary**						
32		13-Sep-89	Buy versus Borrow				
33							
34			Buy	Borrow			
36	Cash costs		1000.00	950.93			
37	Delay costs		279.04	-15.37			
39	Total costs		1279.04	935.56			
40	Advantage of borrowing			343.48			
43	**Model of supporting calculations**						
44							
45	Basic calculations						
46		Beginning				Discount	
47	Period	Balance	Interest	Principal	Depreciation	factor	
49	0	0	0	0	0	1.00	
50	1	1000.00	100.00	163.80	200.00	0.89	
51	2	836.20	83.62	180.18	200.00	0.80	
52	3	656.03	65.60	198.19	200.00	0.71	
53	4	457.83	45.78	218.01	200.00	0.64	
54	5	239.82	23.98	239.82	200.00	0.57	
56	Totals		318.99	1000.00	1000.00		
57							
58	--						
59			Costs of cash (buy versus borrow)				
60							
61		Present value of				Present value of	
62	Period	Buy payment			Borrow payments	Borrow payments	
64	0	1000.00			0.00	0.00	
65	1	0.00			263.80	235.53	
66	2	0.00			263.80	210.30	
67	3	0.00			263.80	187.77	
68	4	0.00			263.80	167.65	
69	5	0.00			263.80	149.69	
71	Totals	1000.00				950.93	
72	--						

(continued)

	A	B	C	D	E	F	G
73							
74		Delay costs of borrowing					
75							
76		Principal			Present value of		
77	Period	Payments	Depreciation		Payments	Depreciation	
79	0	0	0		0.00	0.00	
80	1	163.80	200		146.25	178.57	
81	2	180.18	200		143.64	159.44	
82	3	198.19	200		141.07	142.36	
83	4	218.01	200		138.55	127.10	
84	5	239.82	200		136.08	113.49	
86	Totals	1000.00	1000.00		705.59	720.96	
87	Delay costs	-15.37					
88	--						
89							
90		Delay costs of buying					
91							
92					Present value of		
93	Period	Payments	Depreciation		Payments	Depreciation	
95	0	1000.00	0.00		1000.00	0.00	
96	1	0.00	200.00		0.00	178.57	
97	2	0.00	200.00		0.00	159.44	
98	3	0.00	200.00		0.00	142.36	
99	4	0.00	200.00		0.00	127.10	
100	5	0.00	200.00		0.00	113.49	
102	Totals	1000.00	1000.00		1000.00	720.96	
103	Delay costs	279.04					
106	**Verify area**						
108		3000	Verification sum				
109	If an error appears here, check below and then the appropriate area of						
110	the spreadsheet. (Be sure you have recalculated the whole model.)						
112		1000	Total principal in model intermediate calculations				
113		1000	Total principal in delay costs of borrowing				
114		1000	Total depreciation in delay costs of buyiny				

The Model RAISES

When you prepare the department's budget, one of the most important items is the salary of those in the department. Balancing a newly hired employee's wages with an experienced veteran's, making sure the overall average increase stays within guidelines, knowing when you will have to fight to get someone an extra raise, and knowing what a six month review's salary revision will mean all require having your finger on the pulse of the department's salaries.

RAISES allows you to monitor these conditions and plan your next year in complete detail. The spreadsheet not only provides a helpful summary report, it provides a detailed monthly report that could be copied into the full departmental budget.

	A	B	C	D	E	F	G
1	**RAISES**	5 September 1989	J. M. Nevison				
2	® Copyright 1989 by John M. Nevison						
3	13-Sep-89	Date printed					
5	**Description**						
6		Compute the budgetary effects of the timing and the					
7		amounts of salary raises.					
9	**To use**						
10		1. Vary initial data and see how it affects the department's totals.					
11		2. "Hire" someone by using raise month as hire month and					
12		new annual salary as starting salary. (Original salary is zero.)					
13		3. "Lose" someone by using raise month as loss month and setting					
14		new annual salary to zero.					
16	**Reference**						
17		John M. Nevison, "Excel Spreadsheet Design,"					
18		New York, NY: Brady Books, 1990.					
20	**Contents**						
21		Introduction: title, description, contents					
22		Initial data					
23		Raises model					
24		Verify area					
27	**Initial data**						
28					New		
29		Annual	Raise		Annual		
30	Person	Salary	Amount	Month	Salary		
32	DAM	25,000	3.5%	2	25,875		
33	JAN	33,000	7.5%	4	35,475		
34	AGD	22,000	8.5%	1	23,870		
35	JFM	14,000	3.0%	12	14,420		
36	EKN	44,000	5.0%	7	46,200		

The Introduction tells you what the purpose of RAISES is and gives you directions on how to use it. The Initial Data Area shows what the fundamental elements of the spreadsheet are: old and new salaries, raise amounts, and the month the raise goes into effect. The "New Annual Salary" is a formula based on the "Annual Salary" and the "Raise Amount." You may override the formula when hiring or losing someone in midyear.

	A	B	C	D	E	F	G
39	Raises model						
40	13-Sep-89				New	Earned	
41		Annual	Raise		Annual	For	
42	Person	Salary	Amount	Month	Salary	Year	
44	DAM	25,000	3.5%	2	25,875	25,802.08	
45	JAN	33,000	7.5%	4	35,475	34,856.25	
46	AGD	22,000	8.5%	1	23,870	23,870.00	
47	JFM	14,000	3.0%	12	14,420	14,035.00	
48	EKN	44,000	5.0%	7	46,200	45,100.00	
50	Totals	138,000			145,840	143,663	
51	Averages	27,600	5.5%		29,168	28,733	
52							

The summary model shows information similar to the Initial Data Area with the addition of averages and the "Earned For Year" information. With the average information, you can adjust your salaries so that they give as much as possible to those who deserve it, while still observing the departmental guidelines. The summary information tells you what the overall effects are and gives you a way to double-check the individual results.

An interesting consequence of playing with the initial spreadsheet, which took its summary numbers from the detailed monthly model shown below, was the realization that the summary number "Earned For Year" can be computed without reference to the monthly summary. You can use the following formula.

<earned for year> = (<raise month> - 1)/12 * <old annual salary>

+ (13 - <raise month>)/12 * <new annual salary>

The monthly model still does, however, tell you a great deal about the details of the department's salary.

	A	B	C	D	E	F	G
53	Detailed monthly salaries						
54	Tricky formula:						
55	monthly entry = (if current month number < raise month number,						
56	then old salary,else new salary)						
57							
58	Person			Current month number			
59		1	2	3	4	5	6
61	DAM	2083.33	2156.25	2156.25	2156.25	2156.25	2156.25
62	JAN	2750.00	2750.00	2750.00	2956.25	2956.25	2956.25
63	AGD	1989.17	1989.17	1989.17	1989.17	1989.17	1989.17
64	JFM	1166.67	1166.67	1166.67	1166.67	1166.67	1166.67
65	EKN	3666.67	3666.67	3666.67	3666.67	3666.67	3666.67
67	Totals	11655.83	11728.75	11728.75	11935.00	11935.00	11935.00
68							
69		7	8	9	10	11	12
71	DAM	2156.25	2156.25	2156.25	2156.25	2156.25	2156.25
72	JAN	2956.25	2956.25	2956.25	2956.25	2956.25	2956.25
73	AGD	1989.17	1989.17	1989.17	1989.17	1989.17	1989.17
74	JFM	1166.67	1166.67	1166.67	1166.67	1166.67	1201.67
75	EKN	3850.00	3850.00	3850.00	3850.00	3850.00	3850.00
77	Totals	12118.33	12118.33	12118.33	12118.33	12118.33	12153.33
80	**Verify area**						
82	143663.33 Verification number is from the model's total earned.						
83	If ERR appears here, check the appropriate place(s) in the spreadsheet.						

The detailed monthly model begins with an informative note on the formula used to make the model, the IF function in Excel. Below each month are the monthly totals (should you wish to add a Graph Area and graph them). Finally comes the Verify Area, where you can double-check to be sure that the model's assumptions remain intact after you use it.

Here's what RAISES looks like when one person is new (JAN) and one chooses to leave (AGD).

	A	B	C	D	E	F	G
27	Initial data						
28					New		
29		Annual	Raise		Annual		
30	Person	Salary	Amount	Month	Salary		
32	DAM	25,000	3.5%	2	25,875		
33	JAN	0	0.0%	4	36,000		
34	AGD	22,000	0.0%	2	0		
35	JFM	14,000	3.0%	12	14,420		
36	EKN	44,000	5.0%	7	46,200		
39	Raises model						
40	13-Sep-89				New	Earned	
41		Annual	Raise		Annual	For	
42	Person	Salary	Amount	Month	Salary	Year	
44	DAM	25,000	3.5%	2	25,875	25,802.08	
45	JAN	0	0.0%	4	36,000	27,000.00	
46	AGD	22,000	0.0%	2	0	1,833.33	
47	JFM	14,000	3.0%	12	14,420	14,035.00	
48	EKN	44,000	5.0%	7	46,200	45,100.00	
50	Totals	105,000			122,495	113,770	
51	Averages	21,000	2.3%		24,499	22,754	
52	---						

You see how even though JAN's new salary is slightly higher, he costs the department less in this plan because he doesn't start until April. If AGD leaves at the end of January, the department has plenty of room to hire someone else and still stay within the limits of the original plan.

The Model Template JMNRULE

Most of the spreadsheets in this book began as a template. FULLRULE, at the end of Chapter 4, is a good one to use if you have no other. However, it is not necessary that you begin with exactly this template. You should modify it to fit your common personal needs. For example, here is the author's personal, abbreviated version of FULLRULE, JMNRULE.

	A	B	C	D	E	F	G	H
1	**JMNRULE**	17 July 1993	John M. Nevison					
2	(C) Copyright 1989 by John M. Nevison							
3		TITLE TO TELL						
4	13-Sep-89	: Date printed						
5		MAKE A FORMAL INTRODUCTION						
7	**Description**	DECLARE THE MODEL'S PURPOSE						
8		Provide a framework with which to begin building models.						
10	**To use**	GIVE CLEAR INSTRUCTIONS						
11		Call it up,						
12		change its name,						
13		save it with its new name,						
14		and edit to your purpose.						
16	**Reference**	REFERENCE CRITICAL IDEAS						
17		John M. Nevison, *Microsoft Excel Spreadsheet Design*,						
18		New York, NY: Brady Books, 1990.						
20	**Contents**	MAP THE CONTENTS						
21		Introduction: title, description, contents						
22		Initial data						
23		Model						
24		Report area						
25		Graph area						
26		Verify area						
29	**Initial data**							
30		IDENTIFY THE DATA						
31		SURFACE AND LABEL EVERY ASSUMPTION						
34	**Model**							
35		MODEL TO EXPLAIN						
36		POINT TO THE RIGHT SOURCE						
39		FIRST DESIGN ON PAPER						
40		TEST AND EDIT						
41		KEEP IT VISIBLE						
42		SPACE SO THE SPREADSHEET MAY BE EASILY READ						
43		GIVE A NEW FUNCTION A NEW AREA						
46	**Report area**							
47		REPORT TO YOUR READER						

(continued)

	A	B	C	D	E	F	G	H
50	Graph area							
51			GRAPH TO ILLUMINATE					
54	Verify area							
55			VERIFY CRITICAL WORK					
56		0	Verification sum					
57	If an error appears here, check below and then the appropriate area of							
58	the spreadsheet. (Be sure you have recalculated the whole model.)							
59								
60		0	Reference to spreadsheet					
61		0	Reference to spreadsheet					

Because my work does not require that I use certain areas very much, I have removed the Import Area, the Active Area, the Macro Area, and the Sample Submodel. The table of contents was adjusted to reflect these changes. (If I have a job that requires any of these areas, I simply begin with the original FULLRULE.)

The Title Area was rearranged to suit my personal taste. I substituted my name for Mother Goose. I rearranged the placement of the rules to make them easier to erase, but I left them in because erasing them is an instructive nuisance: I like to remind myself of the rules by reading them before I clear them. The Verify Area was expanded because I think it is important and I wanted to encourage myself to use it. JMNRULE represents a comfortable tool that I find both handy to use and a helpful start to my spreadsheet building.

The Model TODO

When you have a tool such as Excel that you use all the time to get your work done, you should not hesitate to use it to help you in unusual ways. One of the most helpful things a spreadsheet can do is move cells around and copy the contents of cells in new locations. These editing features of Excel make it an ideal tool for writing short lists, outlines, and even an occasional memo. The model TODO is Simple Simon's "To Do" list.

Because he followed the rules of style, Simple Simon was able to construct a tool that can serve him in some surprising ways. Here is his spreadsheet for 1 April 1620.

	A	B	C	D	E	F	G
1	**TODO** 1 April 1620 S. Simon						
2	® Copyright 1989 by John M. Nevison						
3	13-Sep-89 : Date printed						
5	**Description**						
6	Manage activities with a "to do" list.						
8	**To Use**						
9	1. Delete items done yesterday (or move into archive at the bottom).						
10	2. Add notes pencilled on yesterday's sheet to today's list (and new						
11	phone numbers to Phone List).						
12	3. Check "Things to do soon" list						
13	4. Insert new rows for new items.						
14	5. Number the items with today's priority (and sort).						
15	6. Put down specific times for appointments.						
16	7. Copy the value of the current date to indicate when the item						
17	first appeared on your list.						
18	8. Print out a paper copy for your work. (Scribble notes on it						
19	throughout the day.)						
21	**Contents**						
22	Introduction: title, description, directions, contents						
23	To do list						
24	Telephone list						
25	Archive of completed tasks						
28	**To do list**						
29	1-Apr-20 : Today's date						
30	Scheduled events						
31	11:00 Meet pieman						
32	1:00 Attend fair						
33	Things to do						
34	1 Get penny						
35	2 Taste pieman's wares						
36	3 Fish for whale						
37	4 Look if plums grow on thistle						
38	5 Get Salt						
39	6 Catch a dickey bird						
40	7 Get sieve						
41	8 Fetch water						

(continued)

	A	B	C	D	E	F	G
42			Phone calls to make				
43			FAIR ticket agency 368-4321				
44			WATER company 368-5436				
45			Thistle farm 368-2435				
46		Things to do soon (but not today)					Date due
47			Jump candlestick				
48			Review water bill				
49			Buy ice cream for party				4-Apr-20
52	Telephone list						
53			BLUE Boy Blue 368-9867				
54			FAIR ticket agency 368-4321				
55			PEEP Bo peep 368-9868				
56			SALTWORKS 368-1234				
57			WATER company 368-5436				
60	Archive of completed tasks						
61		Activity					Date Completed
62		Chased sheep out of meadow					25-Mar-20
63		Chased cows out of corn					22-Mar-20

Notice that the Introduction contains a very helpful set of instructions on how to use the list. By following along the list, one can be sure not to overlook any handy details. Simple Simon has been using the list for several days already and has begun to accumulate a Telephone List; he includes it in his instructions on use so he does not forget to capture any handy numbers he scribbled on his list of the day before.

He deletes old rows of completed items. He inserts new rows on which to add items. He copies and moves cells to put items in today's list and file special completed items in his archive of completed activities.

Today is the first day of the Fair and the list he prints out looks like this:

```
To do list
    1-Apr-20 : Today's date
                Scheduled events
                    11:00  Meet pieman
                    1:00  Attend fair
                Things to do
                    1  Get penny
                    2  Taste pieman's wares
                    3  Fish for whale
                    4  Look if plums grow on thistle
                    5  Get Salt
                    6  Catch a dickey bird
                    7  Get sieve
                    8  Fetch water
                Phone calls to make
                    FAIR ticket agency 368-4321
                    WATER company 368-5436
                    Thistle farm 368-2435
                Things to do soon (but not today)              Date due
                    Jump candlestick
                    Review water bill
                    Buy ice cream for party                    4-Apr-20
```

Simon has four major areas on the list he prints out: "Scheduled events," for meetings with a definite time; "Things to do," for what he wants to get done; "Phone calls to make," so that when he gets on the phone he can efficiently work down his whole list of calls; and "Things to do soon (but not today)," for those things he does not want to forget, but are not on his immediate list. Sometimes Simon notes a date beside an item to remind him of when it must be completed.

One of Simon's handy discoveries was that he could speed up his rearranging by adding a column in front of his list where he could number things in the order he wished to do them and then use the Sort command to quickly rearrange the list in the new priority.

Simon's April 1 was like most of our days. He had his day interrupted many times, new items had to be added to the list, and others had to be put off. Frequently he jotted notes on his list.

The next day his list looked like this:

```
To do list
     2-Apr-20  : Today's date
                     Scheduled events
                         8:00  Meet pieman
                         9:00  Attend fair
                     Things to do
                         1  Taste pieman's wares
                         2  See fair
                         3  Get Salt
                         4  Catch a dickey bird
                         5  Review water bill
                     Phone calls to make
                         SALTWORKS 368-1234
                         WATER company 368-5436
                         BLUE Boy Blue  368-9867
                     Things to do soon (but not today)            Date due
                         Jump candlestick
                         Buy ice cream for party                   4-Apr-20
```

From this list we can see that Simple Simon is planning on going back to the fair. It's clear that he has earned a penny (at least it's no longer on his list). It's also clear that he did not get everything done on April 1 that he thought he would—he's still trying to get salt to catch a dickey bird. One of his "Things to do soon," "Review water bill," made it onto his list for the present day of April 2.

His new "Phone calls to make" shows he is planning a new adventure with his friend Little Boy Blue. Looking at the part of the spreadsheet he probably did not print, we can gather some additional information.

	A	B	C	D	E	F	G
48	Six month goals (before 30 September 1620)						
49	1. Plant and harvest both corn and squash.						
50	2. Plan next year's fair.						
51	3. Complete building new barn for hay.						
54	Telephone list						
55	BLUE Boy Blue 368-9867						
56	FAIR ticket agency 368-4321						
57	PEEP Bo peep 368-9868						
58	PIEMAN Paul Pieman 368-6666						
59	SALTWORKS 368-1234						
60	THISTLE farm 368-2435						
61	WATER company 368-5436						
64	Archive of completed tasks						
65	Activity						Date Completed
66	Chased sheep out of meadow						25-Mar-20
67	Chased cows out of corn						22-Mar-20
68	Caught whale in a pail						1-Apr-20

His augmented phone list shows he has picked up Paul Pieman's phone number and the Thistle Farm's number. (We know he had past adventures from surveying his "Archive of completed activities.")

We also see that Simon has hit on yet another use for TODO. He has started a new section with his "Six month goals." It shows things he hopes to get done by September 30. By keeping his list of goals near his list of things to do, he will be reminded to concentrate on those activities that will help him to achieve his goals.

8

The Wider World

GOING TO ST. IVES
As I was going to St. Ives
I met a man with seven wives.
Every wife had seven sacks,
Every sack had seven cats,
Every cat had seven kits.
Kits, cats, sacks, and wives,
How many were going to St. Ives?

Sometimes, even while you are building a spreadsheet, you know it is destined for others to use. You know that when your work goes public, it will suffer the trials and tribulations of the wider world.

The wider world asks you to extend your concern for the reader and user of your work. The wider world is unfortunately a more uncertain world. Who will use your work? How will your work be used? Who may eventually modify your work? The answers to these questions grow less clear as the future's horizon retreats. As the author of the spreadsheet, you must acknowledge this uncertainty, but you need not entirely surrender to it. What you owe the future's wider world is your best guess of likely alternatives and your prudent attention to those present details that may have future consequences.

It almost goes without saying that the goal of all spreadsheet activity is better decisions. The decision maker who will be using your spreadsheet needs a spreadsheet that works correctly. One of the ways your behavior will change as you prepare for the wider world is that you will do more to convince the eventual user that the spreadsheet has remained, is, and will remain, correct.

The Work Group and Its Concerns

A good framework for thinking about the concerns of the wider world is to imagine a work group of four to seven people who will use your spreadsheet. Imagine the environment they will be working in. Anticipate and avoid as many of their problems as possible. You should revisit each of the areas of your spreadsheet and test it against the work group's use.

The results of your revisit may mean further work on your spreadsheet. Past experience indicates that getting a spreadsheet ready to go public is hard work. Be prepared to spend as much time revising to go public as you spent writing.

Because correctness is the deep obsession, a Verify Area becomes a must for all but the most simple spreadsheets. Even in a simple spreadsheet, defensive formulas that set off "error" warnings should be employed wherever possible. The future user who sees a spreadsheet with a Verify Area and columns labeled "check sums" has visible testimony to the original author's commitment to a correct spreadsheet.

The work group's use requires that the Model Area meet the highest standards of clarity. If the user cannot understand what the model does, he or she will be reluctant to use it. Someone once said, "A person would rather live with a problem he cannot solve than adopt a solution he does not understand." Be sure that your model's equations will be clear to the average reader in the work group, not just the brightest reader.

The reports and graphs were originally crafted for a specific audience and will probably need no revision. Remember, however, that someone in the work group will be maintaining these areas and review your instructions to be sure they are clear and complete.

The Active Area and the Macro Area may get completely reworked after you seriously consider the work group's use of your model. When you carefully review which parts of the model will be used frequently and which will not be used much at all, you may wish to smooth the user's path with an Active Area or an appropriate macro. When you add these features, you must also go the second mile and provide sufficient explanations and instructions so that an average user will not only be convinced of the activity's correctness, but feel confident that he or she can modify the model appropriately and maintain its correctness.

A potent weapon in your arsenal is the submodel. When you can match a submodel to a work group activity that you anticipate may change over time, you will ensure that the changes to the model can be carried out in a contained area. By isolating the area likely to change, you protect the rest of the spreadsheet from unnecessary disturbances. A portion that is not disturbed will not have errors introduced into it. With Excel, your work can be considerably aided by placing new areas, and especially new submodels, on fresh spreadsheets.

After you have reworked the body of the spreadsheet to meet the work group's needs, you will return to the Initial Data Area and the Introduction. Here, you will need the help of the real, or imaginary, spreadsheet library and its librarian.

The Librarian's Requirements

The spreadsheet librarian is responsible for enforcing the work group's standards on the spreadsheet. Even if you have neither work group standards nor a librarian, pretend for the moment that both exist and review your program from that point of view.

Ask yourself what the standards of a librarian might be. Here is a possible checklist.

The Spreadsheet Librarian's Checklist

Everything in the basic spreadsheet introduction

Title, date, name of author
Alterations, date, name of reviser
Purpose
Directions
References
Contents and map

Special details on how this fits with work group practices and procedures

Telephone numbers of people who will answer questions about this spreadsheet
Supporting documents, files, procedures, or people

External documentation (if the spreadsheet is one of a system of spreadsheets)

Details of the supporting technical environment including:

The computer the spreadsheet will run on
The operating system the spreadsheet will run on
The software the spreadsheet will run on
The disk (physical location and name) that contains the spreadsheet
The file folder (physical location and name) with the paper copies of the spreadsheet

Operating limitations

Who the assumed user is
What the assumed user knows
When and how the spreadsheet should be used
When the spreadsheet should **not** be used
Warnings and cautionary notes

Working through this checklist and being sure that your Introduction addresses what it covers will enhance your spreadsheet's contribution to your work group's real productivity. Remember what you write once will be read many times by a strange reader. Common courtesy requires that you anticipate your reader's likely questions and answer them before they ask. The above list can affect the way you arrange and describe your Initial Data Area and whether or not you wish to include an Input Area in your spreadsheet. Make sure your Initial Data Area gives the user a strong foundation of confidence in the whole spreadsheet.

(If your work group has not yet set up standards and practices for spreadsheets and is using them quite heavily, you may want to initiate the discussion about what standards might make sense. Retain your senses of humor and proportion when you set up these standards and be prepared to revise them in the light of your collective experience.)

If your work group has a set of standards for spreadsheets, it probably already has an informal library of spreadsheets in a central location. That library should require at least three things of any spreadsheet that wishes to be considered for inclusion:

1. A disk with the spreadsheet (or system of spreadsheets) on it—and a second, backup disk.

2. A full printed copy of each spreadsheet with a set of data that helps explain how the spreadsheet works.

3. A second, complete, printed copy of each spreadsheet that shows all formulas in full as they are arranged on the spreadsheet.

Final Moves

After you have completed the revision of your spreadsheet for the wider world, give it a few final reality checks. The spreadsheet will face the challenge of explaining itself to an uninformed user, so before you approve it for use, have it proofread by someone other than the original author. To get the most out of this proofreading, give the model to the intended user. If possible, give it to a second reader as well. If the spreadsheet will be used by several people, include as many of them as possible as proofreaders.

Listen to your proofreaders' comments. Incorporate improvements that you think will answer their criticisms and return it to them for review. After your readers think they understand the printed spreadsheet, ask one of them to make mock use of it—to take it out for a test drive. The user may vary an assumption and play "what if?" with the model. The user may add another month's data to the Initial Data Area. The user may simulate the end-of-year activity when the model's data must be stored and the model revised for a whole new year. The user can try an independent set of initial data to see if the spreadsheet really works. The more testing the model gets, the better your final spreadsheet will be.

After you believe you have done everything that can be done to prepare your spreadsheet for the wider world, you must temporarily assume the role of spreadsheet librarian. Take your spreadsheet as an author and set it down on the desk. Walk around the desk. Pick the spreadsheet up as the librarian. Perform the librarian's review of the spreadsheet vigorously even though the author in you may not like what it hears. After you have completed the librarian's review, set the results back down on the desk. Walk around the desk the other way and see how you did as an author. Repeat this exercise until both of you are satisfied with the results.

You will be finished when you can look at your work and say to yourself, "I would be happy to use this spreadsheet." Given Solomon's remark that "time and chance happeneth to them all," someday you may find yourself being the surprised user of your own work. Make the user in you grateful to the author in you.

Annotated References

Nevison, John M., *Executive Computing: How to Get It Done on Your Own*, Reading, MA: Addison-Wesley, 1981.

This work presents stories about many of the business ideas discussed in this book. The examples all use computer programs written in BASIC. Nevison [1986] gives examples of spreadsheets.

Simon, Herbert, *The Sciences of the Artificial*, Cambridge, MA: MIT Press, 1969.

This is a collection of lectures by a man who is a distinguished management scientist (Nobel Prize in Economics) and an outstanding computer scientist (Turing Award). The talks are a thought-provoking and informative introduction to the problems of design.

Strunk, William, Jr., and E. B. White, *The Elements of Style*, Second Edition, New York: Macmillan, 1972.

The second book to read when you want to write good spreadsheets. The first book to read when you want to write.

Tufte, Edward R., *The Visual Display of Quantitative Information*, Cheshire, CN: Graphics Press, 1983.

The third book to read when you want to write good spreadsheets. The first book to read when you want to display quantitative information.

Zeisel, Hans, *Say It with Figures* (5th Ed. Rev.), New York: Harper & Row, 1968.

This work is a classic in the field of social science analysis. Read it when you want to know how to get to the root causes of business activity, how to ask the questions, and how to look at the answers.

References

Abegglen, James C., and George Stalk, Jr., *KAISHA, The Japanese Corporation*, New York: Basic Books, 1985.

Allen, George B., *A Note on the Boston Consulting Group Concept of Corporate Analysis and Corporate Strategy*, Boston: Intercollegiate Case Clearing House, Soldiers Field, #9-175-175, President and Fellows of Harvard College, 1975.

—*Note on the Use of Experience Curves in Competitive Decision Making*, Boston: Intercollegiate Case Clearing House, Soldiers Field, #9-175-174, President and Fellows of Harvard College, 1975.

Blake, George B., "Graphic Shorthand as an Aid to Managers," *Harvard Business Review* (March-April 1978).

The Boston Consulting Group, *Perspectives on Experience*, Boston: The Boston Consulting Group, 1972.

Brown, Robert Goodell, *Smoothing, Forecasting and Prediction of Discrete Time Series*, Englewood Cliffs, NJ: Prentice-Hall, 1963.

Copeland, Thomas E., and J. Fred Weston, *Financial Theory and Corporate Policy, Third Edition*, Reading, MA: Addison-Wesley, 1988.

Daellenbach, Hans G., and John A. George, *Introduction to Operations Research Techniques*, Boston: Allyn and Bacon, 1978.

Frank, Judith M., *Managing Business Microcomputer Systems*, New York: Brady, Simon & Schuster, 1987.

Halfart, Erich A., *Techniques of Financial Analysis (4th Ed.)*, Homewood, IL: Richard D. Irwin, 1977.

Hirshman, Winfred B., "Profit From the Learning Curve," *Harvard Business Review* (January-February 1964).

Kemeny, John G., et al., *Finite Mathematics with Business Applications (2nd Ed.)*, Englewood Cliffs, NJ: Prentice-Hall, 1972.

Kepner, Charles H., and Benjamin B. Tregoe, *The New Rational Manager*, Princeton, NJ: Princeton Research Press, 1981.

Levy, F. K., G. L. Thompson, and J. D. Wiest, "The ABC's of the Critical Path Method," *Harvard Business Review* (1963): 98-108.

Miller, Robert W., "How to Plan and Control with PERT," *Harvard Business Review* (March-April 1962).

Moesteller, Frederick, and John W. Tukey, *Data Analysis and Regression: A Second Course in Statistics*, Reading, MA: Addison-Wesley, 1977.

Nevison, John M., *1-2-3 Spreadsheet Design*, New York: Brady, 1989.

—*The Elements of Spreadsheet Style*, New York: Brady, 1987.

—*Executive Computing: How to Get It Done with Spreadsheets and Graphs*, Atlanta, GA: Association for Media-Based Continuing Education for Engineers, 1986.

—*The Little Book of BASIC Style: How to Write a Program You Can Read*, Reading, MA: Addison-Wesley, 1978.

Porter, Michael E., *Competitive Strategy*, New York: The Free Press, 1980.

Raiffa, Howard, *Decision Analysis*, Reading, MA: Addison-Wesley, 1978.

Woolsey, Robert E. D., and Huntington S. Swanson, *Operations Research for Immediate Application: A Quick & Dirty Manual*, New York: Harper & Row, 1975.

Appendix A: Checklists for Action

This appendix is intended to give you step-by-step, generic instructions on several small but important techniques you may employ in your Excel work. The phrasing is heavily influenced by the commands of Macintosh Release 2.2. If you have any trouble with a command as you read, please check the manual of your version to be sure of the correct syntax.

A Word on Building the Initial Data Area and the Model Area

When writing a new model, one way to develop the initial data is by beginning with a template like NEW and building the Model Area first. When you write a formula with a constant in it (for example, King Henry's 23 percent tax rate in Chapter 1), you can stop, write, and label the assumption up in the Initial Data Area, return to the model, and rewrite the formula with a reference to the Initial Data Area.

So the old formula may have looked like this

B30 = A30*.23

and the new formula looks like this

B30 = A30*$B$5

and B5 and C5 look like this

23% tax rate

As you continue building the model, you may find a row or column of raw numbers. Again, you move the raw numbers up to the Initial Data Area and change the model entry to a one-term formula that refers to the raw data.

Thus, you will have changed the old model

B36 = 18,346

to the new model

B36 = B15

where the new initial data is

B15 = 18,346

The result of these efforts will be a Model Area that is entirely formulas. Such efforts will force you to think about the spreadsheet's use while the spreadsheet model is being built. The final spreadsheet will benefit from this extra thought.

How to Link Cells

Suppose that the value 10 percent is in the cell A1 on a spreadsheet. Ten percent represents the percentage interest that your firm is using in its financial models. You wish to use this figure at several other locations on your spreadsheet, in particular in cell B20.

To link cell B20 to A1 do the following:

1. Go to cell B20.

2. Enter the formula =A1.

3. Check your work by varying the value in A1 and be sure the value in B20 varies.

To link a block of cells, for example the six-cell block A1:B3, to another block of cells do the following:

1. Copy A1:B3.

2. Select the upper-left corner, B51, of the block B51:D53 .

3. Paste Link.

4. Format the cells in the linked area.

When you are done,

A1:B3 might contain   and look like

   .10   .12   .15   10%   12%   15%

   8   5   10   8.0   5.0   10.0

and B51:D53 would contain: and look like:

   =A1 =A2 =A3   10%   12%   15%

   =B1 =B2 =B3   8.0   5.0   10.0

By linking single cells or whole blocks of cells, you can link parts of a Model Area to the values in the Initial Data Area. When you link to a single value, you will probably want it to be an absolute reference. When you Paste Link to a block, column, or row of cells, the reference will also be absolute.

Linking Labels

Every version of Excel allows you to link labels as well as values. Because linking to a label reduces the chance for an error to enter your work and increases the ease with which you can change a label, you should always link to a label when you have the chance.

How to Protect Your Spreadsheet

In Excel, the Cell Protect commands provide a variety of ways to "protect" a cell. The general effect of this protection is that the user is prevented from inadvertently altering the contents. Excel also provides password protection on the whole spreadsheet with Protect Document.

These protection schemes are merely good first lines of defense. They should not, however, be taken for more than they are. They are not insurance that no one will change your spreadsheet. They are not a guarantee that no one will accidentally alter your sheet. (Someone with the password can turn the protection off and forget to turn it back on, and someone else can make a mistake moving data around.) They are not an excuse for failing to document the whole spreadsheet. ("Because this is protected, the user doesn't have to understand it," is a bad excuse.)

In fact, protection schemes offer so little protection, that you should treat your spreadsheet as if it were going to be handled in an unprotected fashion. Do protect it wherever possible, but don't kid yourself about how much protection you have provided.

When You Protect

1. Begin by unprotecting those areas you wish to allow the user to change with Cell Protection. By unprotecting you force yourself to think about each area you wish to open and you err on the side of overprotecting the spreadsheet when you forget something.

2. Turn on protection for the whole spreadsheet with Protect Document.

3. Password the spreadsheet.

4. Test the spreadsheet to be sure you have correctly protected it.

How to Print a Spreadsheet as Formulas

If you are preparing a paper copy of your work for your files, you will want to have a copy of your spreadsheet with the formulas in their proper location in the spreadsheet. Because some of your formulas may be long, the columns they appear in will necessarily be wide. In fact, be prepared for the formula version of your spreadsheet to be quite large.

You may purchase various programs to print the formulas in your spreadsheet. If you choose to purchase one, try it out at the store (or try a friend's copy) to be sure it works to your satisfaction.

When you are ready to print your spreadsheet as formulas:

1. Call up a copy of your spreadsheet that you will either throw away or save under a separate name.

2. Use the Display command to convert the display to all formulas.

3. Widen each column until all formulas in it are completely visible.

4. Print a paper copy.

5. Assemble the paper copy into one large copy and review it carefully to be sure all formulas are visible.

6. Store it with the regular printed copy of your spreadsheet.

Future New Products for Spreadsheets

Spreadsheets have a great variety of companion products. Some of these tools can substantially aid the user as he or she works with a spreadsheet.

If you don't just use spreadsheets, but create spreadsheet applications for others to use, you should:

1. Acquaint yourself with these products.

2. Decide if, how, and where you will use them in your work.

3. Decide how to inform the reader of a printed copy of the spreadsheet about any extra products you use. (Perhaps you create small remarks in various areas of the spreadsheet, perhaps you create a new area, perhaps you do both.)

Appendix B:
Business Spreadsheets—Templates for Action, Tools for Use

The spreadsheets in this book serve two functions. First, they are examples of spreadsheet form and style. Second, they are examples of spreadsheet function, of what spreadsheets can be used for. As examples of function they can be templates for your action, tools for your own work.

The spreadsheets in this book that can be used as tools form a basic toolkit.

The Business Spreadsheet Toolkit

Management Tools	
Financial Tools	Strategic Business Tools
Personal Business Tools	
Other Spreadsheet Tools	

Figure B-1.

283

Management Tools	• ACTIVITY	(Chapter 7)
	• TASKTIME	(Chapter 7)
	• RAISES	(Chapter 7)
	• PROGRESS	(Chapter 6)
	• RAINCOAT	(Chapter 7)
	• PIETEST	(Chapter 7)
	• QUEST	(Chapter 7)
	• LADY	(Chapter 7)
Strategic Business Tools	• GROWTHA	(Chapter 6)
	• NEWBUD	(Chapter 5)
	• PLANA	(Chapter 2)
	• PLANB	(Chapter 2)
	• PLANC	(Chapter 2)
	• PLAND	(Chapter 2)
Financial Tools	• BUYBORRO	(Chapter 7)
	• INFLATE	(Chapter 4)
	• PAYMENTS	(Chapter 7)
	• SIMPLPAY	(Chapter 7)
	• PRESENT	(Chapter 7)
	• SEASON	(Chapter 7)
	• NEWBUD	(Chapter 5)
Personal Business Tools	• FULLRULE	(Chapter 4)
	• JMNRULE	(Chapter 7)
	• NEW	(Chapter 2)
	• SMALLNEW	(Chapter 2)
	• TRAVEL	(Chapter 2)
	• TODO	(Chapter 7)
	• RAINCOAT	(Chapter 7)
	• QUEST	(Chapter 7)
	• SALES	(Chapter 4)
Other Spreadsheet Tools	• FAMILY	(Chapter 5)
	• GNP	(Chapter 4)
	• MANPOWER	(Chapter 4)
	• QUARTRLY	(Chapter 4)
	• MYTHPETS	(Chapter 4)
	• SILBELLS	(Chapter 2)
	• SHEEP	(Chapter 2)
	• SIXPENCE	(Chapter 1)

Figure B-2.

Management Tools	• ACTIVITY	(Chapter 7)
	• TASKTIME	(Chapter 7)
	• RAISES	(Chapter 7)
	• PROGRESS	(Chapter 6)
	• RAINCOAT	(Chapter 7)
	• PIETEST	(Chapter 7)
	• QUEST	(Chapter 7)
	• LADY	(Chapter 7)

Management Tools

ACTIVITY

Plan and control a set of project activities through several overlapping phases. Keywords: Project management, Project planning, Project control, Activity tracking, Project phase analysis, Graphs.

TASKTIME

Estimate the total time to complete a set of tasks, all of uncertain duration. Keywords: Critical path, Probability, Standard deviation, Project estimation, Time estimation, Cost estimation, Scheduling, Beta distribution.

RAISES

Alter the amount and the timing of raises for each member of the department to determine the timing and amount of the overall budget required. Keywords: Salary, Raises, Compensation, Budget planning.

PROGRESS

Integrate your business unit's budget, current plan, and actual figures to show how much progress has been made to date. Keywords: Budget, Forecast, Actual, Departmental planning, Departmental reporting, Graphs, Smoothing data.

RAINCOAT

Weigh alternatives that have risk and uncertainty associated with them. Keywords: Decision, Probability, Utility theory, Decision tree, Market research costs.

PIETEST

Decide whether a market research effort is worth the cost. Keywords: Decision, Probability, Utility theory, Decision tree, Market research costs.

QUEST & LADY

Select among alternatives with several decision criteria. Keywords: Decision theory, Alternative evaluation, Weighted decision criteria, Adverse consequence analysis.

References

Levy, F. K., G. L. Thompson, and J. D. Wiest, "The ABC's of the Critical Path Method," *Harvard Business Review* 41 (1963): 98–108.

Kemeny, John G., et al., *Finite Mathematics with Business Applications (2nd Ed.)*, Englewood Cliffs, NJ: Prentice-Hall, 1972.

Kepner, Charles H., and Benjamin B. Tregoe, *The New Rational Manager*, Princeton, NJ: Princeton Research Press, 1981.

Miller, Robert W., "How to Plan and Control with PERT," *Harvard Business Review* (March-April 1962).

Nevison, John M., *Executive Computing: How to Get It Done on Your Own*, Reading, MA: Addison-Wesley, 1981.

Raiffa, Howard, *Decision Analysis*, Reading, MA: Addison-Wesley, 1978.

Strategic Business Tools	• GROWTHA (Chapter 6) • NEWBUD (Chapter 5) • PLANA (Chapter 2) • PLANB (Chapter 2) • PLANC (Chapter 2) • PLAND (Chapter 2)

Strategic Business Tools

GROWTHA (GROWTH is old version)

Estimate how experience curve competition plays out in a strategic market. Keywords: Experience curve, Market share, Market growth, Competition, Cost curve, Price curve, Debt policy, Ten-period (year or quarter) simulation, International competition, Spreadsheet revision.

NEWBUD (BUDGET is old version)

Connect quarterly working division budgets to annual statements and test the consequences of working decisions on the annual bottom line. Keywords: Executive budget, Manufacturing budget, Sales budget, Cash budget, Income statement, Balance sheet, Ratio report, Working budgets, Annual reports, Budget integration.

PLANA, PLANB, PLANC, & PLAND

Project a five-year income statement and test its performance against your business assumptions. Keywords: Income statement, Sales forecast, Profit forecast, Five-year plan, Sensitivity analysis.

References

Abegglen, James C., and George Stalk, Jr., *KAISHA, The Japanese Corporation*, New York: Basic Books, 1985.

Allen, George B., *A Note on the Boston Consulting Group Concept of Corporate Analysis and Corporate Strategy*, Boston: Intercollegiate Case Clearing House, Soldiers Field, #9-175-175, President and Fellows of Harvard College, 1975.

—*Note on the Use of Experience Curves in Competitive Decision Making*, Boston: Intercollegiate Case Clearing House, Soldiers Field, #9-175-174, President and Fellows of Harvard College, 1975.

The Boston Consulting Group, *Perspectives on Experience*, Boston: The Boston Consulting Group, 1972.

Halfart, Erich A., *Techniques of Financial Analysis, (4th Ed.)*, Homewood, IL: Richard D. Irwin, 1977.

Hirshman, Winfred B., "Profit from the Learning Curve," *Harvard Business Review* (January-February 1964).

Nevison, John M., *Executive Computing: How to Get It Done on Your Own*, Reading, MA: Addison-Wesley, 1981.

—*Executive Computing: How to Get It Done with Spreadsheets and Graphs*, Atlanta: Association for Media-Based Continuing Education for Engineers, 1986.

Porter, Michael E., *Competitive Strategy*, New York: The Free Press, 1980.

Financial Tools	• BUYBORRO	(Chapter 7)
	• INFLATE	(Chapter 4)
	• PAYMENTS	(Chapter 7)
	• SIMPLPAY	(Chapter 7)
	• PRESENT	(Chapter 7)
	• SEASON	(Chapter 7)
	• NEWBUD	(Chapter 5)

Financial Tools

BUYBORRO (Buy or Borrow)

Analyze whether to borrow or buy a capital item. Keywords: Discount factor, Interest rate, Corporate cost of capital, Depreciation schedule, Time horizon, Net present value.

INFLATE

Work out price increases that preserve profit when cost components are rising at different rates of inflation. Keywords: Cost inflation, Variable rates of cost component growth, Price increase, Margin preservation, Time horizon.

PAYMENTS

Explore the repayment schedule of a loan with even monthly payments. Keywords: Even payment, Outstanding balance, Interest payment, Principal payment, Monthly schedule.

SIMPLPAY (Simple Payments)

Explore the repayment schedule of a loan with even yearly payments. Keywords: Even payment, Outstanding balance, Interest payment, Principal payment.

PRESENT

Calculate the present value of a future stream of cash payments. Keywords: Inflation rate, Discount factor, Discounted cash flow, Present value, Net preset value (NPV), Internal rate of return (IRR).

SEASON

Adjust seasonal data to see true annual patterns and use the results to predict the next value of some seasonally adjusted data. Find the "least squares" best-fitting line through a set of points. Keywords: Estimation, Projection, Least squares method, Linear regression, Line fitting, Seasonal adjustment.

NEWBUD

Connect quarterly working division budgets to annual statements and test the consequences of working decisions on the annual bottom line. Keywords: Executive budget, Manufacturing budget, Sales budget, Cash budget, Income statement, Balance sheet, Ratio report, Working budgets, Annual reports, Budget integration.

References

Brown, Robert Goodell, *Smoothing, Forecasting and Prediction of Discrete Time Series*, Englewood Cliffs, NJ: Prentice-Hall, 1963.

Copeland, Thomas E., and J. Fred Weston, *Financial Theory and Corporate Policy (3rd Ed.)*, Reading, MA: Addison-Wesley, 1988.

Daellenbach, Hans G., and John A. George, *Introduction to Operations Research Techniques*, Boston: Allyn and Bacon, 1978.

Halfart, Erich A., *Techniques of Financial Analysis (4th Ed.)*, Homewood, IL: Richard D. Irwin, 1977.

Nevison, John M., *Executive Computing: How to Get It Done on Your Own*, Reading, MA: Addison-Wesley, 1981.

Personal Business Tools	• FULLRULE	(Chapter 4)
	• JMNRULE	(Chapter 7)
	• NEW	(Chapter 2)
	• SMALLNEW	(Chapter 2)
	• TRAVEL	(Chapter 2)
	• TODO	(Chapter 7)
	• RAINCOAT	(Chapter 7)
	• QUEST	(Chapter 7)
	• SALES	(Chapter 4)

Personal Business Tools

FULLRULE

Provide a template for beginning spreadsheet work. Keywords: Template, Style, Rules.

JMNRULE

Provide a template for beginning spreadsheet work that has been adjusted to personal needs. Keywords: Template, Style, Rules, Personal Versions.

NEW

A more modest template for starting a spreadsheet. Keywords: Template, Style.

SMALLNEW

A template for beginning a one-page spreadsheet. Keywords: Template, Style.

TRAVEL

Prepare a travel expense report. Keywords: Travel costs, Expense report, Mileage, Template.

TODO

Keep track of what activities need to be done today. Keywords: Personal time management, Priority setting, Goal setting, Daily activity management.

RAINCOAT

Weigh alternatives that have risk and uncertainty associated with them. Keywords: Decision, Probability, Utility theory, Decision tree, Market research costs.

QUEST

Select among alternatives with several decision criteria. Keywords: Decision theory, Alternative evaluation, Weighted decision criteria, Adverse consequence analysis.

SALES

Plot the present sales against past years in order to look at the comparison. Keywords: Sales, Graphs, Performance summary.

References

Blake, George B., "Graphic Shorthand as an Aid to Managers," *Harvard Business Review* (March-April 1978).

Kepner, Charles II., and Benjamin B. Tregoe, *The New Rational Manager*, Princeton, NJ: Princeton Research Press, 1981.

Nevison, John M., *Executive Computing: How to Get It Done with Spreadsheets and Graphs*, Atlanta, GA: Association for Media-Based Continuing Education for Engineers, 1986.

Woolsey, Robert E. D., and Huntington S. Swanson, *Operations Research for Immediate Application: A Quick & Dirty Manual*, New York: Harper & Row, 1975.

Other Spreadsheet Tools	• FAMILY	(Chapter 5)
	• GNP	(Chapter 4)
	• MANPOWER	(Chapter 4)
	• QUARTRLY	(Chapter 4)
	• MYTHPETS	(Chapter 4)
	• SILBELLS	(Chapter 2)
	• SHEEP	(Chapter 2)
	• SIXPENCE	(Chapter 1)

Other Spreadsheet Tools

FAMLY (Family Individual Finance, FAMLYFIN is old version)

See how family members can each have control over a part of the total family financial plan.

GNP

A look at the portion of a large spreadsheet that an economic policy maker might be interested in.

MANPOWER

The output of a manpower planning exercise that wants to know what's coming down the road soon.

QUARTRLY

Some report forms for looking at reports on quarterly performance.

MYTHPETS (Mythical Pets)

An illustrative example of the table relationship between row causes and column effects.

SILBELL (Silver Bells)

An illustration of various title area formats for spreadsheets.

SHEEP

How one spreadsheet combined database activity and reports on the activity.

SIXPENCE

How the King combined Model Area and Report Areas to report on the income and disbursements of his government.

Reference

Zeisel, Hans, *Say It with Figures* (5th Ed. Rev.), New York: Harper & Row, 1968.

Index

Active Area, 91, 92, 93, 94, 260, 268, 269
activity tracking, 285
actual figures, 285
additional forms, 55-96
additional functions, 55-96
adverse consequence analysis, 286
alternative evaluation, 286
annotated book references, 273
annual reports, 287, 289
Apply Names commands, 33
assumptions, 28, 31-33, 164
asterisks, 64, 65, 208
"average" row, 214

balance sheet, 287, 289
bar charts, 143
basic forms, 11-46
blocks, 48
book references, 275-276
budget integration, 287
budget planning, 285
building a spreadsheet, 129-155
building the Initial Data Area, 41, 277-278
building the Model Area, 41, 277-278
business functions, 57, 58, 105
business spreadsheet toolkit, 283
business spreadsheets, 283-292

cash budget, 287, 289
cell name label, 84
Cell Protect command, 279
cell references, 58, 84

cells, 38, 79
check sums columns, 198, 203, 268
collecting macros, 83
collections of spreadsheets, 127
column results, 62
columns, 48, 58, 75, 217
compensation, 285
competition, 286
complete printout of formula, 33, 36
computer graphing, 67
computer programmers, 89
computer programming and macros, 88-91
computer programs, 56
constant names, 37
constants, 33, 39
control panel, 81
controlling macros, 82-91
corporate cost of capital, 288
cost curve, 286
cost inflation, 288
Create Name command, 22, 33
cross-checking results, 198
cross-checks, 80, 81
cursor, 25
custom menus, 90
cut-out submodels, 104

daily activity management, 290
databases, 43, 45, 48, 56
debt policy, 286
decision, 285, 290
decision structure, 88
decision theory, 286

decision tree, 285, 290
defensive formulas, 80
Define Name command, 22
departmental planning, 285
departmental reporting, 285
depreciation schedule, 288
description feature, 12
dialog boxes, 90
direction feature, 12
discount factor, 288
discounted cash flow, 288
Display command, 280
displaying results, 39
"Do...While" structure, 88
documenting macros, 83
double-entry bookkeeping, 79

editing your spreadsheet, 49-51, 134,
    173
entering data, 98-104, 134, 135
Entering Data Area, 98, 103, 104, 105,
    127
equations, 43
ERR message, 171, 172
error comments, 139
error warnings, 80, 81, 82, 268
estimation, 289
even payment, 288
evolutionary control of submodels, 105
Excel commands
    Apply Name, 33
    Cell Protect, 279
    Create Name, 22, 33
    Define Name, 22
    Display, 280
    Goto, 22
    Protect Document, 279
    Sort, 263
Excel formulas, 39
Excel macro functions, 88
Excel Reference Manual, 82, 90
executive budget, 287, 289
Exit Area, 99

exiting data, 99
expense report, 290
experience curve, 175, 178, 182, 186,
    192
experience curve formula, 192-193
Experience Curve Mathematics, 182,
    192-194
explaining calculations, 39
explanation of ideas, 174-175

financial tools, 283, 284, 288-289
five-year plan, 287
fixing old spreadsheets, 173
focusing model's activity, 91-94
formatting column headings, 131
forms, 55-96
formulas, 3, 4, 5, 25, 31, 33, 34, 35, 37,
    101, 170
full model example, 187-191
function arguments, 89
functions, 55-96
FV function, 236

generic behavior, 56
generic commands, 89
generic functions, 89
giving instructions, 17-19
giving new functions new areas, 55-58,
    173
goal setting, 290
Goto command, 22
Graph Area, 130, 164, 199, 217, 219, 257
graph names, 71
graphics, 56,
Graphing Area, 55, 56, 57, 69, 70, 71,
    75, 77, 141, 145, 146, 164
graphing tools, 69
graphs, 55, 56, 66-78, 130, 142, 168, 285,
    290
Graphs tool, 285

identifying the data, 26-31
IF function, 257

IF statement, 171
"If...Then... Else" structure, 83
Import Area, 79, 260
importing data, 78-79, 173
income statement, 287, 289
initial data, 27, 28, 91, 92, 242
Initial Data Area, 11, 25, 26-33, 37, 39,
        40, 41, 43, 55, 91, 92, 98, 101, 103,
        104, 105, 127, 134, 146, 164, 165,
        171, 178, 183, 197, 198, 199, 201,
        214, 246, 256, 269, 271, 272, 277,
        279
initial mode, 27
initial test data, 222
Input Area, 271
integrated model, 175, 185
intellectual control of submodels, 105,
        126
interest payment, 288
interest rate, 288
intermediate error, 104
international competition, 286
Introduction, 11-33, 39, 55, 146, 164,
        165, 168, 196, 200, 214, 219, 256,
        262, 269
IRR function, 234, 257, 288

keeping data visible, 51

labels, 69, 75, 84
labelling assumptions, 31-33, 173
least squares method, 289
legends, 73
line fitting, 289
linear regression, 289
linking cells, 278-279
linking labels, 279
logical forms, 88
loops, 88

Macro Area, 55, 56, 57, 260, 268
macro sheet, 55, 56, 57, 58, 83, 88
macros, 55, 58, 82, 90, 269

macros and computer programming,
        88-91
management tools, 283, 284, 285, 286
manufacturing budget, 287
mapping the contents, 20-25, 169
maps, 20, 23, 25, 55
margin preservtion, 288
market research costs, 285, 290
mean, 65
mileage, 290
Model Area, 11, 25, 28, 29, 33-41, 43,
        55, 71, 88, 90, 101, 135, 214, 216,
        221, 237, 242, 278, 279
model implications, 186-191
model results, 184-186
models, 15-17, 29, 31, 33, 48, 55
modifying a spreadsheet, 155-194
monthly schedule, 288
"must" criteria, 202
"must" objectives, 201

names, 58, 84
NPV function, 234, 236, 288

on-line help, 82
other spreadsheet tools, 283, 284, 291-
        292
    FAMLY, 291
    GNP, 292
    MANPOWER, 292
    MYTHPETS, 292
    QUARTRLY, 292
    SHEEP, 292
    SILBELL, 292
    SIXPENCE, 292

"paper" spreadsheet design, 47-49
password protection, 279
performance summary, 290
personal business tools, 283, 284, 286-
        287
personal time management, 290
personal versions, 290

physical control of submodels, 105
PMT function, 237
present value, 288
price increase, 288
principal payment, 288
printing formulas, 37
printing reports, 134
printing spreadsheets as formulas, 280
priortity setting, 290
probability, 285, 290
profit forecast, 287
programming structures, 88, 89
project control, 285
project estimation, 285
project management 285
project phase analysis, 285
project planning, 285
projection, 289
proofreading your spreadsheet, 271-
    272
Protect Document command, 278
protecting macros, 85
protecting your spreadsheet, 279-280
PV function, 236, 237

raises, 285
ratio report, 287, 289
raw numbers, 31,
Reference feature, 12
referencing, 19-20, 38-39
relations, 33
relative error, 81
repetition structure, 88
Report Area, 36, 39, 40, 91
report example, 60
report information, 59
report style, 59
reporting date, 141
reports, 58-66, 130, 131, 134, 142
reusing submodel tools, 104-113
rows, 48, 58
rules, 290

salary, 285
sales, 290
sales budget, 287, 289
sales forecast, 287
seasonal adjustment, 289
sensitivity analysis, 287
separate graphing area, 69, 71
sequence structure, 88
smoothing data, 285
spacing the spreadsheet, 52-54
spreadsheet borders, 60
spreadsheet companion products, 281
spreadsheet design, 47-54
spreadsheet example: ACTIVITY, 224-
    228, 284, 285
    activity tracking, 285
    Graphs, 285
    project control, 285
    project management, 285
    project phase analysis, 285
    project planning, 285
spreadsheet example: BUYBORO, 246-
    254
    "basic calculations," 249
    corporate cost of capital, 288
    depreciation schedule, 288
    discount factor, 288
    Initial Data Area, 246
    Model Area, 248
    net present value, 288
    time horizon, 288
    Verify Area, 250
spreadsheet example: GROWTH, 155-
    194
    assumptions, 164
    ERR message, 171, 172
    experience curve, 175, 178, 182, 186,
        192, 286
    experience curve formula, 192-193
    Experience Curve Mathematics,
        182, 192-194
    explanation of ideas, 174-175

first work session, 165-167
fixing old spreadsheets, 173
formulas, 170
full model example, 187-191
FULLRULE template, 164, 165
Graph Area, 164
Graphing Area, 164, 170
graphs, 168
IF statement, 171
Initial Data Area, 164, 165, 171, 178, 183
Introduction, 164, 165, 178
integrated model, 175, 185
mapping the contents, 169
Model Area, 164, 165, 170, 171
model implications, 186-191
model results, 184-186
original spreasheet example, 156-194
Report Area, 164, 165, 167, 170, 171
revise references, 169
second work session, 168-170
spreadsheet model GROWTH, 175-183
SUM functions, 172
table of contents, 169
third work session, 170-173
Verify Area, 169, 170, 171, 172
spreadsheet example: GROWTHA, 286
    competition, 286
    cost curve, 286
    debt policy, 286
    experience curve, 286
    international competition, 286
    market growth, 286
    market share, 286
    price curve, 286
    spreadsheet revision, 286
    ten-year simulation, 286
spreadsheet example: INFLATE, 288
    cost inflation, 288
    margin preservation, 288

price increase, 288
time horizon, 288
variable rates of cost component growth, 288
spreadsheet example: LADY, 200-204
    adverse consequence analysis, 286
    alternative evaluation, 286
    check sums column, 203
    decision theory, 286
    Initial Data Area, 201
    Introduction, 200
    "must" criteria, 202
    "must" objectives, 201
    "want" criteria, 202
    "want" objectives, 201, 202
    weighted decision criteria, 286
spreadsheet example: NEWBUD, 287
    annual reports, 287, 289
    balance sheet, 287, 289
    budget integration, 287, 289
    cash budget, 287, 289
    executive budget, 287, 289
    income statement, 287, 289
    manufacturing budget, 287, 289
    ratio report, 287, 289
    sales budget, 287, 289
    working budgets, 287, 289
spreadsheet example: PAYMENTS, 288
    Even payment, 288
    interest payment, 288
    monthly schedule, 288
    outstanding balance, 288
    principal payment, 288
spreadsheet example: PIETEST, 209-211
spreadsheet example: PRESENT, 229-236
    discount factor, 288
    discounted cash flow, 288
    FV function, 236
    inflation rate, 288

IRR function, 234, 288
NPV function, 234, 236, 288
PV function, 229-236, 288
"rate," 234
tricky formulas, 232, 233
"values," 234
spreadsheet example: PROGRESS,
    129-155
    actual figures, 285
    bar charts, 143
    budget, 285
    DEPARTMENT name, 129
    departmental reporting, 285
    entering data, 134, 135
    error comments, 139
    forecast, 285
    formatting column headings, 131
    formatting psuedo numbers, 131
    FULLRULE template, 129
    Graph Area, 130, 133
    Graphing Area, 141, 145, 146
    graphs, 130, 131, 133, 134, 142, 143,
        285
    Initial Data Area, 134, 146
    Introduction, 146
    Model Area, 135
    model example, 148-154
    printing the reports, 133
    Report Area, 130, 133, 134
    reporting date, 141
    reports, 130, 131, 134, 142,
    smoothing data, 285
    testing and editing, 133
    Verify Area, 139, 141
spreadsheet example: QUEST, 195-200,
    290
    adverse consequence analysis, 286
    alternative evaluation, 286
    check sums column, 198
    cross-checking results, 198
    decision theory, 286
    Graph Area, 199

Initial Data Area, 197, 198, 199
    Introduction, 196, 199
    "What If" questions, 199
    weighted decision criteria, 286
spreadsheet example: RAINCOAT,
    204-209
    asterisk, 208
    decision, 285
    decision tree, 285
    Initial Data Area, 208
    market research costs, 285
    probability, 285
    utility theory, 285
spreadsheet example: RAISES, 255-258
    "Annual salary," 256
    budget planning, 285
    compensation, 285
    "Earned for Year" data, 256
    Graph Area, 257
    IF function, 257
    Initial Data Area, 256
    Introduction, 256
    "New Annual Salary" formula, 256
    "Raise Amount," 256
    raises, 285
    salary, 285
    Verify Area, 257
spreadsheet example: SALES, 290-291
    Graphs, 291
    performance summary, 290
    sales, 291
spreadsheet example: SEASON, 212-
    217
    "average" row, 214
    estimation, 289
    Graph Area, 217
    Initial Data Area, 214
    Introduction, 214
    least squares method, 289
    line fitting, 289
    linear regression, 289
    Model Area, 214, 216

projection, 289
seasonal adjustment, 289
TREND function, 216
spreadsheet example: TASKTIME,
218-223
beta distribution, 285
cost estimation, 285
critical path, 285
Graph Area, 219
Initial Data Area, 219
initial test data, 222
Model Area, 221
probability, 285
project estimation, 285
Report Area, 219
scheduling, 285
standard deviation, 285
time estimation, 285
tricky formulas, 223
spreadsheet example: TODO, 260-265
"Archives of completed activities"
area, 265
daily activity management, 290
goal setting, 290
Introduction, 262
"Phone calls to make" area, 263, 264
personal time management, 290
priority setting, 290
"Six month goals" area, 265
Sort command, 263
telephone list, 262
"Things to do" area, 263, 264
"Things to do soon" area, 263
To do" list, 260
spreadsheet example: TRAVEL, 290
expense report, 290
mileage, 290
template, 290
travel costs, 290

spreadsheet examples: PLANA,
PLANB, PLANC, and PLAND,
287
five-year plan, 287
income statement, 287
profit forecast, 287
sales forecast, 287
sensitivity analysis, 287
spreadsheet examples: SIMPLPAY and
PAYMENTS, 236-246
even payment, 288
initial data, 242
interest payment, 288
Model Area, 237, 242
"nper," 237
outstanding balance, 288
PMT function, 237
principal payment, 288
"pv," 237
"rate," 237
Verify Area, 242
spreadsheet form, 1, 2, 8
spreadsheet functions, 8, 58
spreadsheet instructions, 277-281
spreadsheet librarian, 269, 272
spreadsheet librarian checklist, 270,
271
spreadsheet librarian requirements,
269-271
spreadsheet models, 2, 3, 4, 5, 6, 7, 8,
80, 129-194, 195-265
spreadsheet revision, 286
spreadsheet template: JMNRULE, 258-
266
Active Area, 260
FULLRULE, 258, 260
Import Area, 260
Macro Area, 260
sample submodel, 260

Title Area, 260
Verify Area, 260
spreadsheet template: NEW, 290
    style, 290
    template, 290
spreadsheet template: SMALLNEW, 290
    style, 290
    template, 290
spreadsheets without Model Areas, 42-45
staging area, 79
standard deviation, 50, 65
strategic business tools, 283, 284, 286-287
style, 290
subblocks, 48
submodels, 48, 52, 58, 97-127
    cells of, 98
    Entering Data Area and, 98, 103, 104, 105
    "Entering from" area of, 104
    entrances of, 98
    evolutionary control of, 105
    exits of, 98
    focusing attention and, 113-126
    Initial Data Area and, 98, 103, 104, 105
    intellectual control of, 105, 126
    intermediate error in, 104
    intermediate partitioning of, 101
    Model Area and, 101
    physical control of, 105
    raw initial data area of, 104
    reuse of submodel tools, 104-113
SUM functions, 172
surfacing assumptions, 31-33

table of contents, 12, 20, 21, 23, 55, 88, 169

templates, 2, 23, 48, 96, 290
ten-period simulation, 286
test data, 50
testing your spreadsheet, 49-51, 134, 173
time horizon, 288
title area, 14
title lines, 12-15
titles, 60
travel costs, 290
TREND function, 216
tricky formulas, 216, 223, 232, 233
two-dimensional tables, 62

using basic forms, 39-41
utility theory, 285, 290

value of formula, 33, 34
variable rates of cost component growth, 288
verification sum, 81, 82
Verify Area, 81, 82, 126, 139, 141, 142, 169, 170, 171, 172, 242, 250, 257, 260, 268
verifying critical work, 79-82, 173

"want" criteria, 202
"want" objectives, 201, 202
warning lights, 81
weighted decision criteria, 286
"What If" questions, 199
Work Area, 93
work group concerns, 268-269
work groups, 268-269
working budgets, 287, 289
working through spreadsheet examples, 129-194
writing macros, 83
written explanation of formula, 33, 34

Put the dynamic features of Excel to work for you!

Understanding and Using Microsoft Excel

From basic skills to advanced program customization, *Understanding and Using Microsoft Excel* (MS-DOS version) unlocks the secrets of this best-selling spreadsheet for every user. Follow it from start to finish to become a master of Excel, or dive in wherever you like to learn about the program's powerful functions and techniques.

Beginning with the basics of spreadsheet use, the book builds on consistent examples that facilitate learning. The major topics covered include:

° The Basics (data entry, formula creation, using functions)
° Printing
° Report Generation (design, presentation)
° Macros and Programming
° System Development
° Windows and Data File Integration

This guide's unique approach to Excel makes it more than just a tutorial and better than a simple reference.

ISBN: 0-13-942103-3

Look for this and other Brady titles at your local book or computer store, or order direct by calling: 1(800) 624-0023, Visa and MasterCard accepted.

Fast Access
Microsoft Excel

Become an instant Excel master with the turn of a page. *Fast Access/Microsoft Excel* gets you started and keeps you going without overwhelming you with irrelevant details. Written in plain English, *Fast Access/Microsoft Excel* explains all the major system features and commands in short keystroke *you/system* instructions to guide you to instant solutions.

Find ready help with:

- The Windows user interface.
- Most commonly used Excel commands and functions— organized alphabetically for instant use.
- Formatting, charting functions, and database essentials.

Brady's *Fast Access* series of unique quick-reference guides gives you immediate mastery of the key features of many popular software programs. Regardless of the software's complexity or your experience, *Fast Access* gives you clear explanations and precise advice right away! For information that's both thorough and convenient, look no further than Brady's *Fast Access*!

ISBN: 0-13-307596-6

The Winn Rosch Hardware Bible

"Enhancing a computer is a matter of fitting connectors together and, at most, operating a screwdriver—almost anyone can do it, and that includes you."

—From the Introduction

PC journalist Winn Rosch walks you safely through the hardware jungle ... from processors to ports, from displays to storage. More than a guided tour, *The Hardware Bible* is hands-on all the way. Whether you want to just get along with your current system, or you're ready to enhance, upgrade, or even build a new machine.

- Covers the IBM PC, PC compatibles and IBM PS/2 hardware.
- Explains PC design and technology—you'll save time and money by making the right decisions up front.
- Spells out standards for settings, adjustments, and compatibilities.
- Offers step-by-step install procedures with worry-free instructions.

ISBN 0-13-160979-3

About the Author

John M. Nevison consults with business on building and maintaining inspired teams that contribute to bottom-line performance.

He has written six books about business and computing, among which are *Executive Computing* (Addison-Wesley, 1981), *The Elements of Spreadsheet Style* (Brady), and the present work. Nevison is a Phi Beta Kappa mathematics graduate of Dartmouth College. He is past Chairman of the Greater Boston Chapter of the Association For Computing Machinery.

He has been featured in articles in *The Wall Street Journal*, and his comments have appeared in *Personal Computing*, *U.S. News and World Report*, *Time*, and *Science*.

He lives with his wife and two daughters in Concord, Massachusetts. His phone number is (508) 369-8029.

Microsoft® Excel Spreadsheet Design

Copyright © 1990, John M. Nevison

22 Rules for Better Spreadsheet Style

1. Make a Formal Introduction

2. Title to Tell

3. Declare the Model's Purpose

4. Give Clear Instructions

5. Reference Critical Ideas

6. Map the Contents

7. Identify the Data

8. Surface and Label Every Assumption

9. Model to Explain

10. Point to the Right Source

//|||Brady

Handy removable reference card. Tear along perforations and keep by your computer

22 Rules for Better Spreadsheet Style

11. First Design on Paper

12. Test and Edit

13. Keep It Visible

14. Space the Spreadsheet for Easy Reading

15. Give a New Function a New Name

16. Report to Your Reader

17. Graph to Illuminate

18. Import with Care

19. Verify Critical Work

20. Control All Macros

21. Focus the Model's Activity

22. Enter Carefully

//// Brady